PAUL AND THE LANGUAGE OF FAITH

PAUL
and the
Language *of* Faith

Nijay K. Gupta

WILLIAM B. EERDMANS PUBLISHING COMPANY
GRAND RAPIDS, MICHIGAN

Wm. B. Eerdmans Publishing Co.
4035 Park East Court SE, Grand Rapids, Michigan 49546
www.eerdmans.com

© 2020 Nijay K. Gupta
All rights reserved
Published 2020

ISBN 978-0-8028-7343-9

Library of Congress Cataloging-in-Publication Data

Names: Gupta, Nijay K., author.
Title: Paul and the language of faith / Nijay K. Gupta ; foreword by James D. G. Dunn.
Description: Grand Rapids : Wm. B. Eerdmans Publishing Co., 2020. | Includes bibliographical references and index. | Summary: "This book will root Paul's love language in its context in the ancient world, where love was seen as affection, loyalty, and generosity; Paul's use is remarkable in making the emphasis one where love is understood as generosity and this, in a culture of reciprocity and mutual expectation"—Provided by publisher.
Identifiers: LCCN 2019026589 | ISBN 9780802873439 (paperback)
Subjects: LCSH: Bible. Epistles of Paul—Theology. | Faith—Biblical teaching. | Pistis (The Greek word)
Classification: LCC BS2655.F2 G87 2020 | DDC 227/.06—dc23
LC record available at https://lccn.loc.gov/2019026589

Contents

Foreword by James D. G. Dunn	ix
Acknowledgments	xi
Abbreviations	xiii

1. Beyond Belief — 1
- Faith as Opinion — 2
- Faith as Doctrine — 3
- Faith as Passive — 3
- The Old Testament Foundation of Paul's Use of Πίστις — 5
- Faith or Faithfulness? — 7
- Is This a Book about the Πίστις Χριστοῦ (Faith of Christ) Debate? — 13
- Πίστις and the Divine and Human Agency in Paul Debate — 14
- A Question of Method — 17
- Looking Ahead — 19
- How to Navigate This Book: A Note for Different Readers — 20

2. Faith in Paul — 21
- Early and Medieval Use of Faith Language — 22
- Luther and Calvin on Faith — 24
- Modern Scholarship on Paul and Christian Faith — 28
- Teresa Morgan's *Roman Faith and Christian Faith* — 33
- Conclusion — 37

3. Πίστις in Ancient Non-Jewish and Jewish Literature — 39
- Pagan Hellenistic Literature — 40

Hellenistic Jewish Literature:
   Septuagint and Pseudepigrapha   46
Hellenistic Jewish Literature: Philo   50
Hellenistic Jewish Literature: Josephus   52
Conclusion   56

4. Will He Find Faith on Earth?   58
Repent and Believe: Faith Language in Mark   58
Seek, Trust, and Obey: Faith Language in Matthew   60
Will the Son of Man Find Faith on Earth? The Gospel of Luke   71
Belief in the Gospel of John   73
Conclusion   75

5. Faithfulness Is Better   77
Plutarch and Odysseus's Silent Friends   77
First Thessalonians   80
Philippians   86
Revelation   91
Conclusion   94

6. Strange Wisdom   95
Faith Language in 1 Corinthians   96
Strange Wisdom, Humble Faith (2:5)   97
Paul and the Gift of Πίστις (12:9; 13:2)   108
Faith, Hope, Love: Is Faith Eternal? (13:13)   110
Conclusion   114

7. On Faith and Forms   115
Second Corinthians and the Corinthian Situation   116
The Theology of Idolatry   119
Second Corinthians 4:1–5:10   122
Conclusion   132

8. Covenantal Pistism   134
Πίστις and the Quest for Paul's Soteriology   134
Covenantal Nomism or Covenantal "Pistism"?   141

Πίστις in Galatians	143
The Christ-Relation in Galatians	147
Covenantal Pistism and the Agency Debate	153
Conclusion	154

9. And the Righteous Will Live by Trust — 156

Romans 1:16–17: A Brief Exegetical Analysis	158
The Background of Habakkuk 2:4 and Its Early Reception	160
Whose Πίστις?	163
Trust, Faith, or Faithfulness? Translating and Interpreting אמונה and Πίστις	165
From Πίστις to Πίστις	168
Conclusion	169

10. Revisiting "The Faith of Christ" — 171

Other Possible Readings of Πίστις Χριστοῦ	173
Πίστις Χριστοῦ and the Centrality of the Christ-Relation	174
The Translation Question	175
Importance of Human Faith in the Christ-Relation	175

11. Faith beyond Belief — 177

Obeying Faith	178
Believing Faith	178
Trusting Faith	179
Πίστις as a Tensive Symbol in Early Christian Discourse	181
Influences on Pauline Πίστις Language	182
What Has Works to Do with Faith?	183
Divine and Human Agency: Believing, Trusting, and Doing	185
How Did Christians Come to Be Called Believers?	191

Bibliography	193
Index of Names and Subjects	217
Index of Scripture and Other Ancient Texts	220

Foreword

This is a fascinating study that begins with a stimulating discussion of πίστις and faith language, whether faith is active or passive, whether the reader should translate πίστις "faith" or "faithfulness," and how they relate to each other. In his review of the history of faith-talk Nijay K. Gupta notes that the movement toward a doctrinal use of faith language ("Christian faith," "confession of faith") was already evident in Augustine. Primary attention is given appropriately to Luther's emphasis on "faith as active dependence on the Christ-relation," as "dependence on Christ."

Gupta notes particularly the richness of Matthew's faith language—seeking faith, trusting faith, faithfulness/loyal faith—and has some interesting reflections on why John uses the verb πιστεύω frequently (I might add very frequently!), but not the noun πίστις. By drawing on related material from contemporary literature and from subsequent Christian reflection on the New Testament texts, Gupta succeeds in drawing out the depth and breadth of the πίστις concept in a remarkably rich way. So, for example, in 1 Thessalonians and Philippians it should regularly be translated "loyalty" or "faithfulness." And he has a challenging reflection on the relation between faith and wisdom in 1 Corinthians 1–4—the "gift of foolish faith."

On Galatians he proposes replacing "covenantal nomism" by "covenantal pistism," as summarizing Paul's reaction to the former and promotion of the latter. It is good to see such a firm objection to the idea of πίστις as "nonwork, a kind of passive reliance on Christ" and the alternative of a "relational dynamic of the covenant . . . that expects fidelity and mutuality with trust as its core"—a stimulating and provocative reading of Galatians.

Chapter 9 has a further interesting discussion in effect on whether πίστις should be translated "faith" or "faithfulness"—illustrating the danger of treating them in an either-or way, whereas in the Greek the one merges into the other. The final chapter offers helpful clarifications of what the Pauline

FOREWORD

contrast between faith and works is all about and whether πίστις Χριστοῦ is best rendered as "faith in Christ" or "the faith of Christ." The final synthesis and conclusion takes the issue further, recalling the opening discussion and suggesting a range of translations—faith, trust, and faithfulness/loyalty—but all bound up in πίστις.

This is a clear discussion of the biblical, particularly Pauline concept of faith, its breadth and its specifics. Reading it with care will strengthen and perhaps correct the reader's understanding of faith. Who could ask for more?

JAMES D. G. DUNN
October 2018

Acknowledgments

First and foremost, I am grateful for the counsel and friendship of Michael Thomson. We have been friends for many years now, and I deeply appreciate his backing of this book project. I am also indebted to Chuck Conniry and Roger Nam for their leadership at Portland Seminary and their endless support for my scholarship. Portions of this material were presented in the Biblical Ethics program of the Society of Biblical Literature annual meeting, at Regent College, at the Tyndale House summer conference, and at a doctoral seminar at Southern Baptist Seminary hosted by Jonathan Pennington. On all of these occasions, questions and comments sharpened and sometimes corrected my thinking. And several people graciously read parts of the manuscript and supplied invaluable feedback: Matt Bates, James D. G. Dunn, Michael Gorman, Patrick Schreiner, and Kent Yinger. Last but not least, I couldn't have written this book without the encouragement of my family, especially my wife Amy. And my children regularly tell me that they love to see their names in print, so here's to you: Simryn, Aidan, and Libby, my little treasures.

This book is dedicated to Prof. James D. G. Dunn (aka Jimmy). Many years ago, I applied to study with Jimmy for my PhD. He informed me that he had retired, so formal supervision was not a possibility. I still went to Durham to work with two excellent supervisors, Stephen Barton and John Barclay. But Jimmy agreed to meet with me regularly over coffee to talk about all things Paul. Needless to say, I was richly blessed by all of my interactions with Jimmy and his wife, Meta. Jimmy, I read your monographs and commentaries in seminary with deep admiration and appreciation—no one has inspired me more as a New Testament theologian than you. You are a gentleman, a gracious mentor, an incisive dialogue partner, and a fellow lifelong student of that enigmatic figure Paul. I look forward to reading more books by JDGD, but I am also hopeful that my work can carry on your legacy of careful and penetrating Pauline scholarship.

Abbreviations

ASV	American Standard Version
BDAG	Danker, Frederick W., Walter Bauer, William F. Arndt, and F. Wilbur Gingrich. *Greek-English Lexicon of the New Testament and Other Early Christian Literature*, 3rd ed. Chicago: University of Chicago Press, 2000.
CEB	Common English Version
ESV	English Stanard Version
KJV	King James Version
LCL	Loeb Classical Library
LXX	Septuagint
NASB	New American Standard Bible
NET	New English Translation
NET	New English Translation
NETS	New English Translation of the Septuagint
NIV	New International Version
NLT	New Living Translation
NRSV	New Revised Standard Version
RSV	Revised Standard Version

1 Beyond Belief

Paul's Dynamic Faith Language

I believe in, *credo in*, means that I am not alone. In our glory and in our misery we men are not alone. God comes to meet us and as our Lord and Master. He comes to our aid.... One way or other, I am in all circumstances in company with Him.... Of ourselves we cannot achieve, have not achieved, and shall not achieve a togetherness with Him; that we have not deserved that He should be our God, have no power of disposal and no rights over Him, but that with unowed kindness, in the freedom of His majesty, He resolved of His own self to be man's God, our God.

—Karl Barth, *Dogmatics in Outline*

To have faith is to be open, vulnerable. It is also to wince and to withdraw. For this reason, faithfulness has a plodding quality. It is more stick-to-itiveness than it is power and glory. The key to faith is persistence. In the face of sin—be it outright evil or simple distraction—it is very difficult to persevere in faith. In the presence of temptation—be it desire or disaster—it is difficult to remain faithful. Yet, for the religious Jew, there is only teshuvah, repentance or re-turning, as the compass needle always returns toward the north.

—David Blumenthal, "The Place of Faith and Grace in Judaism"

In St. Augustine's sermon on John 20, in view of the resurrection appearances of Jesus to his disciples, he addresses the obvious problem of a human (risen) Jesus passing through a wall to present himself to his disciples. *How is this possible?* Augustine made appeal to the uniqueness of Jesus even before his death and resurrection (whereby, for example, he could walk on water, though he had normal body weight). But he finishes his thought with a striking notion: "Where reason fails, faith builds up."[1] Augustine himself was far from being opposed to reason,[2] but there has admittedly been a problematic tension in the history of Christianity between faith and reason. There is, of course, very good reason why the term "faith" has become a distinctively Christian word. After all, the word πίστις, the Greek word often translated "faith," is found hundreds of times in the New Testament (and over thirty-five times in Romans alone). Important words like "faith," though, when overused, tend to get flattened out and have meanings and connotations attributed to it that do not go back to the faith language of Scripture, or do not represent the depth and richness of that word (group). There are three problematic trends in the way Christians (and others) use faith language in religious ways.

Faith as Opinion

A few years ago, I taught a course that introduced the basics of Christianity to first-year college students. Not long after day one, students began debating issues like the historical reliability of the Gospels and the ability to prove the resurrection or divinity of Jesus. I was particularly taken aback when a student tried to end a debate by saying, "I don't care about proving what I believe. I believe it by faith, and that should be enough." As the course went on, I began to notice a trend whereby students used the language of faith in a way someone would use the word "opinion." In that sense, faith became a means of occluding conversation of an academic nature by removing any grounds for debate. "I believe it by faith," in that context, meant that reasons were not needed, even perhaps that *reason* wasn't needed. But is that what Paul meant when he talked about faith? I am afraid that many unknowingly buy into Mark Twain's facetious dictum: *faith is believing what you know ain't so*. We must return to the New Testament, and especially Paul, to see how a proper conception of Christian faith operates. What is the relationship between faith and reason?

---

1. Augustine: "Ubi deficit ratio, ibi est fidei aedificatio"; Sermon 247, author's translation.

2. Mark Boespflug makes a cogent case for understanding Augustine's conception of faith to be rational rather than suprarational; see "Is Augustinian Faith Rational?" *Religious Studies* 52 (2016): 63–79.

Faith as Doctrine

A second typical use of faith language in modern religious vocabulary pertains to things like faith statements and faith traditions. Undoubtedly, we get this terminology from the early creeds—doctrinal statements that begin "I believe" (Latin *credo*). Thus, faith can be nearly synonymous with the language of doctrine or religion, as in "interfaith dialogue." This is not an unreasonable association based on certain language in the New Testament (e.g., 1 Tim 4:6), but this kind of thinking, where faith equals doctrine, could degenerate into a kind of checklist mentality. This can turn faith into something sterile, purely cerebral, and even gnostic. In his book *The Creed*, Luke Timothy Johnson makes the point that πίστις is often translated "faith" in English versions of the New Testament, but, in fact, the Greek word has a broad range of meaning that covers a wide spectrum: belief, trust, endurance, loyalty, obedience. When we translate πίστις *only* as "belief," the polyvalent nature of the term is suppressed and the cognitive dimension often dominates. Johnson finds this way of flatly translating or understanding πίστις deeply problematic in view of understanding the true nature of Christian confession and life.

> One can hold a belief that something is true without letting the belief matter to one's life. The entire Christian creed can be treated as a set of beliefs that amount to no more than interesting opinions. This is the sort of faith that the letter of James scorns: "You believe that God is one. You do well. Even the demons believe—and shudder!" (Jas 2:19 NRSV).[3]

Alternatively, Johnson explains that πίστις involves a "response of the whole person."[4] Part of what I wish to call for, then, is a patient (re)reading of Paul, the most πίστις-focused writer in the New Testament, in order to understand best how and why he employed πίστις terminology.

---

3. Luke Timothy Johnson, *The Creed* (New York: Doubleday, 2003), 45. Johnson is concerned with a proper understanding of the church's ecumenical creeds; but he bases the foundation of the faith language of the creeds (*credo, credere*) on the importance of πίστις in the New Testament, which is made clear in this quotation.

4. Johnson, *Creed*, 44.

Faith as Passive

You might not be surprised to know that Martin Luther was fond of using faith language in reference to his conception of Christianity. In narrating his own epiphany about the true nature of righteousness through Christ, Luther writes:

> At last, by the mercy of God, meditating day and night, I gave heed to the words, namely, "In it the righteousness of God is revealed, as it is written, 'He who through faith is righteous shall live.'" There I began to understand that the righteousness of God is revealed by the gospel, namely, the passive righteousness with which a merciful God justifies us by faith, as it is written, "He who through faith is righteous shall live." Here I felt that I was altogether born again and had entered paradise itself through open gates. There a totally other face of the entire Scripture showed itself to me.[5]

As Alister McGrath explains, Luther understood justification to involve the transference of an alien righteousness to unrighteous persons by faith: "We are passive, and God is active, in our justification. Grace gives, and faith gratefully receives—and even that faith must itself be seen as a gracious gift of God."[6]

The heart of this notion of a passive receipt of righteousness seems close to how some characterize the nature of faith itself (though I do not think Luther himself ultimately favored a notion of "passive faith"; see 24–27). For example, Old Testament scholar Walter Kaiser summarizes the nonmeritorious acceptance of God's grace in view of the exemplary faith of Abraham:

> God does the accounting; God does the reckoning; God does the crediting; God does the justifying—the declaring of this man to be just. Abraham does nothing. God gave the promise which Abraham had only to receive. Sometimes the question is asked, Is believing a work in itself? Do we have "faith in faith"? Can we pull ourselves up by our own bootstraps? The answer, of course, is that faith is passive. It is a passive act. It is like receiving a Christmas present: we put out our hands to take, to accept, to receive.

---

5. Martin Luther, *Commentary on Romans*, Luther's Works, ed. Jaroslav Pelikan and Helmut T. Lehmann (Philadelphia: Fortress, 1972), 34.336–38.

6. Alister McGrath, *Studies in Doctrine* (Grand Rapids: Zondervan, 1997), 390.

> There is nothing more than a passive act here. We don't earn our Christmas presents. The same is true with faith.[7]

The New Testament writers clearly believed that God gave a gift in his grace that no one deserves. Thus, it is fitting to talk about believers as *recipients*. But does the language of *passivity* fit the nature of Pauline πίστις? Did the word πίστις in Paul's time communicate nonactivity, passivity, even a passive act?

One might appeal to Pauline language that juxtaposes faith and works (Rom 3:21–31; 9:32; Gal 2:16; cf. Eph 2:8–9). However, because of the complex history of the interpretation of Paul in the church and Western society, it is best to set a discussion of the Pauline language of faith (πίστις) on the right track by beginning with the Old Testament. Through a study that takes a particularly *Jewish* perspective on the language of faith, we can understand Paul's theology in a way that goes beyond (merely) belief.

The Old Testament Foundation of Paul's Use of Πίστις

Two times Paul quotes Hab 2:4 ("the righteous will live by faith") in order to make a point about a Christian life determined by πίστις (Gal 3:11; Rom 1:17). That should be a key indicator that his own understanding of faith was highly (though not exclusively) influenced by the Septuagint, the Greek translation of the Old Testament that was, for all intents and purposes, what Paul read as Scripture.[8] Thus, in order to make the most sense of what Paul meant when he used the language of πίστις, it is necessary to investigate how the Septuagint translators used this word, especially in view of Hebrew/Aramaic terms and ideas. A substantial discussion of the use of πίστις is coming in chapter 3, but at this juncture it is crucial that a proper perspective on the scriptural use of faith language is adumbrated.

A study of the relationship between the Greek Septuagint and the Hebrew Old Testament demonstrates that, while the Septuagint translators

---

7. Walter C. Kaiser, *The Christian and the Old Testament* (Pasadena CA: William Carey Library, 1998), 54; cf. Grant Osborne, *Romans* (Downers Grove, IL: InterVarsity, 2004), 281: "Faith is not a 'work,' but a passive opening of oneself up to the work of the Spirit within."

8. See especially T. Michael Law, *When God Spoke Greek* (Oxford: Oxford University Press, 2013).

used πίστις in relation to a number of Hebrew words, the three most common are אמונה, אמן, and אמת. The first word, אמן, means "trust" or "reliability." The second, אמונה, is quite similar.⁹ In contexts related to human relationships, אמונה "often refers to those who have the capacity to remain stable (i.e., faithful) amid the unsettling circumstances of life, realizing God's truth has established them."¹⁰ For example, the term is used of Moses's hands as Aaron and Hur supported him on the hill of Rephidim (Exod 17:12). Thus, his hands were *firm, steady, reliable*.

The third term, אמת, can be translated "faithfulness" or "dependability."¹¹ Isaiah 38:3 furnishes a helpful example. Here Hezekiah, having taken ill, pleads before God with these words: "Remember now, O LORD, I implore you, how I have walked before you in *faithfulness* [אמת] with a whole heart, and have done what is good in your sight" (NRSV).

Walter Brueggemann stresses how the Old Testament language of faith is everywhere associated with covenant relationship. Within this construct, faith has less to do with theological ideas per se than with the nature and integrity of a relationship of trust. Brueggemann writes:

> "Faith" concerns attentive engagement in a promissory relationship. Only rarely does the Old Testament suggest that "faith" is a body of teaching that Israel is to "believe." Israel's faith does not necessarily lack normative substance nor is it vacuous, but the relationship is more elemental than the substantive teaching which reflects upon that relationship. That in the Old Testament faith is regarded as "trust in" is more elemental than "assent to" is a matter often discounted in formal theological articulations, but "trust" is not to be understood primarily in emotive terms. Trust is a practice that entails obedience to Torah [the law] and its specific requirements. Israel's fidelity to Yahweh, not unlike fidelity in marriage, thus consists of concrete acts that take the other party with defining seriousness.¹²

---

9. See James D. G. Dunn, *The Theology of Paul the Apostle* (Grand Rapids: Eerdmans, 1998), 373n159.

10. Marvin Wilson, *Our Father Abraham* (Grand Rapids: Eerdmans, 1989), 183.

11. T. F. Torrance linked this Old Testament term to the expression of "the reality of God in covenant-relationship"; see "One Aspect of the Biblical Conception of Faith," *Expository Times* 68 (1957): 111–14 at 112.

12. Walter Brueggemann, *Reverberations of Faith* (Louisville: Westminster John Knox, 2002), 78.

This brief glance at faith language in the Old Testament offers enough evidence to put into question all three of the problematic ways that many modern readers of Paul view such terminology. Faith is neither mere religious opinion nor only doctrinal ideas. And certainly no Israelite or Jew reading the Hebrew Old Testament or the Greek Septuagint would find the word "passive" applicable to the use of such words in the faith semantic category.

Faith or Faithfulness?

Given that the Hebrew terms behind the use of πίστις in the Septuagint (chap. 3) refer to words that are often best translated "faithfulness" (or loyalty, reliability, commitment), why is it that where πίστις appears in Paul it is usually rendered "faith" by most English translations?[13] This question is central to the concerns of this book and one, I hope, that every student of Paul will examine carefully.

Since the default translation of πίστις in most English translations is "faith," it is instructive to observe where deviations tend to occur within these translations. First of all, nearly all translators are prone to translate πίστις "faithfulness" when it relates to the nature and activity of God. In Rom 3:3, for example, Paul writes, "What if some were unfaithful [ἠπίστησάν]? Will their unfaithfulness [ἀπιστία] nullify God's faithfulness [πίστις]?" Almost every modern English translation renders πίστις "faithfulness" here, as it is in reference to the loyalty and reliability of God (e.g., NASB, NIV, ESV, RSV, NRSV, NET; cf. Hos 2:22 LXX).

A second example in the letters of Paul is instructive, this time from Galatians. Near the close of the epistle, Paul contrasts the obvious works of the flesh (e.g., impurity, idolatry, hatred, jealousy, factions) with the "fruit of the Spirit": love, joy, peace, patience, kindness, goodness, *faithfulness* (πίστις), gentleness, and self-control (5:22–23). Richard Longenecker summarizes what is probably the perspective of most scholars who translate πίστις "faithfulness" here (but tend to render it "faith" everywhere else in Galatians):

> *Pistis*, though used repeatedly elsewhere in Galatians to signify a person's response of trust regarding God's salvation provided in Christ Jesus, here undoubtedly means the ethical virtue of "faithfulness." . . . Here . . . the

---

13. See Varghese P. Chiraparamban, "The Translation of Πίστις and Its Cognates in the Pauline Epistles," *Bible Translator* 66 (2015): 176–89.

subject is the believer and the context is determinative. For situated, as it is, amid eight other nouns in a list of human virtues, *pistis* must here be understood as well as the human virtue of faithfulness, that is produced in the believer's life by the faithful God through his Spirit.[14]

Longenecker states that faith (as a "response of trust") is the sort of default meaning for πίστις in Paul and that such a meaning is something sensibly distinct from faithfulness (which he implies is a less-common meaning of πίστις as it pertains to the believer). This appears similar to comments that Douglas Moo makes regarding the language of faith in Romans.[15] It is almost as if there is a preference for viewing the operation of faith for Paul, almost by default, as something essentially internal (after all, Christians believe with their hearts and minds; Rom 10:10) or nonactive insofar as faithfulness would seem *too* active or *too* externally involved.[16]

In his commentary on Philemon, Markus Barth offers an interesting excursus on the interpretation of πίστις in Paul with a view toward whether the apostle means faith or faithfulness. Barth notes that it is not uncommon for Philemon commentators to treat the reference to πίστις in Phlm 5 as "faith" unto the Lord Jesus: "I hear of your love for all the saints and your faith [πίστις] toward the Lord Jesus" (NRSV). As expected, all of the major English translations have "faith" here (e.g., ASV, NASB, NIV, ESV, RSV, NRSV, NET). In that case, the impression is that Philemon is commended for his love for his Christian brothers and sisters and for his "belief/faith" in Jesus Christ. Barth observes that, while the idea of belief is important for Paul, translating πίστις as "faith" on this occasion may be missing his rhetorical and theological point. Because πίστις can have the meaning "fidelity" or "loyalty," we must entertain the possibility that this is what Paul refers to here.[17] Appealing to texts like 1 Thess 1:3 ("work of faith") and Rom 1:5 ("obedience of faith"), Barth underscores the critical point that in many cases obedience and faith are not as neatly separable human operations as some interpreters of

---

14. Richard N. Longenecker, *Galatians*, World Biblical Commentary 41 (Grand Rapids: Zondervan, 1990), 262.
15. Douglas J. Moo, *The Epistle to the Romans*, New International Commentary on the New Testament, 2nd ed. (Grand Rapids: Eerdmans, 2018), 245–46.
16. One often sees this worked out in interpretations of Rom 4:5, where faith and work are ostensibly put at odds.
17. Markus Barth, *The Letter to Philemon*, Eerdmans Critical Commentary (Grand Rapids: Eerdmans, 2010), 273.

Paul presume them to be. With that in mind, when Paul uses ἀγάπη + πίστις, Barth surmises that these are not meant to be treated separately (i.e., *love* for saints, *faith* in the Lord Jesus). Rather, it makes more sense to see them together, perhaps even as a hendiadys: "steadfast love which you have for the Lord Jesus and for all the saints."[18] Is Barth correct about this active nature of πίστις in Phlm 5? Should πίστις be best understood in this context as "belief" (something essentially cognitive) or "faithfulness" (something active and encompassing the whole person and blending into the concept of obedience)?

Part of the confusion comes from the polyvalent nature of the word πίστις itself. To simplify an explanation of how πίστις can stretch to cover either belief or faithfulness, we might look at the key cognate Greek words that appear in the New Testament. On the one hand the verb πιστεύω means "I believe" (and almost never "I obey" or "I show faithfulness").[19] On the other hand the adjective πιστός means "faithful."[20] In the New Testament, πίστις can cover the spectrum of these cognate words. Thus, πίστις can have at least two distinct (but related) meanings in Paul's letters: belief and faithfulness.

Meaning #1: Believing Faith (Πίστις as "Belief")

While I express caution regarding the treatment of πίστις as a passive form of faith, there is sufficient evidence in Paul (and elsewhere in the New Testa-

---

18. Barth, *Philemon*, 271–74.

19. On this point, see R. Barry Matlock, "Detheologizing the ΠΙΣΤΙΣ ΧΡΙΣΤΟΥ Debate: Cautionary Remarks from a Lexical Semantic Perspective," *Novum Testamentum* 42 (2000): 13–15.

20. There are a few interesting deviations from this in certain translations. In Gal 3:9, some translators prefer to render τῷ πιστῷ Ἀβραάμ as "Abraham the believer" (NET) or "man of faith" (ESV) rather than the more natural translation "the faithful Abraham" (KJV, ASV). Even though the most straightforward translation of πιστός is "faithful," most translations opt for "faith" or "believer" because Paul places the emphasis in Galatians, not on Abraham's covenant faithfulness, but precisely on his initial faith and trust in God. Thus, even though "Abraham the believer" makes sense in 3:9 contextually, such an English translation flattens out the almost provocative use of the word πιστός in his argument. For a discussion of the nuances involved in this word choice, see Paul Trebilco, *Self-Designations and Group Identity in the New Testament* (Cambridge: Cambridge University Press, 2012), 87. See also chap. 8 below on Galatians.

ment) to establish a connotation of πίστις focused on cognition, the proper operation of the mind and heart with respect to revelation and truth, what Markus Barth refers to as "an epistemological and hermeneutical sense."[21] When πίστις is used in this way, the emphasis falls on the proper method of perception, which is at odds with worldly knowledge and mere human ways of seeing reality (see chap. 6 on 1 Corinthians and chap. 7 on 2 Corinthians). Barth, quite appropriately, appeals to Heb 11:1, where πίστις is defined as "the assurance of things hoped for, the conviction of things not seen" (NRSV).[22] When used in this way, πίστις represents a kind of divinely enabled extrasensory perception, a second way of seeing and knowing. One can have confidence in what appears invisible—not because it is mere hunch or opinion, but because he or she has been given access to a perceptual key that unlocks a divine reality. Perhaps the best example of this, for Paul, comes in 2 Cor 5, where he proclaims "we walk by faith, not by sight" (5:7 NRSV). Paul commends a faith that goes beyond appearances, the mind must activate a new lens of perception.[23] In chapters 6–7 below, I highlight occasions where Paul employs πίστις with more emphasis on this kind of semantic nuance.

Meaning #2: Obeying Faith (Πίστις as "Faithfulness")

For this second shade of the meaning of πίστις, Barth appeals to the concept of covenant in the Old Testament and how faithfulness is a social platform central to the divine-human relationship, a relationship that expects love, goodwill, mutuality, and loyalty from both sides.[24] It will be a major burden

21. Barth, *Philemon*, 273.
22. Barth, *Philemon*, 273.
23. David Garland expresses the heart of Paul's point in 2 Cor 5:6–8 regarding the proper perspective on his apostolic weakness: "Living by faith and not by sight means that as we walk with God we have no literal pillar of cloud or fire to guide us as Israel of old had. Paul believed that our life is hidden, so he cannot prove it from outward appearances. And those who judge things only by outward appearances (physical weaknesses, suffering, near death experiences) cannot see the whole truth about him or any other Christian. Only faith can take measure of the unseen eternal realities of the next aeon, where all this present weakness and mortality will be transformed into something sublime"; see *2 Corinthians*, New American Commentary (Nashville: Broadman & Holman, 1999), 265.
24. Barth, *Philemon*, 273.

of this book to make this case more extensively (see chap. 5), but for this brief description, let us look at Matt 23:23. In a denunciation of the disingenuous behavior and myopia of the scribes and Pharisees, Jesus makes this accusation: "Woe to you, experts in the law and you Pharisees, hypocrites! For you give a tenth of mint, dill, and cumin, yet you have neglected the weightier provisions of the law: justice, mercy, and faithfulness [πίστις]; but these are the things you should have done without neglecting the other" (NET).[25] Ulrich Luz summarizes the perspective of most commentators on why πίστις here ought to be translated "faithfulness" (and not "faith"):

> "Faithfulness/faith" here cannot mean faith in Jesus, nor can it meant the faith of prayer or the active faith that performs works of love, for faith is never for Matthew the essence of the requirements of the law. Instead, we are to understand [πίστις] in the tradition of biblical language, but also as is understandable for Greeks, as "faithfulness."[26]

Some resistance against this interpretation offered by Luz appears in the discussion of this passage by Matthean commentators W. D. Davies and D. C. Allison. They argue that πίστις cannot mean faithfulness because Matthew never really means it that way elsewhere. Thus, it should be translated "faith."[27] What Davies and Allison seem to be missing, though, is that the Matthean Jesus implies that justice, mercy, and πίστις are things that the scribes and Pharisees have failed to *do* (ποιέω). Elsewhere in Matthew (when he refers to "*believing* faith"), verbs of *doing* (like ποιέω) are not associated with πίστις, but it would be altogether appropriate in 23:23, where there is an ethical core to how πίστις is being used.[28]

While I have only touched on the meaning of πίστις as "obeying faith," something that one *does*, it should prove sufficient for now to demonstrate the more *active* nature of πίστις at least in some instances.

The challenge with the polyvalent nature of πίστις, though, is not that

---

25. Most translations render πίστις "faithfulness" here (NASB, NIV, ESV, NET), but a few prefer "faith" (KJV, RSV, NRSV).

26. Ulrich Luz, *Matthew 21–28*, Hermeneia (Minneapolis: Fortress, 2005), 124.

27. See W. D. Davies and Dale C. Allison, *Matthew*, International Critical Commentary (Edinburgh: T&T Clark, 1997), 3:294.

28. R. T. France should be given credit for this insight; see *The Gospel according to Matthew*, New International Commentary on the New Testament (Grand Rapids: Eerdmans, 2007), 873–74.

it can mean two different things (a similar situation is seen with παῖς, which can mean "servant" or "child"; it obviously means only one or the other in virtually all circumstances, so context usually clarifies which meaning is intended in a particular discourse). Πίστις is far more complex. The two possible meanings (*believing* faith and *obeying* faith) of this word are related and sometimes, perhaps often, blended or indistinguishable in usage. Thus, we inevitably must account for this by bringing in a third meaning or value of πίστις, which somehow meets the two meanings in the middle or perhaps widens to overlap them both.

Meaning #3: Trusting Faith (Πίστις as "Trust")

It is helpful to think of the meaning of πίστις not in isolated zones, but rather along a kind of spectrum:

Faith (cognitive)   Faithfulness (socially active)
|--|

The problem is that most of the time Paul is not wanting to refer to just one extreme of this semantic line, though there is this possibility. Where Paul's meaning in any given contextualized usage lies must be determined on a case-by-case basis. Instead of thinking about the semantics of πίστις in zone terms, we must consider that his meaning may *modulate*, moving across this spectrum according to his intended meaning.

If Paul does not always want to land on one side of this pole, how should we represent that? There may be times (I would argue *many* times) where we must recognize a meaning of πίστις in Paul that tries to encapsulate both of these polarized values. We can call this "*trusting* faith":

                --------------- Trust ---------------
Faith   Faithfulness
|--|

Why the choice of the word "trust"? After all, it is relatively unpopular as a rendering of πίστις in English translations of the Bible. Richard Hays advocates for the use of the English word "trust" to represent πίστις (generally speaking) precisely because it heals the breach, so to speak, between the cognitive aspects of the word's possible meaning and the active (behavioral/practical) valence of the word. Hays remarks that he prefers "trust" over "have faith" especially because there is a tendency to read faith/belief language as a "subjective attitude of the individual believer" that could mislead readers of Paul into thinking that the apostle places his soteriological emphasis on held beliefs rather than relational *trust*.[29] Hays finds "trust" especially appropriate to articulate Pauline πίστις because it can carry at the same time the cognitive dimensions of choosing to think rightly about God as well as the covenantal dimensions of commitment to obedience.

While it is difficult to parcel out the differences between belief, trust, and faithfulness in any precise way, I artificially use the following model for heuristic purposes:

- Believing faith is cognitively active: believing is something you do with your mind. It is a function of thought (cf. Matt 21:32).
- Obeying faith is relationally active: faithfulness is understood in this discussion as an active form of loyalty and obedience. As noted above, scholars tend to associate it with virtues and ethical practices like love and perseverance. Insofar as it may be observed, we can say it is a function of the active self, the self-in-relationship where loyalty can be demonstrated.
- Trusting faith is volitionally active: volition, or will, is a calculated word choice for trusting faith because we use the word "will" in English to represent something preactive ("will to act") and also sometimes active in itself ("goodwill"). The work of the will appears central to the relational commitment of a person to another and, thus, perfectly captures how Paul seems to use πίστις in a large number of cases.

While it would prove difficult in some circumstances to designate a particular occurrence of πίστις as one of these options in a neat way, still it helps the reader of Paul theoretically to keep in mind the unique way that πίστις operates as a polyvalent noun that can modulate across a spectrum of semantic nuances.

---

29. Richard B. Hays, "Lost in Translation: A Reflection on Romans in the Common English Bible," in *The Unrelenting God*, ed. David J. Downs and Matthew L. Skinner (Grand Rapids: Eerdmans, 2014), 92–94.

Is This a Book about the Πίστις Χριστοῦ (Faith of Christ) Debate?

When I first began research for this book and I shared with colleagues my interest in exploring Paul's language of faith, the most common response was: *so you are writing on the πίστις Χριστοῦ debate?* That certainly says something about the longevity and intensity of that particular scholarly discussion, but that has never been a direct interest of mine.[30] First and foremost, I find that scholars and armchair readers of Paul often gloss over Paul's faith language, presuming what he means ("religious beliefs") rather than examining it in its unique semantic breadth and theological depth. Second, I want to place, as it were, Paul's use of πίστις in relation to how Jews and pagans used the same word within and outside of religious discourse. It is easy to assume that faith is primarily a religious term, even a *Christian* term. But the reality is that Paul was largely influenced in his faith language by the Septuagint and the Jesus tradition. Now, of course, Paul was a dynamic thinker, so he was bound to put some fresh thought into the nature of faith, but it was far from a neologism.

When it comes to πίστις Χριστοῦ, I decided not to address this issue as a central matter of this work, because my desire is to step back and take a panoramic perspective on Paul's faith language without getting too bogged down in this particular academic squabble. Chapter 8 on Galatians gives some attention to this discussion, but for those interested in my interpretation of πίστις Χριστοῦ and the nature of the debate, see chapter 10.

Πίστις and the Divine and Human Agency in Paul Debate

At the risk of neglecting the πίστις Χριστοῦ debate, I focus on what Paul's faith language has to say about his understanding of the believer's relationship with God and with Jesus Christ. Paul's use of πίστις can inform the lively academic discussions that are taking place especially regarding "divine and human agency" in Paul.[31] On that matter, scholars look at Paul's language of salvation, works, justification, and grace. Unfortunately, πίστις has not been

---

30. Peter Oakes contends that the πίστις Χριστοῦ debate created a logjam in the study of faith language in Paul; see "Πιστις as Relational Way of Life in Galatians," *Journal for the Study of the New Testament* 40 (2018): 255–75 at 257.

31. See John M. G. Barclay and Simon Gathercole, eds., *Divine and Human Agency in Paul and His Cultural Environment* (London: T&T Clark, 2006).

given much attention.[32] Some argue that Paul's use of faith points to the (passive) acceptance of salvation, apart from works. Others posit that faith refers *not* to something humans do but to the faithfulness of Christ, such that human faith is not really that important in Paul's soteriological framework. In both of these cases, it is as if soteriological agency is viewed as a mathematical equation: [human input] + [divine input] = [salvation]. In the minds of some scholars, any attempt to take πίστις seriously as something humans *do* automatically *decreases* the amount one can put in the divine category and therefore could be labeled "(semi-)Pelagian" or "synergistic." But how reasonable is the assumption that Paul thought of salvation as a zero-sum equation? Again, a more thorough study of Paul's use of πίστις has some very important things to say about this issue, and we will have several occasions to reflect on this.

One major consideration pertaining to Pauline religion and the divine-human relationship involves how πίστις relates to the notion of covenant. It is often said that the word "covenant" plays little to no role in Paul's thought, and this appears to be true when we look at his meager use of διαθήκη in particular (Gal 3:15, 17; 4:24; Rom 9:4; 11:27; 1 Cor 11:25; 2 Cor 3:6, 14; cf. Eph 2:12). But it is instructive to look at patterns and developments in early Judaism and its Greek literature, where we see a limited use of διαθήκη in nonbiblical Jewish literature (see chap. 3) and a desire among Jewish writers to use more generic relational language (including πίστις) to refer to a covenantlike religious sociology. An important and instructive example comes from the Septuagint, specifically Neh 10:1 (2 Esdr 19:38, numbered 20:1 in some versions of the Septuagint).

To give a brief bit of context, Neh 8–10 recounts the covenant-renewal ceremony that preceded the dedication of the rebuilt walls of Jerusalem for the returned exiles. In 9:38 the signatories proclaim:

> Because of all this we make a firm agreement in writing, and on that sealed document are inscribed the names of our officials, our Levites, and our priests. (NRSV)

---

32. Although there are some important recent treatments; see Benjamin Schliesser, *Was Ist Glaube? Paulinische Perspektiven* (Zurich: Theologischer Verlag, 2011); and Teresa Morgan, *Roman Faith and Christian Faith: Pistis and Fides in the Early Roman Empire and the Early Churches* (Oxford: Oxford University Press, 2015).

And in regard to all these circumstances we make a covenant, and write *it*, and our princes, our Levites, *and* our priests, set their seal to *it*. (LXX, trans. Brenton)

καὶ ἐν πᾶσι τούτοις ἡμεῖς διατιθέμεθα πίστιν καὶ γράφομεν, καὶ ἐπισφραγίζουσιν πάντες ἄρχοντες ἡμῶν, Λευῖται ἡμῶν, ἱερεῖς ἡμῶν. (Rahlfs)

The Hebrew phrasing here for "make a covenant" is כרתים אמנה, which literally means "to cut a firmness." This is unusual phrasing; normally you "cut" a covenant (ברית). Here אמנה appears to serve as a kind of circumlocution for the expected word "covenant." The Septuagint sometimes took a very mechanical and rigid approach to translating the Hebrew text. So πίστις would have been a natural choice. But why did the *Hebrew* writer choose אמנה in the first place? To be honest, it is unclear, but one explanation is that here we do not have the institution of a brand new covenant but rather a renewal ceremony.[33] Be that as it may, why would the author use כרת then?

The Greek translator chose a word for establishing (διατιθέμεθα) to clarify the general contractual nature of the situation, and then did what was rather comfortable by rendering אמנה as πίστις. Despite the strange phrasing of the Hebrew text (which is only slightly less awkward in Greek), we can conclude that in the postexilic period אמנה could serve to represent a relational bond, something similar to a covenant.[34] The use of πίστις here corresponds to pagan and mundane use of πίστις in antiquity, where it often refers to relationships of trust, fidelity, and goodwill. It makes sense, then, that πίστις became a term that approximated the covenantal bond, both in the Septuagint and in other Hellenistic Jewish literature (see chap. 3). This might help us consider why Paul does not use explicit covenant language in a formative or central way in the letters, and we also might entertain the thought that Paul's faith language may overlap significantly with the Jewish concept of covenant. This has great potential to inform conversations about divine and human agency in Paul. Consider how biblical scholars reflect on the concept of covenant in the Old Testament and how that might inform or reshape how we approach the divine-human relationship in Paul, espe-

---

33. Philip Noss and Kenneth Thompson, *A Handbook on Ezra and Nehemiah* (New York: United Bible Societies, 2005), 461.

34. See Andrew E. Steinmann, *Ezra and Nehemiah* (St. Louis: Concordia, 2010), 530. L. H. Brockington is more confident that this can refer to a covenant; see *Ezra, Nehemiah, and Esther*, New Century Bible (London: Nelson, 1969), 177.

cially regarding the tendency to quantify agency. Biblical covenants are not business contracts that operate according to a quid pro quo social economy. In the Jewish covenants, God committed himself to Israel out of love (Deut 7:8), and despite Israel's agreeing to obedience, sin was not a deal breaker, so to speak. This statement captures well the covenantal dynamic:

> If the relationship between Israel and Yahweh had been the kind conveyed in a modern contract, Yahweh's commitment would have been contingent upon Israel's keeping of its obligations. In the covenant relationship, Yahweh honors his part (the promises) because of his love and because he is God. The Lord may punish Israel for disobedience, and may even chasten whole generations for stubborn disbelief. But the covenant remains in force—simply because of God's nature.[35]

Contracts depend on legal compliance and sanctions—that is not a bad thing when it comes to legal rights and commercial transactions. But that is not how the Jewish holy covenants operated. They involved what David Blumenthal refers to as a fusion of faith and grace: "Grace evokes faith and faith evokes grace; acts of unmerited love call forth acts of faithfulness, while acts of faithfulness call forth acts of unmerited love—in all dimensions of existence. Thus, god loves us in grace and we are faithful to him and, vice versa, we are faithful to him and he loves us in covenantal grace."[36] Blumenthal sums up by quoting Abraham Heschel: "*Faith is sensitivity, understanding, engagement, and attachment.*" One can see immediately from such a perspective how this Jewish way of thinking about faith and covenant can illuminate Paul's use of faith language. Passive is never a way that an Israelite or Jew would have thought of faith in God. When we encounter what seems like nonactive expressions of faith language, we might be better off speaking of faith as an "active mode of receptivity," or a will that welcomes, invites, defers, and receives with attentiveness and responsiveness.[37]

---

35. William S. LaSor, David Allan Hubbard, and Frederic William Bush, *Old Testament Survey* (Grand Rapids: Eerdmans, 1982), 122.

36. David Blumenthal, "The Place of Faith and Grace in Judaism," in *A Time to Speak*, ed. James Rudin and Marvin R. Wilson (Grand Rapids: Eerdmans, 1987), 104-14 at 111.

37. See Walther Eichrodt, "Covenant and Law," *Interpretation* 20 (1966): 302-21 at 310.

A Question of Method

What is the best way to go about this study of Paul's faith language? Anything that attempts to be exegetical theology will, of necessity, be multidimensional in approach. Below are the operating principles and methods with which I work throughout the book.

A Semantic-Domain Approach to Word Meanings

Many traditional lexicons and dictionaries work with a haphazard approach to the delineation of word meanings. To understand and make meaning of how words are *used*, we do well to think in terms of semantic categories or domains and words like πίστις clearly demonstrate a breadth of usage that covers several broader domains. In their introduction to *Greek-English Lexicon: Based on Semantic Domains*, J. P. Louw and Eugene Nida note that traditional lexicons do not recognize that "the different meanings of a single word are relatively far apart in semantic space." Using the example of πνεῦμα, they point out eight different semantic nuances that cross several broader categories.[38] This is crucial for our study of πίστις; as already noted, Paul could use this word to talk about several different kinds of things: a way of thinking, trust in Jesus Christ, social fidelity to another person, and so on.

Cultural Linguistics

This study adheres to the notion that the words that humans choose are deeply connected to their cultural heritage and assumptions. When we talk about πίστις in Paul, we must do the best we can to place the usage of that term into its wider encyclopedia in a particular time and culture. This does not dictate the exact meaning of the word in a given situation, but it does tie the word to its history of usage and expected connotations in a general sense.

---

38. Johannes P. Louw and Eugene Albert Nida, *Greek-English Lexicon of the New Testament: Based on Semantic Domains* (New York: United Bible Societies, 1996).

Contextualized Meaning

One of the obstacles to studying key words in Paul (generally) is the way readers can flatten out the use of a word and ignore the specific text's literary context. But, of course, this is precisely the most important factor for discerning the exact meaning of a word like πίστις in any given occasion. Therefore, I examine several uses of πίστις in Paul with close attention to his communicative purposes in their discrete contexts. This will allow the nuances of that situation to color πίστις in different ways. That does not prevent one from stepping back and observing broader patterns and repeated theological themes, but the temptation to make general statements ought not to shortcut the process of case-by-case, passage-by-passage, examination.

Looking Ahead

Before diving into Paul's letters, I begin our study in chapter 2 with a brief history of the interpretation of πίστις and faith language in Paul. It is probably no surprise that Luther and Bultmann played pivotal roles in shaping how Protestant scholarship read and interpreted πίστις in biblical discourse. Next (chap. 3) I offer various soundings in the ways that πίστις is used in pagan and Jewish Greek texts of antiquity. This offers a perspective on the breadth of usage and also interesting patterns and developments specifically in Jewish literature. After that I examine πίστις in the Jesus tradition (chap. 4). In some ways this might seem anachronistic, since 1 Thessalonians and Galatians almost certainly predate the canonical Gospels. Still, given how central faith language is to the Jesus tradition, we can assume that this would have played some formative role in how Paul thought about and used faith language.

These initial chapters set the stage for a series of studies on πίστις and faith language in individual Pauline texts. In chapter 5 I examine selections from 1 Thessalonians and Philippians, letters that tend to prefer a meaning of πίστις that is close to that notion of (human) faithfulness. Chapters 6 and 7 respectively cover faith language in the two Corinthians epistles. While there is not one consistent meaning for πίστις in any of Paul's letters, nevertheless, I make the case that the more cognitive nuance of πίστις is showcased well in some specific cases in the Corinthian letters, especially as faith relates to wisdom and epistemological transformation. Chapter 8 is a lengthy study of πίστις in Galatians and addresses with more detail how Paul's faith language relates to divine and human agency and what has come to be known as "covenantal nomism." Chapter 9 addresses Rom 1:17 in relation to the quotation of Hab 2:4 ("the *righteous* will live by faith"). This case study offers an opportunity to focus on a leading thesis statement in Rom 1:16–17 and also an Old Testament text central to Paul's theology of faith. Within these chapters on Paul's letters (chaps. 5–9), it would be impossible to catalog and discuss each and every use of πίστις. What I provide is a series of vignettes that highlight a verse or section of an epistle that can serve as a focal point for reflection on how he uses πίστις language semantically and rhetorically.

Chapter 10 engages with the πίστις Χριστοῦ debate. In chapter 11, I bring together the different threads of insight from the previous chapters and address at a broader level how this might shape how we approach Paul and his language of faith.

How to Navigate This Book: A Note for Different Readers

When I wrote this book, I had in mind the academic conversations about Paul's theology that happen in the guild of Pauline studies. There is much misunderstanding about Paul's use of faith language and ignorance about both the Jewish and pagan use of πίστις in antiquity as well as the early reception of Paul's faith language; thus, the first two main chapters (chaps. 2–3) are necessarily lengthy and technical. I encourage scholars to read that material carefully and patiently.

There may be other readers who are interested in Paul's theology but do not want to wade through some of the more dense material at the beginning. For those, I give you permission to skip ahead to chapter 4. Of course, this book builds the chapters on Paul's letters on those preliminary discussions and arguments, but I think the rest of the chapters are readable. If someone wishes to pick up on the main arguments I make in this book about Paul's use of faith language and how it relates to his theology—especially his understanding of divine and human agency—some readers might do well to read the conclusion (chap. 11) *first* and then turn to the main chapters.

2 Faith in Paul

A Brief History

> We . . . are not made upright through our own wisdom or understanding or piety or the deeds which we have done with a devout heart—but through faith, through which the all-powerful God has made all these people upright, from the beginning of the age. To him be the glory forever and ever.
>
> —1 Clement 32.4

> "The faith of Christ" is the faith which is alive in the fellowship with the spiritual Christ, and it is "faith-in-God" identical in content with the faith which Abraham in the sacred past had held, that is to say, unconditional trust in the living God in spite of all temptations to doubt.
>
> —Adolf Deissmann

How does one begin to summarize the history of the development of the study of biblical faith language? Answer: unsuccessfully! Nevertheless, it is still a helpful exercise to get a sense for how theologians and biblical scholars have used faith language throughout the centuries. Perhaps most crucial is to see the rapid development of the move toward a focus on the cognitive dimensions of this language (within a few centuries after Paul) and the impact that Luther—more accurately Lutheran interpretation—had on how modern Western readers of Paul use and interpret faith language. We begin with the apostolic fathers and move through early and medieval Christian history quickly, and slow down a bit as we enter the Reformation period and modern scholarship.

Early and Medieval Use of Faith Language

As I mentioned in the introduction, modern readers of Paul tend to treat his faith language as primarily cognitive: *we believe or have faith with our hearts and minds.* Christianity moved in this direction rather early on in the history of its existence, but if we look at the apostolic fathers, we don't see that development quite *yet*, and certainly not comprehensively.

Clement's lengthy letter to the Corinthians (1 Clement) includes several occurrences of πίστις.[1] Rather frequently Clement uses this language in relation to how Christians ought to endure and suffer as believers in Christ. He gives the example of the apostle Paul, who faced many imprisonments and survived torment and yet remained resilient in faith (5.5–6). Clement also commends two women by the names of Danaids and Dircae who also endured torture but finished the "race of faith" with steadfastness (6.2).

Clement makes it a point as well to commend those figures who showed respect and obedience to God even at great risk or uncertainty, specifically in the area of "faith and hospitality." Abraham, demonstrated faith in the form of hospitality, and he was rewarded with a son (10.7). Likewise, Rahab was blessed by God for her "faith and hospitality" (12.1). In these instances, it is not immediately clear what Clement means when he refers to faith, but later he refers to the example of Abraham, who performed acts of righteousness and truth *through faith* (31.2). Clearly Clement was not equating faith with act, but it appears to be more than something purely or even primarily cognitive. Clement's usage fits with a *volitional* sense of that which moves in human will to become obedience.

At other times, Clement could make a clear and fine distinction between faith and works. He explains to the Corinthians: "We . . . are not made upright through our own wisdom or understanding or piety or the deeds which we have done with a devout heart—but through faith, through which the all-powerful God has made all these people upright, from the beginning of the age. To him be the glory forever and ever" (32.4). That does not mean that Clement did not also view πίστις as a virtue. He lists πίστις as something for the Christian to pray for alongside patience, longsuffering, self-control, purity, and sobriety (64.1). In the company of these items, πίστις takes on the quality of something like loyalty or commitment.

---

1. All quotes come from Bart Ehrman, *The Apostolic Fathers*, vol. 1: *I Clement, II Clement, Ignatius, Polycarp, Didache*, LCL 24 (Cambridge: Harvard University Press, 2003).

A Brief History

Ignatius's employment of πίστις in his *To the Ephesians* follows a similar range of usage. Like other apostolic fathers, Ignatius favored pairing πίστις with ἀγάπη as twin dispositions toward Christ (1.1). If faith is the foundation for one's relationship with God, though, Ignatius believed (probably based on 1 Cor 13) that love is the ultimate goal (14.1). In a manner that parallels or echoes the Johannine Epistles, Ignatius could use πίστις to contrast belief and unbelief as ways of indicating spirituality and carnality (8.2). We start to see the makings of a doctrinal use of πίστις in 16.2, where he refers to the problem of heretical teachings that could undermine faith.

Barnabas likewise pairs love and faith (1.4; 11.8). Barnabas mentions a central spiritual triad. The first element is the "hope of life," which is glossed as the "beginning and completion of our faith" (ἀρχὴ καὶ τέλος πίστεως ἡμῶν; 1.6).[2] Barnabas 2 addresses the necessary attitude for those facing evil and temptation. What faith (πίστις) requires is "fear and patience" as well as "endurance and self-control" (2.2).

Diognetus offers a bit more of an epistemologically weighty use of πίστις overall.[3] Believing in gods visible in rocks and fire is folly because God is invisible, and "he revealed himself through faith, which is the only means by which one is permitted to see God" (8.6).[4] The author presses the reader to see with the eyes of faith and to lean on God's self-revealing grace, a grace that "reveals mysteries" and rewards those who seek truth (11.6). When the eyes and heart are opened, then one can recognize and appreciate the reverent character of the law, the grace of the prophets, "the faith of the gospels" (εὐαγγελίων πίστις), "the tradition of the apostles," and "the joy of the church" (11.6). Here, πίστις appears to refer to belief in Christ. One can clearly see the belief-oriented nuance of πίστις in Diognetus overall, but it is certainly not exclusive. In the previous verse the author could use πίστις in reference to staying within certain religious boundaries, that is, not "break[ing] the pledges of faith [ὅρκια

---

2. The second and third elements are righteousness ("the beginning and end of judgment") and love ("which is the testimony of works of righteousness"); for the English translation, see Michael W. Holmes, *The Apostolic Fathers: Greek Texts and English Translations*, 3rd ed. (Grand Rapids: Baker, 2007), 381, 383.

3. This should not come as too much of a surprise given the clear apologetic purpose of this work—to inspire unbelievers to find the claims of Christianity sensible and the belief in this god compelling; see Michael W. Holmes, *The Apostolic Fathers in English* (Grand Rapids: Baker, 2006), 289–91.

4. Holmes, *Apostolic Fathers*, 297.

πίστεως]" (11.5). This is reminiscent of classic Hellenistic language related to relational fidelity.

We start to see a move toward a more mental or doctrinal use of faith language especially with Augustine. In his *Enchiridion*, Augustine uses the language of "Christian faith" (16.60) and a "confession of faith" (24.96). As far as he is concerned, faith guides the Christian life. When he talks about the Christian triad of faith, hope, and love, he explains that "faith believes" and "hope and love pray" (though later he can also affirm that "faith prays too"; cf. 2.7). Despite this clearly cognitive orientation toward faith language, Augustine is also insistent that *true faith* cannot be *merely* mental or rational. In the *Enchiridion* as a whole Augustine makes much of the Pauline language of faith working through love (Gal 5:6; see *Enchiridion* 7.21; 18.67; 31.117). He dedicates a whole tractate to faith in his *On Faith and Works*. Here he defends a Christian theology of "faith alone"—and affirms that faith involves what one believes—but it cannot be a faith devoid of works. Indeed the true faith of Christian grace is "faith that acts through love" (chap. 16).

Eight hundred years later, Thomas Aquinas dedicates a portion of his *Summa Theologica* to the virtues of faith, hope, charity, prudence, justice, fortitude, and temperance.[5] Aquinas defines faith as "assent of the intellect to that which is believed" (2.2.4). He goes on to explain that two key elements are involved in faith—the object of belief and the intellect, which makes a choice of one thing over another. He associates faith with very specific core doctrines, not only belief in the Godhead but also the incarnation, the sacraments of the church, and the sinful condition. He reflects at length on the relationship between faith and science. By science he means what is known through objective proof. To begin with, Aquinas explains that science is based on knowledge, reason, and logic. Therefore, faith must be scientific because the apostles used logical argumentation to elicit faith (see 2.2.5). At the same time, Aquinas observes that faith necessarily cannot rely on sight, whereas science expects to prove based on observation.

Luther and Calvin on Faith

It should come as no surprise that Luther has a lot to say about faith. Much of what we inherited from Luther's theology of faith and works comes from

---

5. Thomas Aquinas, *The Summa Theologica*, trans. L. Shapcote and D. J. Sullivan (Chicago: Encyclopedia Britannica, 1909-90).

his controversial commentary on Galatians. I always assumed previously that Luther was singularly focused on a narrow way of thinking about and using faith language. But he shows remarkable nuance in his understanding of Paul's theology of faith. He claims that "the Holy Spirit speaks of faith in different ways in the Sacred Scriptures," covering a range of semantic possibilities.[6] He refers, first, to a kind of absolute use of faith that refers to justification (74). Second, he observes how faith is clearly distinguished from works. This faith becomes the foundation for action, but the two must not be equated. Luther talks about a "faithful doing, a doing inspired by faith," that is, "first have faith in Christ, and Christ will enable you to do and to live" (74). Luther is remarkably honest about the challenge of separating faith and works conceptually, even for theological reasons. He writes (apparently with chagrin): "It is not an easy matter to teach faith without works, and still to require works" (143). The third use of faith that Luther discerns pertains to faith as a virtue, for example when it refers to "faith in men" (151).

On the relationship between faith and works, Luther calls faith the "divinity of works." That is, "faith permeates all the deeds of the believer, as Christ's divinity permeated His humanity" (74). Abraham the patriarch was "accounted righteous because faith pervaded his whole personality and his every action" (74). Clearly Luther was intent upon clearly distinguishing faith from works and representing the former as the more central concern, such that "Paul as a true apostle of faith always has the word 'faith' on the tip of his tongue" (96; cf. Gal 3:26).

Luther so associated faith with Christianity that it belonged in the same circle, as it were, with Christ and imputation of righteousness (43). For all intents and purposes, faith *is* Christianity; it constitutes "the highest worship, the prime duty, the first obedience, and the foremost sacrifice" (65). Furthermore, it is "the height of wisdom, the right kind of righteousness, the only real religion" (60). But what *is* this faith, and what exactly does this faith believe? For Luther, the Christian is not someone who is sinless but rather somebody "against whom God no longer chalks sin, because of his faith in Christ" (43).

Luther was also clear about the problem in Galatia: these believers were preyed upon by meddling teachers of work-righteousness who taught that "in

---

6. Martin Luther, *Commentary on the Epistle to the Galatians*, trans. T. Graebner (Grand Rapids, Zondervan, 1965), 74. Subsequent quotations from this commentary are noted by parenthetical page numbers.

addition to faith in Christ the works of the Law of God were necessary unto salvation" (74). Luther is quick to link these ancient works-righteousness teachers with the papists who preach not faith but "self-devised traditions and works that are not commanded by God" (19). This is heresy because no tradition can overcome sin, not even the law, only Christ (74).

Luther is insistent that one must have a clear understanding that mixing faith and works in the gospel creates a false gospel, a "conditional" gospel (32). Works are an important part of the Christian life, but only faith can justify, "because it apprehends Christ, the Redeemer" (32). In one telling statement, Luther explains that human reason, by itself (and without faith), expects to be justified by works of the law, saying, "This I have done, this I have not done." But "faith looks to Jesus Christ, the Son of God, given into death for the sins of the whole world. To turn one's eyes away from Jesus is to turn to the Law" (32).[7]

Based on Galatians, we often assume that Luther treated faith as a codeword for nonwork(s), resting in God and trusting God for justification through Jesus Christ. Given Luther's constant juxtaposition of faith and works, one can see how such conclusions are made. But if one looks carefully at his relentless Christocentricity, it seems that the core of his soteriology and πίστις theology is the notion that faith is active dependence on the Christ-relation.[8] Luther was not intent upon waxing eloquently about "justification by faith alone," even though he obviously cared about this. His essential concern is the treatment of faith as dependence on Christ, that is,

---

7. Siegbert Becker, *The Foolishness of God: The Place of Reason in the Theology of Martin Luther* (Milwaukee: Northwest Publishing, 1999), 69-92, offers an interesting discussion of Luther's view of the relationship between faith and reason. In his reading of Luther, Becker sees Luther's understanding of faith as primarily cognitive, a way of thinking that "governs the intellect" and a "receiving instrument by which the individual believer appropriates the merits of Christ" (88). Conversion renews the imagination, leaving behind the darkened mind as a snake sheds its old skin (89). Bernhard Lohse takes a different approach to Luther's theology of faith, arguing that for the Reformer it was not primarily a matter of the mind (like reason) but of the heart, the active part of the person that responds holistically to pardon and summons from the Word of God; see *Martin Luther's Theology: Its Historical and Systematic Development* (Minneapolis: Fortress, 1999), 200-205.

8. I am indebted to Chris Tilling for the language of "Christ-relation." See Chris Tilling, *Paul's Divine Christology* (Grand Rapids: Eerdmans, 2015), 8-9, 108, 181, 188, 196.

clinging to Christ alone for salvation: "True faith lays hold of Christ and leans on Him alone. Our opponents cannot understand this. In their blindness they cast away the precious pearl, Christ, and hang onto their stubborn works" (32). The reason why this is important is because Luther was vehemently opposed to boiling down Christianity to a correct doctrine or a set of doctrines (of any kind); rather, it is in and through Christ, through *faith* in Christ, that one's sins are forgiven. For Luther, faith is not a thing in and of itself but a means of relating to Christ, connecting oneself to Christ: "We say, faith apprehends Jesus Christ, Christian faith is not an inactive quality in the heart. If it is true faith it will surely take Christ for its object. Christ, apprehended by faith and dwelling in the heart, constitutes Christian righteousness, for which God gives eternal life" (42–43). This explanation of Luther's theology of faith *could* make it appear that Luther had a strong participationistic theology; I do not claim to be an expert on Luther's thought, but it is clear that he could express rather clearly just such a notion: "Faith connects you so intimately with Christ, that He and you become as it were one person" (52).[9]

Calvin was no doubt deeply informed by Luther's reading of faith language in Galatians and Romans. Nevertheless, Calvin's use of the word is obviously more doctrinal. In his *Institutes of the Christian Religion*, Calvin defines faith in terms of "knowledge of God and Christ."[10] He also relates it to key theological concepts such as sin and salvation.[11] Having true Christian faith requires a "firm persuasion of the truth of God,"[12] that is, a certainty is required that is "full and decisive."[13] But Calvin did not treat faith as purely cerebral: "The word is not received in faith when it merely flutters in the brain, but when it has taken root in the heart, and

---

9. For a cogent discussion of Luther and faith, see Stephen Chester, *Reading Paul with the Reformers* (Grand Rapids: Eerdmans, 2017), 175–217, who defines Luther's understanding of faith as that which "grasps hold of Christ and united the believer with him so that his righteousness is received" (215). Tuomo Mannermaa presses for this reading of Luther quite strongly: "In faith, the person of Christ and that of the believer are made one, and this oneness must not be divided; what is at stake here is salvation, or the loss of it"; *Christ Present in Faith: Luther's View of Justification* (Minneapolis: Fortress, 2005), 1–42 at 42.

10. John Calvin, *Institutes of the Christian Religion*, trans. H. Beveridge (repr. Grand Rapids: Eerdmans, 1964), §2.3.

11. Calvin, *Institutes*, §1.313.

12. Calvin, *Institutes*, §3.42.

13. Calvin, *Institutes*, §3.15.

become an invincible bulwark to withstand and repel all the assaults of temptation."[14]

Modern Scholarship on Paul and Christian Faith

Modern scholarship and the understanding of Paul's faith language begins with Rudolf Bultmann, a German biblical theologian who carried forward some of Luther's thoughts (e.g., Luther's works/faith dichotomy), but also developed an existential interpretation of Scripture. In his *Theology of the New Testament*, Bultmann describes faith as "the attitude of man in which he receives the gift of 'God's righteousness' and in which the divine seed of salvation accomplished itself."[15] He contrasts this with his reading of Jewish thought, whereby *works* is central. Faith is closely related to divine revelation and an awakening knowledge, as the believer comes to a new understanding of self (cf. 2 Cor 4:6; 2:14). But that does not mean faith is *only* cognitive. Ultimately, for Bultmann, faith means acceptance of the gospel. Beyond merely mental assent, faith is *response* and even *obedience*.[16] Here Bultmann points to texts in Romans where Paul mentions a faith that is *observable* and lived out (1:5, 8; 16:19).[17]

Karl Barth engages with faith in the New Testament and specifically in Paul in a number of his works, especially his commentary on Romans (see chap. 9 below), but he gives focused attention to the topic in his *Church Dogmatics*.[18] Under the wider umbrella of "The Doctrine of Reconciliation," Barth treats subjects such as the fall and justification. The most concentrated

---

14. Calvin, *Institutes*, §3.36.

15. Rudolf Bultmann, *Theology of the New Testament*, 2 vols., trans. K. Grobel (New York: Scribner, 1951, 1955 (German original: *Theologie des Neuen Testament*, 2 vols. [Tübingen: Mohr Siebeck, 1948–53], 1.314).

16. Bultmann, *Theology of the New Testament*, 1.314. We can see, perhaps, Schlatter as an important influence on Bultmann. Adolf Schlatter's first major monograph was *Der Glaube im Neuen Testament* (Stuttgart: Calwer, 1883). Schlatter argues that Palestinian Jews believed that faith was focused on law obedience, which prioritized works, and that religion took precedence over trust in God. Jesus and Paul taught true faith that concentrated on transformation through encountering God in trust and obedience.

17. Bultmann, *Theology of the New Testament*, 1.318.

18. Karl Barth, *Church Dogmatics*, vol. 4.1: *The Doctrine of Reconciliation*, ed. G. W. Bromiley and T. F. Torrance (Edinburgh: T&T Clark, 1956).

discussions of faith appear in his essays "Justification by Faith Alone" and "The Holy Spirit and Christian Faith."[19] Ultimately, Barth views faith as a response to God.[20] But he can break this response down into four stages: (1) knowledge, which involves a true knowing of Jesus Christ and that he is *for me*; (2) recognition, more specifically the knowing of Christ that leads to a deeper self-recognition: "I see myself as the man I am irresistibly determined by Him, unmistakably stamped by Him, clearly set in His light from the depth, the lowest depth, in which I find myself in relation to Him";[21] (3) confession—public and honest proclamation of faith; and (4) faith as *act*.[22] Barth reminds his readers that mental faith, belief in the gospel of Jesus Christ (i.e., conversion), is certainly the center of faith, but it is not all we must say about faith. While conversion-faith is the center, "the center has a circumference."[23]

Probably one of the more distinctive aspects of Barth's approach to faith is the weight he gives to the notion of humility. By faith mortals are confronted with their own pride and recognize pride's emptiness and impotence. Pride corrupts, and "faith is the abdication of vain-glorious man from his vain-glory."[24]

Ernst Käsemann's approach to Paul's faith language is similar to Bultmann's—one might think about it as Bultmann transposed into an apocalyptic key. Like Bultmann, Käsemann regards Christian faith as a response and decision.[25] Käsemann is more comfortable defining faith as "the acceptance of the divine address."[26] His approach is more traditionally Lutheran with his unique eschatological twist: "The real point is the constantly new

---

19. Barth, *Church Dogmatics*, 4.1.608–42 and 4.1.740–80.

20. Here is one of his more detailed definitions: "The human action that makes a faithful and authentic and adequate response to the faithfulness of God, which does justice to the reality and existence of the justified man created by God's pardon, which meets with the divine approval in its suitability to this object, which is recognized and judged and accepted by Him as right, which therefore the knowledge of justification is a genuinely and concretely human event"; *Church Dogmatics*, 4.1.618.

21. Barth, *Church Dogmatics*, 4.1.770.

22. See Barth, *Church Dogmatics*, 4.1.758.

23. Barth, *Church Dogmatics*, 4.1.618.

24. Barth, *Church Dogmatics*, 4.1.618.

25. Ernst Käsemann, "The Faith of Abraham in Romans 4," in *Perspectives on Paul* (London: SCM, 1971), 79–101 at 83.

26. Käsemann, "Faith of Abraham," 83.

hearing of, and holding fast to, the divine Word, which drives us to constant exodus and always strains forward to what lies ahead, that is to say to God's future."[27] Furthermore, Käsemann underscores that true faith is not doctrinaire, nor is it static and parochial. And it is not something that mortals muster or create; rather, "we are called out of ourselves through God's Word and miracle."[28]

Günther Bornkamm, in line with both Bultmann and Käsemann, describes faith as responsiveness to the gospel.[29] He is insistent, though, that faith is a difficult subject to study on its own because Paul never defines it, and it cannot be treated as an act or disposition per se. It is a reaction to or inclination toward God.

Adolf Deissmann's analysis of Pauline faith is remarkably different than Bultmann's approach. Deissmann defines faith as "union with God which is brought about in the fellowship with Christ."[30] If Bultmann concentrated on responsiveness to God, Deissmann preferred the image of transformative participation: "'The faith of Christ' is the faith which is alive in the fellowship with the spiritual Christ, and it is 'faith-in-God' identical in content with the faith which Abraham in the sacred past had held, that is to say, unconditional trust in the living God in spite of all temptations to doubt."[31]

Joseph Fitzmyer, from a Catholic perspective, also views Pauline faith as an *experience* of God through Christ. With Rom 10 in mind, Fitzmyer describes faith as "an awareness of the difference the lordship of Christ has made in human history."[32] Furthermore, on an individual level faith is a "vital, personal commitment, engaging the whole person to Christ in all his or her relations with God, other human beings, and the world."[33] Again, like Deissmann, Fitzmyer bases this experience in "a new union with Christ," a reality that transcends what even the mind can believe, but transformative in such a holistic sense that the will is actively guided by faith.[34]

27. Käsemann, "Faith of Abraham," 84.
28. Käsemann, "Faith of Abraham," 84.
29. Günther Bornkamm, *Paul*, trans. D. M. G. Stalker (New York: Harper & Row, 1971), 141.
30. Adolf Deissmann, *St. Paul: A Study in Social and Religious History* (New York: Hodder & Stoughton, 1912), 143.
31. Deissmann, *St. Paul*, 142.
32. Joseph Fitzmyer, *Pauline Theology: A Brief Sketch* (Englewood Cliffs, NJ: Prentice-Hall, 1967), 84–85.
33. Fitzmyer, *Pauline Theology*, 85.
34. Fitzmyer, *Pauline Theology*, 85.

Douglas Moo offers his thoughts on faith language in the New Testament with a view toward early Christian use of Gen 15:6.[35] Moo draws a clear distinction between faith and obedience (though he finds the two related). Faith should not be treated as a virtue or act, but a trusting response to God.[36]

Similarly, Thomas Schreiner describes Pauline faith as a gift of God's grace such that one "rests on and believes in what God has accomplished through the crucified and risen Lord."[37] Good works cannot help one to attain a right standing with God. And yet genuine faith is bound to produce fruit in action and obedience.[38]

For what may appear to be an *opposite* perspective, we might appeal to Leander Keck. Keck (closer in thought to Käsemann) regards faith and obedience as nearly coterminous. But this does not assume obedience is a work. Instead, for faith to be the powerful thing it is (as a response to the gospel) it cannot help but have a totalizing effect on the believer. Keck, then, refers to faith as something inherently moral (perhaps even a virtue?): "It energizes the will no less than the mind or feelings; trust is a response of the whole self. When that response is to a word that makes a claim on the hearer, that response can be called obedience."[39]

Michael Wolter offers a rather detailed discussion of faith in his *An Outline of Paul's Theology*. First, he points out how Paul associates faith with the gospel of Jesus Christ (Gal 1:23; Phil 1:27) and the basic narrative of the Christ event (Rom 6:8; 10:9; 1 Thess 4:14).[40] Wolter makes a distinction between merely treating faith as the entry point into Christianity and the way faith is an ethos by which a Christian lives: faith and believing "connote not only the one-time event of conversion that comes about through affirmation of the proclamation of the gospel, but also the permanent adherence to this

---

35. Douglas J. Moo, "Genesis 15:6 in the New Testament," in *From Creation to New Creation: Biblical Theology and Exegesis: Essays in Honor of G. K. Beale*, ed. Daniel M. Gurtner and Benjamin L. Gladd (Peabody MA: Hendrickson, 2013), 147–62.

36. Moo, "Genesis 15:6 in the New Testament," 151.

37. Thomas Schreiner, *Magnifying God in Christ: A Summary of New Testament Theology* (Grand Rapids: Baker, 2010), 185.

38. See too Thomas Schreiner, "Justification apart from and by Works: At the Final Judgment Works Will Confirm Justification," in *Four Views on the Role of Works at the Final Judgment*, ed. Alan P. Stanley (Grand Rapids: Zondervan, 2013), 71–98.

39. Leander Keck, *Paul and His Letters* (Philadelphia: Fortress, 1979), 51.

40. Michael Wolter, *Paul: An Outline of His Theology* (Waco: Baylor University Press, 2015), 73.

affirmation."⁴¹ He refers to faith as a "permanent orientation of life" that goes beyond an individual disposition. Rather, it is necessarily "*community-founding*," a feature that Wolter argues is rather unique to the way Christians used faith language (compared to Jews and pagans in antiquity). By this he means that it was unusual in the first century for a group to co-identify exclusively on the basis of a shared set of religious beliefs.⁴² Evidence can be found throughout Paul's letters, but Wolter puts forward as an example Paul's use of the language of "household of faith" (Gal 6:10).⁴³

Wolter is interested not only in faith as ethos, but also the epistemological elements of Paul's use of πίστις/πιστεύω. He posits that the modern notion of faith as hesitancy rather than assurance is far from Paul's own conception. Faith is not belief without evidence; rather, Christian faith "views certain matters as genuinely factual because these matters—and this foundation makes its *assumption* of reality first and foremost a *certitude of faith*—coincide with reality according to God."⁴⁴ He also comments on how human faith relates to atonement in Paul. For Wolter, the act of Christ is salvific according to Paul, but it becomes a saving reality only when it is interpreted by faith as it "perceives the salvific character of Jesus's death and thereby puts its salvific efficacy into operation."⁴⁵

In his recent work on Paul and mission, Michael Gorman also gives direct attention to Paul's faith language.⁴⁶ Gorman criticizes the way that readers of Paul today often associate faith with intellectual assent only. He promotes the translation "faithfulness" or other robust glosses such as "be-

---

41. Wolter, *Paul*, 81.

42. "Faith is what the Christian minority has in common and what binds them together, and at the same time it denotes the decisive distinction between them and the mainstream social order"; Wolter, *Paul*, 82. Wolter argues that faith binds Christians together the way that Torah did for Jews; he cites as parallel evidence this statement from Josephus: "He receives (i.e., *the one who gives the law*) amicably all who wish to live with us under the same laws, because he intends that there be a membership in a household not only on the basis of lineage, but also on the basis of the way of life"; *Against Apion* 2.165; 2.210.

43. There are some similarities between Wolter's statement's and N. T. Wright's "covenantal badge" approach to human faith in Paul; see *Paul and the Faithfulness of God* (Minneapolis: Fortress, 2013), 848–49.

44. Wolter, *Paul*, 85.

45. Wolter, *Paul*, 105–6.

46. Michael J. Gorman, *Becoming the Gospel: Paul, Participation, and Mission* (Grand Rapids: Eerdmans, 2015).

lieving allegiance," "faithful allegiance," or "trusting loyalty."[47] In terms of definitions, Gorman writes that faith is "a posture of both heartfelt devotion and concrete commitment," a disposition closely in line with how Jews related to the God of Israel.[48] Gorman's reading comes at a time when several scholars are expressing interest in πίστις as an active virtue or way of being.

Here, then, we can also point to Matthew Bates's book *Salvation by Allegiance Alone*.[49] Bates's work is more general in orientation, covering the New Testament at large, but his study takes interest in Pauline language of faith. His approach to New Testament faith is centered on the story of Christ—especially his lordship, where it is natural then to think of his followers as those who profess allegiance (as to a king). Christians are, thus, called to embodied loyalty, not merely a mental assent we might call faith. Perhaps what is most distinctive about Bates's approach is the story-oriented contextualization of how New Testament writers (like Paul) used faith language and the holistic and especially political nature of this language—not politics in a formal sense, but the way πίστις is inevitably caught up in how one lives in relationship not only to Jesus Christ, but consequently to the whole world in everyday life.

Teresa Morgan's *Roman Faith and Christian Faith*

When I first began a conversation with a publisher about the idea of a book on πίστις in Paul, I stated, rather matter-of-factly, that the study of Paul's use of faith language has suffered serious neglect, and nothing very important had been written on the subject in many decades (aside from the πίστις Χριστοῦ debate, which tended to focus more on the genitive syntax of Χριστοῦ than the nature of πίστις itself). That was 2014, and since then a number of important studies have appeared (e.g., Bates's *Salvation by Allegiance Alone* and the multicontributor work *Glaube: Das Verständnis des Glaubens im frühen Christentum und in seiner jüdischen und hellenistisch-*

---

47. Gorman, *Becoming the Gospel*, 90–91.
48. Gorman, *Becoming the Gospel*, 91.
49. Matthew W. Bates, *Salvation by Allegiance Alone: Rethinking Faith, Works, and the Gospel of Jesus the King* (Grand Rapids: Baker, 2017)

römischen Umwelt).⁵⁰ But clearly the most important recent work on Paul's faith language is Teresa Morgan's *Roman Faith and Christian Faith*.⁵¹

When this work came out, I was very interested in Morgan's historical expertise and also her interpretation of Pauline and early Christian use of πίστις. It is important to begin by identifying how Morgan's project is different than my own. Her monograph has a much larger scale, covering basically the entire New Testament (and a bit later beyond as well). And it lumps sections of Pauline material together in cluster chapters. This makes it a bit difficult to compare our respective approaches on Paul and πίστις. I focus here on her context and background material and then give more attention to the sections specifically devoted to the undisputed Pauline epistles (212–306).

Morgan's primary research question is clear: "Why is faith so important to Christians?" (1); more specifically, "Why [did] *pistis* so quickly bec[o]me so important to the earliest followers of Jesus Christ that it already plays a key role in the [New Testament]?" (2). She criticizes popular assumptions that faith is essentially individualistic and propositional. She appeals to a historical approach to πίστις/*fides* that focuses on "the way the cluster of relationships and practices expressed through these lexica operate in the world into which early churches were born" (15). Setting the early Christian writings within the history and context of the Roman world of the early principate, she develops a sociology of πίστις, that is, how it functioned as a term pertaining to the establishment and mediation of relationships of all kinds and at all levels of life (120). She underscores how πίστις was a term that pervaded and undergirded the fabric of social life in the Greco-Roman world. That is, πίστις makes "possible new relationships and communities, new forms of action and social structures" (210). This was also the case within the Jewish communities of the Roman world. Morgan, with special attention to the Septuagint, argues that Jews used πίστις to reinforce the notion of obedience to God and "hope in what Israel's relationship with God will bring."

In her first main chapter on Paul ("*Pistis* and the Earliest Christian

---

50. Jörg Frey, Benjamin Schliesser, and Nadine Ueberschaer, eds., *Glaube: Das Verständnis des Glaubens im frühen Christentum und in seiner jüdischen und hellenistisch-römischen Umwelt*, Wissenschaftliche Untersuchungen zum Neuen Testament 373 (Tübingen: Mohr Siebeck, 2017).

51. Teresa Morgan, *Roman Faith and Christian Faith: Pistis and Fides in the Early Roman Empire and the Early Churches* (Oxford: Oxford University Press, 2016). Subsequent quotations from this source are noted by parenthetical page numbers.

Preaching") she focuses on 1 Thessalonians and 1–2 Corinthians. She observes that, while Paul encourages mutual πίστις among believers, priority is given to πίστις in the divine-human relationship, and that the encouragement of horizontal πίστις flows out of that fountainhead (215; cf. 218, 259). Thus, an "economy of *pistis*" emerges where "a faithful God calls his apostle to *pistis*; the faithful apostle, acting as God's intermediary, calls others to *pistis* toward God, who may themselves inspire yet others, by their example if not by active preaching" (217). Πίστις would have fit comfortably as a social term as Paul portrayed the church as a familial or householdlike community (220–21).

Morgan devotes some attention in this chapter to the nature of πίστις in early Pauline teaching. She argues that πίστις was not merely relational, but included "cognitive and affective aspects" (224, 225–26, 261). In summary she writes, "Early Christian preachers aim to change the hearts, minds, affiliations, and behavior of *hoi pisteuontes* and incorporate them into the household and kingdom of God and a loving, worshipping community on earth" (231).

Morgan's second major Pauline chapter groups together Galatians, Romans, Philippians, and Philemon; her comments on Galatians are the most weighty for her approach to πίστις overall. Here she reinforces how Paul prioritizes the divine-human relationship referring to a "hierarchy of trustworthiness which [πίστις] generates, descending from God through Christ, Paul himself, and those of his coworkers whom he characterizes as *pistoi*" (305). According to Morgan we find some unique developments in these latter epistles. For example, we find a works/faith contrast, but she rightly urges that this should not be read as a "hard antithesis" (270). One of the most important discussions in this chapter relates to πίστις Χριστοῦ in Galatians, Romans, and Philippians. Against the objective genitive interpretation, Morgan mentions (but does not rely too heavily on) the concern of redundancy in places like Gal 2:16. Overall, she finds the subjective genitive reading to be more natural but puts a bit of a spin on her version (see chap. 11 on πίστις Χριστοῦ in Paul). She reads Christ's πίστις ("faithfulness") as running in two different directions simultaneously, toward God *and* toward believers: "Christ is therefore at the centre of a nexus of divine-human *pistis*," thus giving Paul's πίστις a "Janus-faced quality" (273; cf. 272).

It is important to affirm that Morgan's monograph is an absolute treasure trove of historical and semantic riches on πίστις (and its cognates) and also a variety of other key terms she puts in context like δικαιοσύνη. She cogently argues that πίστις was a crucially important word in the Greco-Roman world, signaling networks of relationships of trust and mutuality, though they could function in many different ways based on the situation. When it comes to Paul, Morgan is certainly correct that Christ mediated divine πίστις toward believers, which was then *channeled* horizontally in the church.

I have one major concern with her work, one minor one, and some thoughts on where our separate approaches to Pauline πίστις might intersect and find some synergy. First, Morgan underdevelops the cognitive aspects of how Paul used the language of πίστις and πιστεύω. Clearly a cognition-oriented aspect of Pauline faith language can be detected in places like 2 Cor 4:4, 13; 5:7; and Rom 10:9–10. She overstates the matter with this summary: "Graeco-Roman, Jewish, and Christian sources alike take frustratingly little interest in exploring the nature and internal relationships of *pistis/fides* as an emotion, an act of cognition, and a virtue, and virtually never distinguish between interiority, relationality, and action in portraying its role in society" (472; cf. 455–88).

In her articulation of the interiority of πίστις, she devotes only a few pages to faith and cognition, and even then she does not treat Christian literature at all; and when it comes to Jewish literature she briefly mentions only Josephus.[52] This, to me, misses a crucial element of the dynamic way that Paul used faith language. Yes, the relational dimension is core, but how Paul relates πίστις to a transformed epistemology and a new form of wisdom (i.e., the mind of Christ) is also prominent. Perhaps Morgan underplays this aspect because she was strongly pushing against the propositional assumptions about faith that pervade popular readings of Paul, or because she argues that Pauline faith is not antirational. Where she fails to capture Paul's influences is in the Jewish prophetic and apocalyptic traditions (hence the importance of Isa 53:1) where God's people were called to faith in the invisible work of God—what I call "believing the unbelievable." Of course this feature is rather prominent precisely in those places where Paul was bent on conveying a transformed epistemology, as in 1–2 Corinthians.

Another small concern with Morgan's work is that she does not connect Jewish language of πίστις to Jewish covenant. As I argue in chapter 3, although πίστις doesn't actually *mean* "covenant," it seems to play a role in the Septuagint (and also in writers like Josephus) in referring to that kind of relational platform assumed by Jews. This would have helped Morgan because her articulation of Jewish and Pauline relationships of πίστις seem

---

52. Interaction with Philo would have been an obvious option (see *On the Life of Joseph* 100; *On the Life of Moses* 1.90; *On the Decalogue* 15); see Morgan, *Roman Faith and Christian Faith*, 455–58.

A Brief History

to mirror the same sorts of dynamics and assumptions made in Jewish covenant: cooperation, fidelity, obligation, and goodwill.

In terms of where our approaches to Paul might be brought into dialogue, I am intrigued with Morgan's take on πίστις Χριστοῦ. She leans toward the subjective view, while I lean toward the objective one, but I appreciate her willingness to step beyond the simplistic solutions inherited from the guild-created binary framework and articulate a position that puts Christ at the center but values his πίστις toward believers. By basically rejecting the role of human πίστις in πίστις Χριστοῦ in Galatians, Morgan is less convincing for the reasons proposed by Dunn and others, namely that Abraham is put forward as the exemplar of faith for believers and that Hab 2:4 (on what I consider a plain reading) is brought in to establish the same basic kind of personal relationship of trust in God that was also true of Abraham. Still, this issue notwithstanding, Morgan's take on πίστις Χριστοῦ is remarkably compatible with my view that what Paul refers to here, in a rather generic way, is the *Christ-relation*—that is, the mediatorial role that Christ plays in connecting God to his people—and my inclination is that Paul was intending to refer to the fact and efficacy of that relationship and not necessarily with specificity about which direction is more important.

Conclusion

This short chapter presents a brief and sweeping tour through many centuries of scholarship on faith language in Paul and the New Testament. Many theologians (like Clement and Ignatius) use πίστις in a way that I find similar to the nature and breadth of Paul's own usage. While faith is the term for how one responds to the gospel in belief and trust, these apostolic fathers are quite comfortable treating πίστις as a kind of virtue (not a work) comfortably paired with words like love and hospitality. With Augustine we see evidence of the beginnings of a shift toward a more cognitive use of faith language, emphasizing what the mind believes, and Augustine dwells on the friction between a faith approach to God and a works approach. Aquinas was even more narrowly interested in the cognitive and epistemological dimensions of faith.

Inspired in part by Augustine, Luther also dwells on faith as the illumination of the mind and heart by God to instill belief. In his unique context, though, Luther is also known for his clear delineation of justification by faith apart from works. But (especially in America) Pauline interpreters inherited Luther in such a way that we perhaps do not pick up on the participationistic dimensions of his theology of faith that can be identified even in his Galatians commentary. Throughout the modern period, it is clear that most scholars pick up on faith as a response to God, but some seem to dwell on cognitive transformation and others press more for faith as obedience. The next chapter goes all the way back to Paul's world and examines how πίστις was used in the Hellenistic literature of antiquity.

3 Πίστις in Ancient Non-Jewish and Jewish Literature

Faith Language in Antiquity

> If you want to, you shall preserve the commandments, and to maintain loyalty is a matter of your good pleasure [ἐὰν θέλῃς, συντηρήσεις ἐντολὰς καὶ πίστιν ποιῆσαι εὐδοκίας].
>
> —Ben Sira (Sirach 15:15 NETS)

> If there is room for observing the bond of trust even with one's greatest enemies, it must be most strictly applied to one's friends [ὡς ἥ γε πίστις ἔχουσα καὶ πρὸς τοὺς πολεμιωτάτους τόπον τοῖς γε φίλοις ἀναγκαιοτάτη τετηρῆσθαι].
>
> —Josephus (*Jewish Antiquities* 15.134, trans. Jan Willem van Henten)

We ought not to imagine that the apostle Paul was the first religious person to use πίστις in a meaningful way. While I argue later that Paul had a very distinctive and nuanced theology of faith, as it were, (other) Jews and pagans were as comfortable using this word, not least in relationship to social contexts, arguments, and ideas, as Paul was. Therefore, it behooves us to spend time becoming familiar with how all kinds of ancient people and texts used πίστις to get a feel for the range and popularity of its employment and also to focus more closely on Jewish usage. First we will offer some soundings in pagan Greek literature in regard to πίστις. Then we will turn to Jewish literature, examining the Septuagint, the Old Testament Pseudepigrapha, Philo, and Josephus. What we will find is that πίστις is a remarkably polyvalent word with several translations that can be appropriate depending on the context, meanings that include "opinion," "faithfulness," "pledge of trust," "trust," and "belief." The vast majority of its uses, though, in pagan and Jewish literature, relates to relational fidelity.

ΠΙΣΤΙΣ IN ANCIENT NON-JEWISH AND JEWISH LITERATURE

Pagan Hellenistic Literature

There are literally hundreds upon hundreds of appearances of πίστις in the extant Greek literature of antiquity, and it would be impossible and unnecessary to examine all of these. A great many of these texts are histories that include political and war material where πίστις involves alliances. I will focus on only one history, Dionysius of Halicarnassus's *Roman Antiquities*. Dionysius was born in the first century BCE and wrote his history of Rome shortly before the Common Era. He desired to pay tribute to the nobility of Rome and to persuade Greeks of the virtues of Roman leadership. Originally, Dionysius's document contained twenty books, but now less than half remain.[1]

Dionysius uses πίστις frequently in *Roman Antiquities* 11 as he recounts the end of the decemvirs with special interest in the misdeeds of Consul Appius Claudius Crassus. When Appius is brought before the Senate, he is warned against trickery and the dangers of entering into duplicitous agreements and πίστεις—secret pledges of loyalty (11.11.5).

One of the charges brought against Appius was that he had kidnapped the daughter of a centurion and passed her off as his slave. When this matter was brought to trial, πίστεις was also the term used for the offering of "proofs" in the case (11.34.5)

> When it came time for Appius to acquit himself, he made reference to his illustrious lineage and the many good services he had rendered to the commonwealth, appealing too to the oaths and pledges of good faith, on which men rely when accommodating their differences, [bringing forward] his children and relations, [displaying] even the humble garb of the suppliant, and doing many other things that move the multitude to compassion. (11.49.4, trans. Cary in LCL)

Later in book 11, Dionysius relates what happened after the dissolution of the decemvirs. Consulship passed to Marcus Genucius and Gaius Quintius. At this time the plebeians demanded that there be common voice in the consulship and not just that of patricians. This potentially volatile situation was interrupted by concerns that attacks were imminent from the Aequians and the Volscians. Immediately the Senate approved the dispatching of an army with the consuls in attendance. A plebian tribune, though,

---

1. For a helpful introduction to Dionysius and this work, see H. Hill, "Dionysius of Halicarnassus and the Origins of Rome," *Journal of Roman Studies* 51 (1961): 88–93.

opposed this course of action, seeing this as a deflection of their concerns. The Senate tried to reason with them, promising to return to this matter of consul representation when the threat had been dealt with, but the tribune was unrelenting. They urged that their consulship proposal be accepted provisionally before the army could be sent. Not only did they make this a concern in the Senate, but even in the general assembly of the people, "swearing the oath that to them is the most binding, namely by their good faith [πίστεως]" (ὅρκους, οἵπερ εἰσὶ μέγιστοι παρ' αὐτοῖς, κατὰ τῆς ἑαυτῶν πίστεως διομοσάμενοι; 11.54.4).

These examples from *Roman Antiquities* offer a few of the many shades of meaning of πίστις, especially how it can refer to commitments and vows, promises and pledges. It can also refer to a demonstration or proof in argumentation.

Plutarch's *Dialogue on Love* (*Amatorius*) contains a story narrated by Autobulus, Plutarch's son. The setting is the town of Thespiae where the newly married Plutarch carries on discussions about a wealthy widow (Ismenodora) proposing to a teenage ephebe.[2] At one point, Plutarch is in dialogue with a certain visitor on the matter of how Eros became divine and how society could attribute to love such incontrovertible powers. He makes this statement:

> Pemptides, it is, I believe, a grave and dangerous matter that you are broaching; or rather, you are altogether violating our inviolable belief in the gods when you demand an account and proof of each of them. Our ancient traditional faith is good enough [ἀρκεῖ γὰρ ἡ πάτριος καὶ παλαιὰ πίστις]. It is impossible to assert or discover evidence more palpable than faith.... This faith is a basis, as it were, a common foundation, of religion; if confidence and settled usage are disturbed or shaken at a single point, the whole edifice is enfeebled and discredited. (*Dialogue on Love* 756AB, trans. Helmbold in LCL)

It is fascinating how Plutarch refers to a set of beliefs as πίστις, a rare, but clear instance of religious faith.[3] He goes on to explain it as a foundation

---

2. See John M. Rist, "Plutarch's *Amatorius*: A Commentary on Plato's Theories of Love," *Classical Quarterly* 51 (2001): 557–75.

3. See Daniel Babut, "Du scepticisme au depassement de la raison: Philosophie et foi religieuse chez Plutarque," in *Parerga: Choix d'articles de D. Babut (1974–1994)* (Lyon: Maison de L'Orient Méditerranéen, 1994), 549–81; Benjamin Schliesser, "Faith

for religious piety (πρὸς εὐσέβειαν), recognizing the power it has to hold together a whole structure of religious thought (756B). Later there is mention of how one might appeal to mythology as evidence (πρὸς πίστιν) in the matter. Here Plutarch tells many fables and legends of the hypnotic power of love. He recounts how it is a cultural practice for lovers to visit the tomb of Iolaus, nephew and *eromenos* of Heracles. At his tomb lovers exchange "vows and pledges" (ὅρκους τε καὶ πίστεις) in honor of Iolaus (761E). In another discourse, Plutarch returns to the question of how it is possible that one can lose control of reason and moderation when in love:

> Is not this a plain case of divine possession? Is it not a supernatural agitation of the soul? Is the disturbance of the Pythia grasping her tripod so great? Do the flute, the tambourine, the hymns of Cybele, cause so much ecstasy in any of the devotees? (763A, trans. Helmbold in LCL)

How can it be that many have the same attractive features, but only a certain person is seized by love when looking at that one? It is for these reasons that Plutarch is convinced all over again of the divine influence of Eros. Yes, the senses do tell us scientific things, observable truths, he admits. But there are other ways of knowing. Plutarch states that belief (πίστις) is based on three elements: myth, law, and rational explanation. Put another way, we use our own mind and senses as teachers, but we also rely on legislators, poets, and philosophers for guidance (763C).

Later in the *Dialogue on Love*, Plutarch extols the virtues of love that are inspired by Eros. Among these values are unity and commonness, a reality of those who "though separated in body, forcibly join their souls and fuse them together, no longer wishing to be separate entities, or believing that they are so" (767E). Next, Plutarch refers to self-control and moderation,

---

in Early Christianity," in *Glaube: Das Verständnis des Glaubens im frühen Christentum und in seiner jüdischen und hellenistisch-römischen Umwelt*, ed. Jörg Frey, Benjamin Schliesser, and Nadine Ueberschaer, Wissenschaftliche Untersuchungen zum Neuen Testament 373 (Tübingen: Mohr Siebeck, 2017), 1–50 at 15; Rainer Hirsch-Luipold, "Religiöse Tradition und individuelle Glaube: Πίστις und Πιστεύειν bei Plutarch," in *Glaube*, ed. Jörg Frey, et al., 251–73 at 258–59; cf. also a critical discussion of πίστις in *Amatorius* in Françoise Frazier, "Returning to 'Religious' ΠΙΣΤΙΣ: Platonism and Piety in Plutarch and Neoplatonism," in *Saint Paul and Philosophy*, ed. Gert-Jan van der Heiden, George van Kooten, and Antonio Cimino (New York: de Gruyter, 2017), 189–208. Cf. also Gerhard Barth, "Pistis in hellenisticher Religiosität," *Zeitschrift für die neutestamentliche Wissenschaft* 73 (1982): 110–26.

a necessity of marriage. Eros values and inspires self-control insofar as he honors "mutual trust" (πίστεως μέτεστιν) between the lovers (767E).

A bit later, Plutarch expounds more directly on the subject of sexual love between men. He observes how, culturally, it is looked down upon to enjoy the position of being the "passive partner" and that such men are not considered worthy of friendship or confidence (οὔτε πίστεως μοῖραν οὔτ' αἰδοῦς οὔτε φιλίας νέμομεν; 768E). He goes on to talk about the difference between men-lovers and wives. Plutarch talks about marriage in such a way as to praise the beauty of a pledge of love and commitment found in marriage, a kind of friendship that transcends fleeting pleasure. Marriage daily calls for "respect and kindness and mutual affection and loyalty" (τιμὴ καὶ χάρις καὶ ἀγάπησις ἀλλήλων καὶ πίστις; 769A). Plutarch rejects here any notion that women are weak or incapable of trust and commitment. He asks, "What need is there to discuss their prudence and intelligence, or their loyalty and justice [πίστεως καὶ δικαιοσύνης], when many women have exhibited a daring and great-hearted courage that is truly masculine?" (769B). And again later, Plutarch stands by his argument that male union with woman through love is more powerful than attraction to "boy lovers," because one can enumerate so easily many successful marriages that demonstrate "every sort of fidelity and zealous loyalty" (πάσης πίστεως κοινωνίαν πιστῶς ἅμα καὶ προθύμως; 770C).

We can observe here in *Dialogue on Love* that Plutarch employs πίστις with a variety of nuances, sometimes meaning belief and at other times mutuality and loyalty in marriage.

In two consecutive discourses, *On Trust* and *On Distrust*, Dio Chrysostom instructs on the dangers of being a person who is entrusted with important things. By and large, Dio engages this matter with a focus on the verb πιστεύω.[4] This is telling, as the tendency is for πιστεύω to mean "believe," whereas here it obviously means "(en)trust." Due to this value of πιστεύω, Dio can alternate somewhat fluidly between πιστεύω and πίστις. At the outset, Dio wonders, "Shall we say that all those who were trusted [τοὺς πιστευομένους] themselves derived some good from the trust [τῆς πίστεως]?" (73.3). He proceeds to offer several examples of how various people suffered and were mistreated because of this trust. First he presents cases where being trusted led to the demise of public

---

4. *On Trust* 1: Ἆρά γε τὸ πιστεύεσθαι τοῖς πιστευομένοις ἀγαθόν ἐστι καὶ τοιοῦτον οἷον τὸ πλουτεῖν καὶ τὸ ὑγιαίνειν καὶ τὸ τιμᾶσθαι τοῖς τιμωμένοις καὶ ὑγιαίνουσι καὶ πλουτοῦσιν, αὐτοῖς ἐκείνοις τινὰ φέρον ὠφέλειαν;

figures. He offers the example of Nicias, son of Niceratus. Nicias was inspired to set out on a dangerous expedition because he was entrusted as a protector of his fellow citizens. He made this journey despite being ill, and Dio notes how he died because of this trust (διὰ τὴν πίστιν ταύτην; 73.7). Later Dio comments on private figures. Some might believe that it is far safer to be trusted (πίστις) as a private person—surely the risk is less (73.9). Yet, Dio argues, reality tells us of "untold trouble and labors" and plenty of ingratitude that await anyone in this position, including private citizens. Even if they were to be rewarded with money or goods, some might feel later on that they were overpaid!

In *On Distrust*, Dio indulges a bit of his dark side by arguing that humans cannot trust anyone; not enemies, of course, but neither can they trust friends, and not even themselves. Considering that some even commit suicide, "What kind of trust can one have in dealing with men like these?" (ποία δὴ πίστις πρὸς τοὺς τοιούτους; 74.5).

Later Dio mentions the case of a Spartan who was invited to a party and some guests asked him to make a pact of friendship. They presented the opportunity to name a guarantee (πίστιν) of his choosing. He replied:

> There was only one guarantee [πίστιν], namely, their inability to do harm even if they wished, but all other guarantees were foolish and absolutely good for nothing. That guarantee [πίστιν] alone should one accept from the masses, no other. For the guarantee which consists in phrases, in acquaintanceship, in oaths, in kinship is laughable.[5] (11–12, trans. Cohoon in LCL)

It should be no surprise that πίστις is found commonly in Greek papyri, especially in relation to business matters. For instance, O.Did 415 is a fragmentary letter to a certain Epaphroditos (Didymoi, near Egypt). The letter's author was clearly upset with Epaphroditos (Επαφροδιτω τω μη αξιω χαιρ[ειν]) for reasons not entirely clear, but the two engaged in several transactions. The author refers to broken agreements and a breach of trust (πίστις).[6] Second, famous for its reference to an enema-doctor (ἰατροκλύστης), P.Hib II 268 (260 BCE), another fragmentary document

---

5. μίαν ἔφη πίστιν εἶναι τὸ ἐὰν θέλωσιν ἀδικῆσαι μὴ δύνασθαι, τὰς δὲ λοιπὰς πάσας εὐήθεις καὶ τελέως ἀσθενεῖς. ταύτην μόνην παρὰ τῶν πολλῶν τὴν πίστιν δεῖ λαμβάνειν, ἑτέραν δὲ οὐδεμίαν. ἡ γὰρ ἐκ τῶν λόγων καὶ τῆς συνηθείας καὶ τῶν ὅρκων καὶ τοῦ γένους καταγέλαστος.

6. See Adam Bülow-Jacobsen, "Private Letters," in *Didymoi: Une garnison ro-*

Faith Language in Antiquity

(probably a bill), mentions a pledge/IOU (πίστις) for some purchased item. P.Bad. 2.35 is a note from a certain Johanna to an Epagathos (87 CE; Ptolemais Hermeiou). Epagathos broke a business agreement and Johanna wrote to demand that the principal be returned: "I am astonished that you have become faithless [θαυμαζο, πῶς τὴν πίστιν σου ἤλλαξαι]." Despite how upset Johanna is in this text (often subtitled in scholarship "full of reproaches"), she ends the letter with "above all, take care of yourself, so you may be well."[7]

In another personal letter, an unknown author writes to a certain Zenon, a sponsor, who is helping him to be in the good graces of Nikanor and Hakataios. The author notes how Nikanor was admitted to his full confidence (πᾶσαν πίστιν; P.Col. 4.64).[8] Yet another correspondence (P.Erasm. 1.1), addressed to King Ptolemy (and his queen), offers a plea to the sovereign to punish bad housing tenants, Herakleides and his "accomplice" Horion, for "breaking faith with the trust that adheres among men" (καὶ ἀθετήσας τὴν ἐν ἀνθρώποις ὑπάρχουσαν πίστιν).[9] If that weren't enough trouble, later these same men came to his house seeking a second time to get pledges (ἐνεχυρασίας) so they might rent the property again.

The short letter SB 14.12172, from Ptollas to Isas (7 CE), offers a reminder that Isas borrowed money but has not paid it for two years. Ptollas affirms that the funds were initially given knowing Isas was "trustworthy" (εἰδὼς τὴν σὴν πίστιν) and that he has been trusted to pay it back in full as a person of good faith (πιστὸν).[10]

This sampling opens a small window into daily life in antiquity where we find πίστις used in a variety of relationships, mostly business related, where trust is secured, kept, or broken.[11] The notion was probably widespread in

---

maine dans le désert oriental d'Égypte, vol. 2: *Les textes*, Fouilles de l'Ifao 67 (Cairo: Institut français d'archéologie orientale, 2012), 317–465 at 349–50.

7. Translation from Roger S. Bagnall and Raffaella Cribiore, *Women's Letters from Ancient Egypt, 300 BC–AD 800* (Ann Arbor: University of Michigan, 2006), 291.

8. http://papyri.info/ddbdp/p.col;4;64. See Peter Arzt-Grabner, "Zum alltagssprachlichen Hintergrund von Πίστις," in *Glaube: Das Verständnis des Glaubens im frühen Christentum und in seiner jüdischen und hellenistisch-römischen Umwelt*, ed. Jörg Frey, Benjamin Schliesser, and Nadine Ueberschaer, Wissenschaftliche Untersuchungen zum Neuen Testament 373 (Tübingen: Mohr Siebeck, 2017), 241–49 at 244.

9. http://papyri.info/ddbdp/p.erasm;1;1.

10. http://papyri.info/ddbdp/sb;14;12172.

11. The nuances of πίστις in pagan Greek literature are well documented and described by James H. Moulton and George Milligan, *The Vocabulary of the Greek Testament* (repr., Peabody, MA: Hendrickson, 1997 [originally 1930]), 515; and Ceslas

the Greco-Roman world, as we find cited in Epictetus, that society itself could not function without the virtue of πίστις.[12]

Hellenistic Jewish Literature: Septuagint and Pseudepigrapha

Examination of Hellenistic Jewish literature must begin with the Septuagint, because of the important role it played in the formation of early Judaism and early Christianity.[13] As observed in the introduction, the Septuagint translators chose to render Hebrew words like אמונה as πίστις, but sometimes as ἀλήθεια.[14] Given the meaning of πίστις in pagan literature, πίστις was a sensible choice.[15] In the Pentateuch, we find only one occurrence of πίστις, Deut 32:20, in the Song of Moses where a wicked generation of Israelites are called

---

Spicq, "Πίστις," in *Theological Lexicon of the New Testament*, ed. and trans. J. D. Ernest (Peabody, MA: Hendrickson, 1994), 3.110-17. Sometimes scholars try to distinguish between passive and active meanings of πίστις (i.e., πίστις as quality versus πίστις as behavior), but we do well to heed Spicq's comments: "In normal relationships, when πίστις is used, it is often impossible to distinguish between practical fidelity and good faith" (3.115).

12. Epictetus, *Discourses* 2.4: "Man is born for πίστιν ..., he who subverts fidelity subverts the peculiar characteristic of men" (2.4.1); and *Enchiridion* 24.4-5; as referenced in Suzan Sierksma-Agteres, "The Metahistory of Δικη and Πιστις," in in *Saint Paul and Philosophy*, ed. Heiden, et al., 209-30 at 219; cf. also Schliesser, "Faith in Early Christianity," 12.

13. See Dieter Lührmann, "Pistis im Judentum," *Zeitschrift für die neutestamentliche Wissenschaft* 64 (1973): 19-38; on the Septuagint esp. 20-25.

14. See Frank Ueberschaer, "Πιστις in der Septuaginta," in *Glaube: Das Verständnis des Glaubens im frühen Christentum und in seiner jüdischen und hellenistisch-römischen Umwelt*, ed. Jörg Frey, Benjamin Schliesser, and Nadine Ueberschaer, Wissenschaftliche Untersuchungen zum Neuen Testament 373 (Tübingen: Mohr Siebeck, 2017), 79-107 at 86-95.

15. Louis H. Feldman makes a rather bold—and overstated—claim about the Septuagint writers' choice of πίστις: "In rendering the word אמונה by πίστις, the Septuagint is using a word that in Plato's Republic (7.533E-34A), the most influential of philosophical works during the Hellenistic Age, refers to a mere opinion about real things and is, in fact, the next to the lowest degree of human knowledge"; *Judaism and Hellenism Reconsidered* (Boston: Brill, 2006), 60. More balanced is William S. Campbell's conclusion: "Because of the Romans' misconceptions about the meaning of faith, Paul's major concern in writing to them is with the nature of obedient faith. The translation of a Semitic faith into Hellenistic culture may have allowed the Romans to miss

out as faithless children (υἱοί οἷς οὐκ ἔστιν πίστις ἐν αὐτοῖς). In the historical books, there are about a dozen occurrences of πίστις in the Septuagint, mostly in 1–2 Chronicles. First Samuel 26:23 finds David offering this statement to Saul: "And the Lord will return to each his righteous deeds and his faith [πίστιν], as the Lord gave you into my hand today, and I did not want to bring my hand against the Lord's anointed" (1 Sam 26:23 NETS). Here πίστις has to do with covenant loyalty and relates to maintaining upright behavior in the eyes of the Lord. Extremely common in the historical books is the phrase ἐν πίστει, which is chosen to represent אמונה and sometimes functions as a kind of adverbial prepositional phrase meaning "honestly" or "faithfully" (2 Kgs 12:16). In 1–2 Chronicles, ἐν πίστει takes on the meaning "in [a position of] trust," approximating the way πίστις is used in Dio's discourse *On Trust* mentioned above (see 1 Chr 9:26, 31; 2 Chr 31:12, 15, 18; 34:12).

The poetic books of the Septuagint have another dozen occurrences of πίστις (see below). In Ps 32:4 LXX, God's work is described as being ἐν πίστει, that is, trustworthy or reliable. Proverbs underscores the importance of relational fidelity (3:3), and we see the regular pairing of mercy and loyalty (ἐλεημοσύναι δὲ καὶ πίστεις; 14:22; 15:27) and righteousness and loyalty (καρδίαι δικαίων μελετῶσιν πίστεις; 15:28).

In the prophetic books, we find πίστις mostly in Jeremiah (eight times). The Lord seeks anyone who "practices justice and seeks faithfulness" (ποιῶν κρίμα καὶ ζητῶν πίστιν; 5:1). The occurrence in 9:2 LXX seems closer to the meaning of truth: "And they bent their tongue like a bow; falsehood and not faith [ψεῦδος καὶ οὐ πίστις] grew strong in the land, because they proceeded from evil to evil, and me they did not know" (NETS). One final example is 40:6 LXX's vision of restoration, where the Lord exclaims, "Behold, I am bringing it soundness and healing, and I will make clear to them and heal it and make for them peace and trust [εἰρήνην καὶ πίστιν]" (NETS). The phrase εἰρήνην καὶ πίστιν functions like a hendiadys and means *covenantal peace*.[16]

In the so-called Apocrypha, we find πίστις several times in the Maccabean books. In 1 Macc 10:27, for example, Demetrius writes a letter to Jonathan urging him to maintain their alliance (νῦν ἐμμείνατε ἔτι τοῦ συντηρῆσαι πρὸς ἡμᾶς πίστιν). In 3 Macc 3:3 there is the pairing εὔνοιαν καὶ πίστιν, which is exceedingly common in pagan Hellenistic literature in

---

some of the content πίστις normally carried for those of Jewish background, familiar with the Septuagint"; *Unity and Diversity in Christ* (Cambridge: James Clarke, 2017), 65.

16. This sweeping survey is selective, but more information will be given on the infamous appearance of πίστις in Hab 2:4 in chap. 9 below.

histories and discourses in relation to political friendship. The most extensive usage is in 4 Maccabees. Toward the end of the book, the author praises the piety and courage of the famous mother of the seven Jewish martyrs. She is extolled for having the same mindset (ὁμόψυχον) as father Abraham (14:20). Though she had to endure witnessing the torture and execution of her beloved sons, she did not betray her piety (εὐσεβεία; 15:12). Again, she was forced to watch "the flesh of her children being consumed by fire, their toes and fingers scattered on the ground, and the flesh of the head to the chin exposed like masks" (15:15), but "devout reason, giving her heart a man's courage in the very midst of her emotions, strengthened her to disregard, for the time, her parental love" (15:23). Again, the author explains that she was able to overcome all of these obstacles and afflictions, physical and emotional, because of her faith in God (διὰ τὴν πρὸς θεὸν πίστιν; 15:24). One might equate πίστις here with some notion of belief, but given how πίστις is used in 4 Maccabees overall (cf. 16:22; 17:2), it apparently has more to do with a clash of cultures, and the mother's loyalty to Ἰουδαϊσμός (the Jewish way), which demonstrates piety, rather than a particular set of beliefs per se. Here the crux is not whether Yahweh is real or any given doctrine is true, but whether one is willing to die in allegiance to this god or forsake this deity in view of another.[17]

Aside from the singular occurrence in Wis 3:14,[18] the bulk of usage in the rest of the Apocrypha appears in Sirach. Ben Sira, the sage, offers numerous nuggets of wisdom about honest and shrewd friendship among mortals and the fundamental importance of true loyalty to God. As for the latter, Ben Sira echoes Prov 9:10 with the maxim, "For wisdom and education are the fear of the Lord, and his delight is fidelity and humility [πίστις καὶ πραότης]" (1:27 NETS slightly modified). Ben Sira affirms covenantal obedience by explaining, "If you want to, you shall preserve the commandments, and to

---

17. See Stefan Krauter, "'Glaube' im Zweiten Makkabäerbuch," in *Glaube: Das Verständnis des Glaubens im frühen Christentum und in seiner jüdischen und hellenistisch-römischen Umwelt*, ed. Jörg Frey, Benjamin Schliesser, and Nadine Ueberschaer, Wissenschaftliche Untersuchungen zum Neuen Testament 373 (Tübingen: Mohr Siebeck, 2017), 207–18 at 217.

18. "Blessed also is the eunuch whose hands have done no lawless deed, and who has not devised wicked things against the Lord; for special favor will be shown him for his faithfulness [γὰρ αὐτῷ τῆς πίστεως], and a place of great delight in the temple of the Lord."

keep faith is a matter of [one's own] good pleasure [πίστιν ποιῆσαι εὐδοκίας]" (15:15 NETS).[19]

On a more social level, Ben Sira also gives wise counsel, encouraging the reader to "gain your fellow's trust [πίστιν κτῆσαι] in poverty so that in his prosperity you may be filled as well; in a time of distress stay with him so that in his inheritance you may be a join heir" (22:23 NETS); and later, "He who reveals secrets has destroyed trust [ἀπώλεσεν πίστιν] and will never find a friend for his soul" (27:16 NETS).

Before turning to the Old Testament Pseudepigrapha, I mention again that Neh 10:1 LXX serves as a very insightful occasion where the translator made a choice to use πίστις in relation to the nature of the covenant with God. It is not so much that πίστις could *mean* covenant in a formal sense, but rather its meaning fits that notion of obligation, loyalty, and devotion that made sense within the Hellenistic cultural encyclopedia (more clearly than διαθήκη). Our select survey of the Septuagint usage of πίστις bears this out—the general tendency of the Septuagint translators was to prefer πίστις as the Greek word roughly equivalent to אמונה and אמן, offering that sense of "fest, sicher, zuverlaessig."[20]

In the Old Testament Pseudepigrapha, πίστις is found on occasion, especially in the Sibylline Oracles.[21] In the Testament of the Twelve Patriarchs, πίστις appears as a central priestly virtue alongside righteousness and truth and with the activities of (miraculous) testimony and prophecy (T. Levi 8.2). In an eschatological discourse, the Lord himself is prophesied as gathering together Israel in mercy and ἐν πίστει (T. Asher 7.7). The text known as Pseudo-Phocylides offers the insight of "Phocylides, the wisest of men" (1.13). Among its many sayings, we find "keep a deposit safe, and preserve

---

19. Patrick Skehan and Alexander A. Di Lella capture nicely the meaning of πίστις here: "To be faithful one must keep the Law and so do God's will. Faith in the biblical sense to the word implies not only an act of the intellect, which accepts God's word as true and normative, but also the activity of the will that puts belief into action"; *The Wisdom of Ben Sirach* (New Haven: Yale University Press, 2007), 272.

20. Hans Wildberger, "Glauben, Erwägungen zu האמין," in *Hebräische Wortforschung: Festschrift für W: Baumgartner*, Vetus Testamentum Supplement 16 (Leiden: Brill, 1967), 373. Takamitsu Muraoka offers two meanings for πίστις: "loyalty" and "faith/trust" (559); *A Greek-English Lexicon of the Septuagint* (Louvain: Peeters, 2009), with a submeaning under "faith/trust" of "behaviour, attitude or deed which inspires trust" (such as Jer 9:3 LXX).

21. Given the complex and uncertain Christian influence on the extant Sibylline Oracles, I will not discuss how the oracles use πίστις.

loyalty in everything" (13).²² One of the final sentences of Pseudo-Phocylides emphases friendship: "Love your friends until death; for faithfulness is better [πίστις γὰρ ἀμείνων]" (218).

Hellenistic Jewish Literature: Philo

Jewish philosopher and exegete Philo of Alexandria used πίστις extensively in his massive body of work that exists today, and his usage is more varied than that found in the Septuagint and the Pseudepigrapha.²³ Philo could use πίστις with the common meaning of proof (*Allegorical Interpretation* 3.208) and with the basic sense of loyalty (*On Drunkenness* 40, where it is juxtaposed with ἀπιστία). He sometimes plays on multiple meanings of πίστις even in the same sentence; for example, in *On the Life of Abraham* 273 with the meaning faith and then pledge. In *On the Life of Joseph* 258, the patriarch is praised for demonstrating "excessive good faith and honesty in all his dealings [τοσαύτῃ πίστεως ἐχρήσατο ὑπερβολῇ]" (trans. Yonge), such that it is no wonder he was blessed with unparalleled wealth.

In a different tractate, Philo comments on the interpretation of the Decalogue, and in regard to the fourth word (on false testimony) he lists the vices that belong in this category: "Of not deceiving, of not bringing false accusations, of not co-operating with those who are committing sins, of not making a pretense of good faith a cloak for faithlessness [τὸ μὴ ποιεῖσθαι προκάλυμμα πίστιν ἀπιστίας]" (*On the Decalogue* 172).²⁴

---

22. My translation, based on insights from Walter T. Wilson, *The Sentences of Pseudo-Phocylides* (Berlin: de Gruyter, 2005), 92.

23. See Martina Böhm, "Zum Glaubensverständnis des Philo von Alexandrien," in *Glaube: Das Verständnis des Glaubens im frühen Christentum und in seiner jüdischen und hellenistisch-römischen Umwelt*, ed. Jörg Frey, Benjamin Schliesser, and Nadine Ueberschaer, Wissenschaftliche Untersuchungen zum Neuen Testament 373 (Tübingen: Mohr Siebeck, 2017), 159–81. David Hay helpful offers insight into Philo's use of πίστις: Philo most commonly uses it with the meaning "evidence" but also belief, trust, pledge, loyalty, and a few other nuances; see "Pistis as 'Ground for Faith' in Hellenized Judaism and Paul," *Journal of Biblical Literature* 108 (1989): 461–76; esp. 463.

24. My preferred translation here is from Yonge, but Colson's footnote in LCL on this is worth reading: "I understand this to refer to cases where a man repays a small sum or returns a small deposit in order to induce the other party to entrust him with something greater which he can embezzle.... Possibly, however, it may refer more generally to the false assumption of a truthful air" (91).

Faith Language in Antiquity

On occasion, Philo has opportunity to mention the practice of benefaction and the moral obligation of loyalty. He offers the example of the Xanthians, who refused to side with Brutus after he murdered Julius Caesar. The Xanthians did not give in when Brutus aggressively attacked them. Rather, they endured horrific slaughter but met their end "with a noble and free spirit" for the sake of "freedom and loyalty" (ὑπὲρ ἐλευθερίας ἅμα καὶ πίστεως; see *That Every Good Person Is Free* 118, trans. Yonge). Elsewhere Philo stresses how important it is that loyalty is treated as a virtue all by itself, not simply as a means to some sort of personal gain (*On Planting* 101). He refers to πίστις as "the queen of all the virtues" (*On the Life of Abraham* 270, trans. Yonge).

There are several instances where Philo uses πίστις in reference to belief in God (e.g., *On the Cherubim* 85; *On the Change of Names* 201; *On the Life of Abraham* 268). In *On the Confusion of Tongues* 31 Philo examines Deut 5:31, where the Lord says to Moses, "Stand here with me." Philo interprets this statement as having a meaning beyond location. For Moses to stay put, to stand still, involves the soul's confidence in the Lord, able to don "that surest and most stable quality, faith [ἀποδυσάμενος τὴν ὀχυρωτάτην καὶ βεβαιοτάτην διάθεσιν, πίστιν]."[25] In his study of Gen 15:5, Philo addresses the matter of divine promises from God relating to Abraham's future and family. Abraham, not knowing what will happen in the present, must trust God; this an example of faith by which the soul believes in God with expectation and hope (*On the Migration of Abraham* 43). Elsewhere Philo handles the faith of Abraham again, calling πίστις the greatest of virtues (*Who Is the Heir?* 91) and claiming that only the pure mind can attain to "believ[ing] in the only true and faithful God" (93, trans. Yonge). What did it mean for Abraham's faith to be counted as righteousness? Philo explains: "Nothing is so righteous as to have an unalloyed and entire belief in the only God" (94, trans. Yonge). Again, he can explain that religious piety toward God requires three things (like a ring, armlet, and staff): faith (πίστις), symbiotic union between thought and action, and a proper education (*On Flight and Finding* 152). He contrasts these with things that destroy true piety, namely faithlessness (ἀπιστία), the mismatch between thought and action, and ignorance. We see, perhaps, the most suprarational use of πίστις by Philo in a discourse where he likens the race of the son of promise, Isaac, to the person who

---

25. That this happens to be a more cognitive use of πίστις can be demonstrated by Philo's contrasting faith with doubt and hesitation, which he considers "qualities of the unstable mind" (*On the Confusion of Tongues* 31).

shows true faith in God, insight and belief that involves rationality that is not dependent on the senses (πρὸς θεὸν πίστεως καὶ ἀφανοῦς ὑπολήψεως; *On Dreams* 1.68); hence, such a one can be called "self-taught" (αὐτομαθής; 1.68; cf. *On the Life of Moses* 1.280).[26]

Hellenistic Jewish Literature: Josephus

Because Josephus's use of πίστις is especially interesting and historically important for the study of Paul, it will be beneficial and necessary to examine his work closely. No one has done more work on Josephus's use of πίστις than Dennis R. Lindsay, especially in his monograph *Josephus and Faith*.[27] Lindsay isolates six uses of πίστις in Josephus: (1) trust, faith, confidence, (2) loyalty, fidelity, (3) pledge that gives rise to confidence or trust, (4) that which is entrusted, (5) a treaty or other assurance of political protection, and (6) belief (in the specific sense of credibility).[28] It should be rather obvious by now that this is in line with wider Hellenistic use of πίστις.[29]

In *The Life*, we find the expected use of πίστις whereby it pertains to political fidelity, as in promised loyalty to Rome (τὴν πρὸς Ῥωμαίους πίστιν; *Life* 39)—this is the dominant meaning in the many instances of πίστις in this text. In *Against Apion* he can use πίστεις in reference to arguments

---

26. Böhm, "Zum Glaubensverständnis des Philo," 165.

27. Dennis R. Lindsay, *Josephus and Faith: Πίστις and Πιστεύειν as Faith Terminology in the Writings of Flavius Josephus and in the New Testament* (Boston: Brill, 1993). See too Dennis R. Lindsay, "Πίστις in Flavius Josephus and the New Testament," in *Glaube: Das Verständnis des Glaubens im frühen Christentum und in seiner jüdischen und hellenistisch-römischen Umwelt*, ed. Jörg Frey, Benjamin Schliesser, and Nadine Ueberschaer, Wissenschaftliche Untersuchungen zum Neuen Testament 373 (Tübingen: Mohr Siebeck, 2017), 183–205.

28. Lindsay, "Πίστις in Flavius Josephus," 185. This also mirrors rather closely the conclusions made by Douglas Campbell in relation to Philo and Josephus. Campbell offers these meanings: (1) fidelity or faithfulness, (2) pledge (whether a token of fidelity or something entrusted—in concrete terms quite different entities), (3) trust, (4) belief, (5) proof, and (6) the supervirtue faith (far less commonly). The last of these he also calls the "over-arching virtue." Obviously some of these are more prominent in Philo than Josephus; see *The Quest for Paul's Gospel: A Suggested Strategy* (London: T&T Clark, 2005), 180.

29. So states Campbell, *Quest for Paul's Gospel*, 185.

or logical propositions (1.72) or testimonials (2.18). When talking about πίστις as a social quality, he can draw it into association with virtue (ἀρετή) and graciousness (ἐπιείκεια) (2.42-43). In a discourse in which Josephus praises the wisdom of Moses (likening him to the judicious Minos among the Greek), he explains how Moses had the belief (πίστις) that *his* God was the author of the best laws (2.163). In fact, so convincing was Moses in teaching his fellow people the laws of this God that he "so firmly imprinted this faith in God [περὶ θεοῦ πίστιν] upon all their posterity, that it never could be moved" (2.169).

In *Jewish Antiquities*, there are several more interesting case studies. In reference to the relationship between Joseph and Mariamne, he makes mention of a great trust that had developed between them (μεγάλης αὐτοῖς πίστεως ἐγγενομένη; 15.87). In a discussion of Herod, Josephus talks about his thin skin and his domineering form of governance; how he would dress up in the guise of plebian attire and mingle with common folk to catch word of how they felt about his rule (15.366). For those who openly opposed him, Herod prosecuted them. Overall, his modus operandi was to demand from his subjects oaths of loyalty (ὅρκοις πρὸς τὴν πίστιν) and bound pledges of goodwill (εὔνοιαν; 15.368). Josephus does not shy away from telling us that many indeed offered such allegiance, some out of the hope of political gain, others of fear. There were some, of course, who opposed Herod, but he found a way to get rid of them (15.369). In all these examples, not unlike Plutarch and Philo, Josephus could alternate rather comfortably between social-relational uses of πίστις and more cognitive ones.

An interesting phenomenon that occurs in Josephus's *Jewish Antiquities* involves the use of the plural πίστεις in relation to various contracts and pledges of fidelity that occur on the personal level in the story of Israel and its important leaders. For example, in 1 Sam 20 we find the story of the special bond between Jonathan and David that is called a διαθήκη in the Septuagint (20:8). In the narration of the same general story, Josephus represents this with πίστεις (*Jewish Antiquities* 6.228). It is not that Josephus is averse to using διαθήκη; he does so dozens of times in *Jewish Antiquities*. But, as C. T. Begg explains, because covenant was not a concept that pagans readily understood, Josephus was able to use the very common notion of reciprocal pledges (πίστεις) to approximate the concept of covenantal commitment.[30]

30. Christopher T. Begg, *Josephus' Account of the Early Divided Monarchy (AJ*

Similarly, Josephus refers to a story about Abner and David from 2 Sam 3:12 (*Jewish Antiquities* 7.24). According to the Septuagint, Abner sent messengers to form a covenant (διαθήκη) between Abner and David; Josephus here represents this story with πίστεις, rather than διαθήκη. Another example appears in *Jewish Antiquities* 10.63, which describes how King Josiah called together all the people of Israel, especially the Levites and priests, and compelled them to make "oaths and agreements" (ὅρκους ποιήσασθαι καὶ πίστεις) that they would worship God and keep the laws of Moses (cf. 2 Kings 23:3 // 2 Chron 34:31). Both 2 Kgs 23:3 and 2 Chron 34:31 have διαθήκη, but Josephus prefers πίστεις to communicate the same idea of sworn loyalty. In all these cases, Josephus made a conscious decision *not* to use διαθήκη. The obvious reason for this is that Josephus uses διαθήκη with the meaning "will" (e.g., *Jewish Antiquities* 13.349; 17.1, 53, 78, 146). Josephus was much more comfortable using συνθήκη, as it conventionally carried the meaning "agreement" or "pact." In fact, Josephus's use of συνθήκη seems to be identical to his (sociopolitical) use of πίστεις.

Josephus did not use the language of covenant (in Greek) to talk about Israel's relationship with God, nor did most other Jewish writers in antiquity.[31] Terminologically, this appears to be correct, and a reading of *Jewish Antiquities* bears this out. Therefore, it is difficult to prove that Josephus or any other Jew of his time thought about *one* covenant of Israel with God. In relation to material found in *Against Apion*, John Barclay offers a helpful analysis of how Josephus seems to have understood, or at least portrayed, Jewish identity publicly. Barclay offers several features that constituted Jewish identity, including common ancestry and history, focus on a particular territory (i.e., Judea), a historically Jewish language (Hebrew), a common set of sacred texts, and a centralized temple.[32] Finally, Barclay mentions that Jews shared a unique πολίτευμα,

---

8,212–420) (Leuven: Peeters, 1993), 100–101n609. Lester Grabbe also addresses this matter: "This lack of reference to the biblical covenants [in Josephus] appears very puzzling at first sight. There was plenty of opportunity for Josephus to refer to the various Old Testament covenants, but he avoids them all. One has to conclude that this is deliberate"; "Covenant in Philo and Josephus," in *The Concept of the Covenant in the Second Temple Period* (Boston: Brill, 2003), 251–66 at 257.

31. Grabbe, "Covenant in Philo and Josephus," 258–66.

32. John M. G. Barclay, *Flavius Josephus: Translation and Commentary*, vol. 10: *Against Apion* (Boston: Brill, 2007), lvii–lviii.

which he translates "constitution" (with Moses as the legislator, so to speak). Josephus utilized this political language to portray the life of the Jewish people so as to compare them to Greeks. One important feature of Josephus's description in *Against Apion*, though, is the way that he refers to their government as a "theocracy" (θεοκρατία; *Against Apion* 2.165): God is the highest authority for Jews, Josephus explains, worthy of highest esteem, author of all good things, and the one who answers prays offered by the needy. Furthermore, God sees all, not only actions, but internal dispositions and thoughts as well (2.165–66).

Overall, Barclay explains how Josephus worked hard to describe Jewish life using terms and concepts familiar to Greeks, and it is for this reason that we do not read of a covenant with God.[33] Thus, Barclay urges that Josephus describes Jewish collective identity as a "constitutional nomism" rather than a "covenantal nomism."[34] Paul Spilsbury offers a similar portrayal of how Josephus explains the Jews' relationship with God. Instead of using the language of constitution, Spilsbury frames it in terms of the scheme of Roman patronage. In *Jewish Antiquities* and *Against Apion* especially, Spilsbury suggests that Josephus preferred *not* to use the construct of covenant because he wished to portray the God-Israel relationship as one of patron and client: "In Josephus' view, God functions as Israel's patron by offering numerous benefactions including military alliance and, most importantly, the Law of Moses. As God's favored client Israel is required to express profound gratitude for this benefaction by a life of piety which is defined quite explicitly as obedience to the Law of Moses."[35]

Spilsbury, like Barclay, finds that Sanders's covenantal-nomism pattern is too imprecise for what we see in Josephus; Spilsbury thinks that a proper modification would be "patronal nomism." This suggests that Josephus was interested in transposing traditional Jewish language (of covenant) into a Greco-Roman key.[36] Spilsbury offers sufficient reasoning for why Josephus

---

33. Barclay, *Against Apion*, lx. Grabbe comes to similar conclusions, explaining that Josephus directed his works toward Greco-Roman readers and referencing "covenants would not serve his purposes and might be misunderstood"; "Covenant in Philo and Josephus," 266.

34. Barclay, *Against Apion*, lx.

35. Paul Spilsbury, "Josephus," in *Justification and Variegated Nomism: The Complexities of Second Temple Judaism*, ed. D. A. Carson, Peter T. O'Brien, and Mark Seifrid (Grand Rapids: Baker, 2001), 241–60 at 250; cf. 259.

36. Spilsbury proposes that, by avoiding tradition Jewish covenantal language,

may have preferred Greco-Roman language of political alliance over Jewish covenantal language. Begg presents further ideas.[37] First, the Greek language of διαθήκη carried the meaning "will" (not "covenant") in the common vocabulary of pagans. Second, Begg mentions (as Spilsbury does) the dangers of using exclusive political language that might look suspicious, though Begg considers the possibility that Josephus was concerned with the dangerous ways that *Christians* were using "new covenant" language. Begg observes that in Greek Jewish translations of the Old Testament after the first century CE διαθήκη is largely absent (replaced by circumlocutions). One of the implications that we can draw from this is that Josephus felt comfortable using πίστεις in relation to covenant or covenantlike language in the Old Testament. This was not an arbitrary decision, but guided by a desire to communicate clearly and convincingly to a Hellenistic audience using familiar language of concord and obligation. This insight will be instructive for the way Paul used πίστις language, in the ways he talked about πίστις as a virtue, the πίστις of God or Christ, and πίστις as a way of relating to God.

Conclusion

These soundings in pagan and Jewish use of πίστις help us better understand the world and culture in which the apostle employed faith language. First, there is a popular misunderstanding that this was primarily religious language, but this is obviously not true. Second, it is often argued that Paul used faith language to oppose his Jewish or Jewish Christian opponents' theology of works (or Torah works), but Jews could easily use πίστις to talk about their religious commitments and obligations.[38] While Paul's use of πίστις became distinctive, it did not emerge ex nihilo.

In part because of the Septuagint writers' selection of πίστις for אמונה, and in light of Josephus's intentional preference for πίστεις to approximate or portray Jewish covenantal commitment, we can begin to rethink Paul's

---

Josephus may have skirted any whiff of militaristic messianism; "Josephus," 252.

37. Begg, *Josephus' Account of the Early Divided Monarchy*, 100–101n609.

38. See Lührmann, "Pistis im Judentum," 36: "Im Judentum selber assoziiertdas Wort den Zusammenhang von Gesetz und Treue gegenüber demGesetz als dem Spezifikum der Gottesverehrung, während in der Mission das stichwort »Glaube« diesen Zusammenhang nicht unmittelbar benennen konnte."

use of πίστις, particularly how he used this language to talk about a new type of relationship with God, a new covenant we might say, that occurs via the Christ-relation. While this chapter plays the important role of contextualizing Paul's use of πίστις, it is especially important context and history for what we discuss in chapter 8 in regard to πίστις in Galatians.

4 Will He Find Faith on Earth?

Faith Language in the Jesus Tradition

> Who has believed our message,
> and to whom has the arm of the LORD been revealed?
>
> —John and Isaiah (Isa 53:1 as cited in John 12:38 NIV)
>
> When the Son of Man comes, will he find faith [πίστιν] on earth?
>
> —Jesus (Luke 18:8 NIV)

What were the major influences on Paul's faith language? We can readily see how Paul points to texts like Hab 2:4 to talk about the nature of justification by πίστις (Gal 3:11; Rom 1:17). These matters have been considered by other scholars as impactful on how Paul reflected on the centrality of faith. What is less often discussed is the potential influence of the Jesus tradition on Paul's faith language.[1] Probably a central reason why there is neglect in this area is that Paul's letters predate the composition of the Gospels as we have them. Still, it would be irresponsible not to consider how Paul may have been drawn to faith language because of the way Jesus used such language.

Repent and Believe: Faith Language in Mark

We begin our look at faith language in the Jesus tradition with Mark, since it is probably the earliest extant Gospel. Mark begins his story of Jesus with the belief-centered preaching of Jesus. After John the Baptist was arrested, Jesus

---

1. Maureen W. Yeung, *Faith in Jesus and Paul* (Tübingen: Mohr Siebeck, 2002); cf. Teresa Morgan, *Roman Faith and Christian Faith: Pistis and Fides in the Early Roman Empire and the Early Churches* (Oxford: Oxford University Press, 2015), 347–48.

went to Galilee and proclaimed the good news of God: "The time is fulfilled, and the kingdom of God has come near; repent, and believe in the gospel" (Mark 1:15 NRSV margin). This is the summons of a prophet, urging Israel to turn from sin and return to God.[2] Jesus was carrying forward John the Baptist's message in his absence.[3] He was calling Israel to "abandon a whole way of life, and to trust him for a different one."[4] A new era had dawned, and the rule of God was imminent—participants were inspired to repent, not necessarily because their sins compelled them to, but because God was fulfilling the promise of his reign on earth.[5] John, though, preached repentance but did not call for *belief*.

In the Old Testament, when repentance was urged, the counterpart for turning away from sin would naturally be to commit to God and to do what is right (Jer 34:15; Ezek 18:21). Jesus does not say "repent and *obey* God" but rather "repent and *believe* the good news." That Israel had to *believe* this seems to imply that it was not a matter of accepting a plain fact. It would take *belief*, a suprarational leap of faith, as it were, to live into a reality that Jesus was "the one who discloses God's sovereignty" and that one must respond to him with trust and obedience to the expectations of the kingdom he was inaugurating.[6] As Frank Matera explains, there is a critical *epistemological* quality to the way Mark expresses the nature of faith:

---

2. See Craig A. Evans, "Prophet, Sage, Healer, Messiah: Types and Identities of Jesus," in *Handbook for the Study of the Historical Jesus*, ed. Tom Holmén and Stanley E. Porter (Leiden: Brill, 2010), 1219–22; R. T. France, *The Gospel of Mark*, New International Greek Testament Commentary (Grand Rapids: Eerdmans, 2002), 93. On the subject of repentance and how it relates to faith, see Mark J. Boda, *"Return to Me": A Biblical Theology of Repentance* (Downers Grove IL: InterVarsity, 2015), 163–64, 184 (more generally 145–61 on the theology of repentance in Scripture).

3. See W. D. Davies and Dale C. Allison, *Matthew* (Edinburgh: T&T Clark, 1988), 1:72.

4. N. T. Wright, *Jesus and the Victory of God* (Minneapolis: Fortress, 1996), 258. Wright makes a good case for this nationalistic reading of Jesus's repentance-call, but less convincing is his more specific argument that the problem was "nationalistic violence" (253).

5. See Guy D. Nave, *The Role and Function of Repentance in Luke-Acts* (Leiden: Brill, 2002), 132.

6. See Christopher D. Marshall, *Faith as a Theme in Mark's Narrative* (Cambridge: Cambridge University Press, 1994 [originally 1989]), 44–56 at 54; also Wright, *Jesus and the Victory of God*, 263; Frank Matera, *New Testament Ethics: The Legacies of Jesus and Paul* (Louisville: Westminster John Knox, 1996), 22.

Faith, in Mark's Gospel, is not merely one virtue among others. In the Markan narrative, it is the all-embracing term that describes the moral and ethical life of those who embrace the kingdom of God. Faith is perceiving and understanding, whereas the lack of faith is blindness and incomprehension. Those who believe, perceive, and understand what Jesus says and does can see the presence of God's kingdom in his ministry even though the manifestation of the kingdom is presently hidden and seemingly insignificant. Convinced that the kingdom of God is present, although not yet in power, such people live lives of discipleship in a community of disciples gathered around Jesus. Within Mark's Gospel, people believe in order to see.[7]

For Mark, though, πιστεύω means more than simply *believing* in the good news of the kingdom of God; it also implies immersing oneself wholeheartedly into this good news, tethering oneself to it.[8] As Jack Dean Kingsbury aptly puts it, for Mark "faith connotes radical confidence, an unconditional turning toward the gospel in complete trust."[9]

Seek, Trust, and Obey: Faith Language in Matthew

Matthew shares Mark's interest in the faith language of Jesus.[10] Several episodes and teachings of Jesus are parallel, such as the link between healing and faith in particular miracle stories (cf. Matt 9:2–8 // Mark 2:1–12; Matt 9:18–26 // Mark 5:21–43; Matt 15:21–28 // Mark 7:24–30). Matthew also includes the statement about faith in relation to the cursing of the fig tree (Matt 21:18–22 // Mark 11:20–26). Matthew, though, also inserts faith-miracle episodes not included in Mark (e.g., Matt 9:27–31). Matthew offers a similar storm-stilling episode as Mark, but famously Jesus questions his disciples' meager faith in Matthew (ὀλιγόπιστος; Matt 8:26), whereas Mark's Jesus accuses them of having *no* faith (οὔπω ἔχετε πίστιν; Mark 4:40).

---

7. Matera, *New Testament Ethics*, 23.
8. See France, *Mark*, 94.
9. Jack D. Kingsbury, *The Christology of Mark's Gospel* (Philadelphia: Fortress, 1983), 73.
10. Mary Ann Beavis's excellent short essay on faith in Mark's Gospel underscores this point cogently, although she goes too far in assuming that Matthew and Luke contribute little to the notion of faith in the Synoptics; see "Mark's Teaching on Faith," *Biblical Theology Bulletin* 16 (1986): 139–42.

Faith Language in the Jesus Tradition

If we presuppose as true in Matthew what we identified in Mark—despite more specific nuances to faith language in the Gospel—there is a kind of comprehensive connection made between the good news of Jesus Christ and faith (e.g., Mark 1:14–15). This seems to be implied in Matt 27:42, where the mockers in the crowd jeer at Jesus: "He saved others; he cannot save himself. He is the King of Israel; let him come down now from the cross now, and we will *believe* in him [πιστεύσομεν ἐπ' αὐτόν]" (NRSV). This may be what the crowd said, or perhaps it was something similar and Matthew reframed it in terms of Christian confessional language.[11] Such brief glimpses of belief in Jesus language (cf. Matt 18:6) offers an important reminder that Matthew saw, as the ultimate expression of Christian spirituality, faith in Jesus that was evident in wholehearted discipleship.[12]

Matthew's conception of faith falls into three categories: seeking faith, trusting faith, and loyal faith.

Seeking Faith

Of the seven key episodes where Matthew focuses his faith language, five of them involve the faith of those who seek out Jesus and desire healing/help from him for someone (8:5–13; 9:2–8; 9:18–26; 9:27–31; 15:21–28). As often noted, this πίστις is not the fully formed faith of a disciple of Jesus. Rather, these are people who seek Jesus out as someone who has the power of God at his disposal.[13]

The very first occurrence of πίστις in Matthew is in the story of the healing of the centurion's servant. When Jesus agrees to come and heal this paralyzed man, the centurion stops him: "Lord, I am not worthy to have you come under my roof, but only speak the word, and my servant will be healed. For I also am a man under authority, with soldiers under me; And I say to one, 'Go,' and he goes, and to another, 'Come,' and he comes, and to my slave, 'Do this,' and the slave does it" (Matt 8:8–9 NRSV). Jesus was amazed

---

11. See Davies and Allison, *Matthew*, 3.620; they note similar language in Acts 11:17; 16:31; 1 Tim 1:16.

12. France points to the clear, but unusually rare, Johannine-like quality of belief in Matt 18:6—the only time this specific phrasing occurs in the Synoptic Gospels; *The Gospel according to Matthew*, New International Commentary on the New Testament (Grand Rapids: Eerdmans, 2007), 681.

13. See James D. G. Dunn, *Jesus Remembered* (Grand Rapids: Eerdmans, 2003), 501.

and said, "Truly I tell you, in no one in Israel have I found such faith [πίστις]" (8:10 NRSV). Why does Jesus compare this man's faith to Israel? Matthew is interested in pointing out the slowness of Israel to believe, and also sensitivity of certain gentiles to respond to Jesus.[14] Jews ought to have been the first sort of people to seek Jesus out and place their trust in him—here a pagan, without hesitation, confidently appeals to the authority of Jesus. Jesus appears to be referring to a phenomenon that is alien, unprecedented, operating outside the normal realm of human knowledge and decision making. To borrow language from Paul: "A faith has been revealed apart from the law" (cf. Rom 3:21). Those like the centurion who pursue Jesus, without *normal* reasons, demonstrate a unique kind of faith; one might even call it a sort of sixth sense.[15] Somehow, they *know* this man Jesus is something special. Gerald Hawthorne refers to this kind of faith as "spiritual insight":

> I mean by faith that which gives eyes to the soul (cf. Heb 11), so that the person of faith has the ability to see beyond the limiting barriers of matter and sense, and to penetrate the secret of spiritual reality, to see beyond human predicaments to God, and the goodness and wisdom and power of God, to see beyond the problems to the possibilities that God presents, to see beyond natural limitations to the limitlessness of the omnipotence of God, and to believe God for the solutions to life's problems, for making the possible a reality, for bursting the boundaries of human constrictions.[16]

Jesus marvels, as it were, at a faith that is ahead of everyone else, a few steps beyond where physical evidence leads. With all the privileges that Israel possessed, Jesus implies that they ought to have been the first ones to sense the power of God present in Jesus, but this is simply not the case.[17]

Jesus tells the centurion, "Go; let it be done for you according to your

---

14. Donald A. Hagner, *Matthew*, World Biblical Commentary 33A-B (Grand Rapids: Zondervan, 1993-95): 1.205.

15. Matthew tips us off regarding the origin of this special insight. When Peter confesses Jesus as Messiah, Jesus commends him and explains: "Flesh and blood has not revealed this to you, but my Father in heaven" (16:17 NRSV).

16. Gerald F. Hawthorne, "Faith: The Essential Ingredient of Effective Christian Ministry," in *Worship, Theology, and Ministry in the Early Church*, ed. Michael H. Wilkins and Terence Paige (Sheffield: JSOT Press, 1992), 249-59 at 250.

17. See John Nolland, *The Gospel of Matthew*, New International Greek Testament Commentary (Grand Rapids: Eerdmans, 2005), 356.

faith [ὡς ἐπίστευσας]" (8:13 NRSV). Some downplay the necessity of faith for the healing to take place,[18] but here it should be clear. As Jürgen Moltmann boldly observes:

> The divine power of healing does not come from [Jesus's] side alone. Nor is it simply his own "ministry," as and when he wishes to perform it. It is rather something that happens between him and the people who seek this power in him, and importune him. When Jesus and faith meet in this reciprocal activity, healing can happen.... The healings are stories about faith just as much as they are stories about Jesus. They are stories about the reciprocal relationship between Jesus and the faith of men and women. Jesus is dependent on this faith, just as the sick are dependent on the power that emanates from Jesus.[19]

In Matthew's story of the healing of the paralytic (9:2–8), Jesus is impressed again with faith, and, again, not with the faith of the person in need, but with the faith of those who brought the paralytic to Jesus (9:2). We are reminded that Jesus responds to those who act boldly in pursuit of him. As is true in Mark's Gospel, Matthew's Jesus "measures faith not by its orthodoxy but by its determination, courage, and persistence. It is not the 'i's' dotted or the 't's' crossed but the obstacles overcome that count."[20]

The third episode where Matthew highlights *seeking faith* is that of the bleeding woman (9:18–26). She is desperate (as with the above seekers) to encounter Jesus for help—but this time it is for herself. For some reason she believes that merely touching his garment will suffice (9:21). Despite her efforts to touch his clothes, Matthew notes that Jesus relates her healing to her *faith* (9:22).[21] This is the first time in the First Gospel that Jesus himself

---

18. See Sigurd Grindheim, "'Everything Is Possible for One Who Believes': Faith and Healing in the New Testament," *Trinity Journal* 26 (2005): 11–17.

19. Jürgen Moltmann, *The Way of Jesus Christ: Christology in Messianic Dimensions* (Minneapolis: Fortress, 1993), 111; see also Gerd Theissen, *The Miracle Stories of the Early Christian Tradition*, trans. F. McDonagh, ed. John Riches (Edinburgh: T&T Clark, 1983), 140.

20. Note Alan Culpepper's comments on Mark 2:5; *Mark* (Macon, GA: Smyth & Helwys, 2007), 77; see similarly David M. Rhoads, *Reading Mark* (Minneapolis: Fortress, 2004), 82; cf. Marshall, who refers to faith in Mark's Gospel as "sheer dogged perseverance"; *Faith as a Theme*, 237.

21. See Graham Twelftree, *Jesus the Miracle Worker* (Downers Grove, IL: InterVarsity, 1999), 118–19, 337.

uses the language of salvation (σῴζω) after the prophecy was uttered in 1:21: "She will bear a son, and you are to name him Jesus, for he will *save* [σῴζω] his people from their sins" (NRSV). Jesus is working out his *saving* ministry, but he connects his healing power to the woman's faith.[22]

In another healing passage two blind men call upon Jesus (son of David) to have mercy on them (9:27–31). Jesus responds with a question: "Do you believe that I am able to do this?" (9:28 NRSV). When they reply affirmatively, he touches their eyes and says, "According to your faith let it be done to you" (9:29 NRSV; cf. 8:13; 15:28). This is the only occasion in Matthew where Jesus enquires about human faith.[23]

The final episode is Jesus's discourse with the Canaanite woman (15:21–28). While Jesus was in the region of Tyre and Sidon, this gentile approached fhim out of concern for her daughter, who was possessed by a demon (15:22). At first, the disciples plead with Jesus to send her away ("she is bothering us"; 15:23 NLT), and Jesus proclaims to her, "I was sent only to the lost sheep of the house of Israel" (15:24 NRSV). However, she kneels before him and pleads with him. Jesus appears to rebuff her by telling her that the "children's food" should not be given to "dogs." The Canaanite woman plays along and responds, "Yes, Lord, yet even the dogs eat the crumbs that fall from their masters' table" (15:27 NRSV). Jesus is impressed, answering, "Woman, great is your faith! Let it be done for you as you wish" (15:28a NRSV). Her daughter was instantly made whole again (ἰάομαι). This story underscores significantly Matthew's interest in faith, moreover the faith of gentiles, despite the privileges of Israel. Jesus tests the woman's resilience and she responds with *amazing* faith (μεγάλη σου ἡ πίστις).[24]

What do these stories in Matthew teach us about faith? None of these characters were disciples of Jesus, they did not profess faith in him as Messiah. Yet, the way Matthew portrays them, they are models of faith. What were they modeling to the readers of his Gospel? As noted in the quotation from Gerald Hawthorne above, the Gospels are trying to demonstrate the *strangeness* of faith in Jesus, the backwardness of it. Consider the old Irish

---

22. See Walter T. Wilson, *Healing in the Gospel of Matthew: Reflections on Method and Ministry* (Minneapolis: Fortress, 2014), 217, 224–25.

23. France, *Matthew*, 367.

24. See Twelftree, *Jesus the Miracle Worker*, 134–35. For an insightful reading of the Markan version see Matthew L. Skinner, "'She Departed to Her House': Another Dimension of the Syrophoenician Mother's Faith in Mark 7.24–30," *Word and World* 26 (2006): 14–21 (esp. 18–19).

hymn *Be Thou My Vision*—the version in the hymnal of my youth had a single Scripture verse written at the top: "And when they lifted up their eyes, they saw no one but Jesus only" (Matt 17:8, the Transfiguration). Seeing *only* Jesus, forsaking everything else, *this* is the nature of the faith of the centurion, the Canaanite, and the others. There is a *carelessness* to their faith, a *recklessness*, not unlike selling everything to buy a pearl (13:46).

One notable theory regarding the origins and purpose of Matthew's Gospel involves a community of Jewish Christians who are struggling with an identity crisis toward the end of the first century. As Donald Hagner reasons:

> To their Jewish family they have always had to answer charges such as disloyalty to the religion of Israel, disloyalty to the Mosaic law (or at least of association with others who fail to observe it), and affiliation with an alien, if not pagan, religion, the large majority of whose adherents are Gentiles. ... Matthew's original readers were in an unenviable position, in a kind of "no-man's-land" between the Jews and Gentile Christians, needing to reach back for continuity with the old while at the same time reaching forward to the new work that God was doing in the largely Gentile church—simultaneously answerable, so to speak, to both Jews and Gentile Christians.[25]

To survive in the midst of this identity crisis, *faith* was needed, the kind of faith that forsakes all to see only Jesus. Despite those pursuing healing and help from Jesus *not* being committed disciples, they are held up as role models because of the awkward, unnatural pursuit of Jesus, their shameless faith. The disciples in Matthew's Gospel want to turn these noisy seekers away from Jesus. Jesus calls these seekers forward and commends them for their faith.

Trusting Faith

Because the disciples have some sense of the messianic identity of Jesus (Matt 16:16, 20), the faith that is required of them is *trusting faith*. While the Matthean Jesus does use πίστις in regard to the disciples (17:20; 21:21–22),

---

25. Hagner, *Matthew*, 1:209; see also Donald A. Hagner, "Matthew: Christian Judaism or Jewish Christianity?," in *The Face of New Testament Studies: A Survey of Recent Research*, ed. Scot McKnight and Grant Osborne (Grand Rapids: Baker, 2004), 263–82.

his favorite term for their faith is ὀλιγόπιστος (6:30; 8:26; 14:31; 16:8; 17:20; cf. Luke 12:28). This word does not occur outside of the Synoptic Gospels, and it is employed in Matthew (and Luke) more as a nickname than a description; for example, "Why are you afraid, Little Faith-ers?" (8:26). Again, in Mark, the disciples are accused of having *no* faith, while Matthew allows for a small measure of faith.[26] Ulrich Luz offers an explanation regarding what Matthew might mean by ὀλιγόπιστος: "'Little faith' is the faith of those who set out with Jesus only to lose heart. Little faith is faith mingled with fear and doubt. Little faith is the faith of those who would like to believe but cannot."[27] Similarly, John Meier comments that ὀλιγόπιστος "designates not unbelievers or apostates, but true disciples who panic in a moment of crisis and act as though they did not believe."[28]

We will keep this in mind as we look at the two uses of πίστις vis-à-vis the disciples, both of which occur in the second half of the First Gospel (17:14–21; 21:18–22). Beginning in 16:5, the disciples are given more attention by Matthew (though cf. 13:36). As Daniel Harrington notes, the curing of the demon-possessed boy is followed by a passion prediction. This sequence climaxes with the teaching given to the disciples in Matt 18.[29]

In 17:14–16, a man approaches Jesus and explains that his son, suffering from seizures, could not be cured by the disciples. Jesus responds, "You faithless [ἄπιστος] and perverse generation, how much longer must I be with you? How much longer must I put up with you?" (17:17 NRSV). Immediately, Jesus rebukes the demon and heals the child (17:18). The disciples inquire as to why *they* could not do this (17:19). Jesus explains, "Because of your little faith [ὀλιγοπιστία]. For truly I tell you, if you have faith [πίστις] the size of a mustard seed, you will say to this mountain, 'Move from here to there,' and it will move; and nothing will be impossible for you" (17:20 NRSV).[30]

---

26. See Pheme Perkins, *Introduction to the Synoptic Gospels* (Grand Rapids: Eerdmans, 2009), 187.

27. Ulrich Luz, *The Theology of the Gospel of Matthew*, New Testament Theology (Cambridge: Cambridge University Press, 1995), 68.

28. John P. Meier, *Matthew* (Wilmington: Glazier, 1980), 67; cf. Michael Wilkins, *The Concept of Disciple in Matthew's Gospel as Reflected in the Use of the Term Mathētēs* (Boston: Brill, 1988), 182. For a classic study of Matthew's use of faith language in regards to the disciples, see Gerhard Barth, "Glaube und Zweifel in den synoptischen Evangelien," *Zeitschrift für Theologie und Kirche* 72 (1975): 269–92.

29. See Daniel Harrington, *The Gospel of Matthew*, Sacra Pagina 1 (Collegeville, MN: Liturgical Press, 1991), 259.

30. While faith language was used earlier in Matthew for those *seeking* healing

Faith Language in the Jesus Tradition

What went wrong? Why were these disciples *not* able to perform the healing? One possibility is that they were treating the power to heal as a kind of magic, presuming that they could do this on their own.[31] More likely, though, their faith failed because they were not with Jesus and began to shrink. That is, they were overcome by doubt.[32] An interesting paradox presents itself, though, in this episode. Jesus's nickname for the disciples is "Little Faith," a chiding moniker, and yet he commends faith as small as a mustard seed. Apparently there is a good kind of small faith and a bad kind of small faith.[33] What exactly *is* this good faith of a mustard seed? Looking at Mark's account, Jesus explains, "This kind can come out only through prayer" (Mark 9:29 NRSV). The failure on the disciples' part is not a matter of training but one of *trust*. "The little faith of the disciples is a faith which *understands* and *assents*, but which does not *trust* totally. A faith which trusts God can be, in the world's estimation, as small and unimpressive as a mustard seed. Yet such trust can do the impossible."[34]

The second key episode that concentrates on the faith of the disciples is the cursing of the fig tree (Matt 21:18-22). Jesus, feeling hungry, notices this tree by the road. When he approaches it, he sees no figs, only leaves (21:18-19). He condemns the tree, saying, "May no fruit ever come from you again!" (21:19b NRSV). The fig tree withers. The disciples are amazed and perplexed by its instantaneous desiccation (21:20). Jesus instructs them, "Truly I tell you, if you have faith and do not doubt [ἐὰν ἔχητε πίστιν καὶ μὴ διακριθῆτε], not only will you do what has been done to the fig tree, but even if you say to this mountain, 'Be lifted up and thrown into the sea,' it will be done. Whatever you ask in prayer, you will receive, if you have faith [πιστεύοντες]" (21:21-22 NRSV modified). Here again Jesus relates faith to the moving of mountains (see 17:20; cf. Isa 40:4; 49:11; 54:10). The statement that they can receive whatever they ask harks back to Jesus's teaching in Matt 7: "Ask, and it will be given you; search, and you will find; knock, and the door will be opened for you. For everyone who asks receives, and

---

(for themselves or another), here the emphasis is on the faith of the one performing the healing; see Hagner, *Matthew*, 2:505.

31. See Leon Morris, *The Gospel according to Matthew* (Grand Rapids: Eerdmans, 1992), 448.

32. See France, *Matthew*, 662-63.

33. This paradox was brought to my attention by Frederick Dale Bruner, *Matthew*, vol. 2: *The Churchbook* (Grand Rapids: Eerdmans, 2004), 191.

34. Meier, *Matthew*, 194.

everyone who searches finds, and for everyone who knocks, the door will be opened" (7:7–8 NRSV). While the focus of the asking in the Sermon on the Mount is on God, in the context of the teaching after the cursing of the fig tree, Matthew transitions to the challenging of Jesus's authority by the chief priests and elders (21:23–27). The disciples are called to have faith in God, but Matthew is clear that the faith must center on Jesus (1:23; cf. 18:6; 27:42; 28:18).

What was Matthew trying to teach through these stories about the disciples' little faith and their need to trust and not doubt? Donald Senior is probably correct that the experiences of Christians as Matthew writes drive the way he shapes the gospel story:

> The church believes that its Lord has given it a share in his own power over sin and darkness. But fear and doubt are realities, too, and they seem to smother faith's vitality. Yet even then prayer is not in vain. Even we are "in the boat," we "of little faith" can be lifted from the waves by a merciful Lord....
>
> He chose them, human beings practically identical with the "sick" he came to save. He endured their dullness. He dealt with them honestly, exactingly, but neither his critique nor his commands were ever destructive. The disciples' record was not good. They complained, they misunderstood, they quarreled, they deserted, they denied. Only one was lost. But the part of the story that becomes "gospel"—"good news"—is that in the face of the master they failed, the disciples detected the infinite compassion of God, and they committed this memory to the church.[35]

Loyal Faith

The last occurrence of πίστις appears in the fourth woe of Jesus's denunciation of the Scribes and Pharisees (23:23; see 23:1–36). Jesus condemns them for meticulously tithing on their mint, dill, and cumin but neglecting "the weightier matters of the law," namely justice, mercy, and faithfulness (τὴν κρίσιν καὶ τὸ ἔλεος καὶ τὴν πίστιν). Translators are divided as to how πίστις should be rendered here: some prefer "faithfulness" (NIV, NET, ESV), while others have "faith" (RSV, NRSV, NLT; cf. KJV). Those who opt for the English translation "faith" here attempt to draw 23:23 into Matthew's wider

---

35. Donald Senior, *Jesus: A Gospel Portrait* (Mahwah, NJ: Paulist, 1992), 61.

use of faith language in his Gospel. Robert Gundry, for example, notes that Matthew seems to have placed a distinct emphasis on faith (in God) here, given that the parallel statement by Jesus in Luke 11:42 omits πίστις.[36] Others, however, prefer "faithfulness," because it would appear that Matthew is referring to covenantal faithfulness, acting in a manner of loyalty and obedience in view of what's called for by the covenant.[37] R. T. France makes the important observation that πίστις is used here in an ethical sense as attested by Jesus's referring to such things as being "done"—here πίστις is a virtue, "faithfulness" (cf. Gal 5:22-23).[38]

This use of πίστις presents itself as a third type of faith in Matthew's spirituality—*loyal faith*, or *faith as faithfulness*. This use of πίστις runs parallel to what is often found in pagan Hellenistic literature, where friends and allies (even nations) pledged fidelity to one another (see 40-46). Is Matthew promoting this kind of πίστις within his own Christian readers, or is this condemnation purely a denunciation of the Scribes and Pharisees?[39] Given the significant role that πίστις plays in the First Gospel as a whole, Matthew's underscoring of the centrality of πίστις, it would be seem unlikely that this particular instance would be irrelevant to his readers. Surely if Matthew did *not* want to apply this to his readers, he would have used another word or simply left πίστις out (cf. Luke 11:42).

Jesus, undoubtedly, was contrasting the disobedience of the Jewish religious leaders with Jesus's own true loyalty to God and to God's covenant, as David Bauer observes: "Their unfaithfulness serves as a foil to the faithfulness which is expected of the disciples. Since the disciples are aligned with Jesus, who himself stands over against unrepentant Israel and especially the religious leaders, the disciples are to be like Jesus by being unlike those opponents."[40]

---

36. Robert Gundry, *Matthew: A Commentary on His Literary and Theological Art* (Grand Rapids: Eerdmans, 1982), 463-64.

37. See Hagner, *Matthew*, 2:670. Several scholars consider the possibility that Jesus's statement echoes Mic 6:8; see, e.g., Nolland, *Matthew*, 937-38.

38. R. T. France, *The Gospel of Matthew*, NICNT (Grand Rapids: Eerdmans, 2007), 873-74.

39. D. A. Carson, for example, argues that 23:23 does not address matters pertaining to continuity/discontinuity between the old covenant and the new, but rather only involves "the relative importance of material within the [Old Testament]"; see "Matthew," in *Matthew and Mark*, ed. Tremper Longman and David E. Garland, New Expositor's Bible Commentary (Grand Rapids: Zondervan, 2005), 23-670 at 540.

40. David Bauer, *Structure of Matthew's Gospel: A Study in Literary Design* (London: Bloomsbury, 2015), 106.

Matthew's Jesus, thus, was not only calling his disciples to *believe*—seeing the world in a new light[41]—and not only to *trust*, but also to be *faithful*, the kind of πίστις that is demonstrated in action.

Summary of Matthew's Faith Language

In the Gospel of Matthew, πίστις is a central way in which humans ought to respond to Jesus and God. This is obvious on the surface of the text, but once one examines more closely what Matthew *means* in his use of faith language, there is a richness that is rarely considered carefully. Matthew places a large emphasis on the faith of those who seek out Jesus—those who know virtually nothing about Jesus except that he is special, and yet they have reached the end of their rope and they cling to hope that Jesus can bring healing and help in their desperate hour of need. This is *seeking faith*. Matthew writes primarily to Christians, those who have already sought Jesus in some way. But it should be clear enough that these seekers in the First Gospel are held out as models of *great faith*. What these exemplars of faith demonstrate is a peculiar sensitivity to realizing the uniqueness of Jesus. Matthew commends a faith that is never stagnant, always seeking and reaching, ever in pursuit of Jesus and the kingdom of God.

The second kind of faith Matthew highlights is that of those who need to trust God (*trusting faith*). The disciples, despite having a leg up on the blind religious leaders, are stamped with the label "little faith." They have made a beginning with Jesus but yet do not understand who he is, what he will achieve, and how this will transform all things. Moreover, they do not understand the role they can and should play in this new order. He has called them to do the impossible (17:20), but they can do this only by placing their full trust in God. Given what Jesus taught his disciples in Matt 10, *doing the impossible* in the context of teaching his disciples probably meant both the performing of great works of healing and deliverance (10:1, 8) as well as enduring persecution and rejection in their mission (10:14–39).

Matthew also emphasizes πίστις as *faithfulness* (*loyal faith*; 23:23). What the religious leaders lack is a commitment to covenant faithfulness, *doing* what is right vis-à-vis God's expectations for his people. More or less, this is

---

41. Stephen Westerholm makes an apt analogy using Matthew's lamp lesson (6:22–23): "To know, trust and love God, Jesus says, is like having one's vision suffused with light. To live without God, by way of contrast, is to walk in the dark"; see *Understanding Matthew* (Grand Rapids: Baker, 2006), 39.

Faith Language in the Jesus Tradition

Matthew's way of referring to the will's inclination toward obedience. Faith is not private or hidden, though it may be hard to understand. It is public and active, it is doing and working. It is tethered together with active mercy and active justice. Most modern Western readers of Matthew usually assume that his faith language was focused on *interiority* (i.e., one's beliefs). The inside matters, of course, to Matthew. But, though the gospel's power works inside out, it must finally come out to fulfill its purpose vis-à-vis the good news of God. Stephen Barton addresses this in view of Matthew's emphasis on fruit-bearing and *doing* righteousness.[42] The Gospel according to Matthew, and the nature of its spirituality, is about becoming something new by God's grace by faith. As Barton writes: "In short, the church is to become the embodiment and reflection of the coming kingdom of heaven, on earth in the here and now"—this requires faith, trust, and obedience.[43]

Will the Son of Man Find Faith on Earth? The Gospel of Luke

The faith language found in Luke's Gospel largely follows the same patterns and themes as Matthew's. Like Matthew, Luke links πίστις to forgiveness (Luke 5:20), healing (7:9, 50; 8:48; 17:19; 18:42), and faith in Jesus's person and mission (8:25; 17:5–6). There are a few places where Luke includes material not found in Matthew in relation to faith. At the Last Supper, where Jesus predicts Simon Peter's betrayal, he says, "Simon, Simon, listen! Satan has demanded to sift all of you like wheat, but I have prayed for you that your own faith [πίστις] may not fail; and you, when once you have turned back, strengthen your brothers" (22:31–32 NRSV). The very specific nature of the language of repentance and return (ἐπιστρέψας) helps to narrow the meaning of πίστις. Betrayal in this circumstance is an active breach of loyalty. Furthermore, Peter's rather flippant affirmation of fidelity is noticeably active: "Lord, I am ready to go with you to prison and to death!" (22:33 NRSV).

Another important occurrence of πίστις appears in 18:8, at the close of the parable of the widow and the unjust judge (18:1–8). Jesus comments on this parable by saying that God wastes no time upholding justice for the sake of his

---

42. For righteousness as a *leitmotif* of Matthew's Gospel, see Benno Przybylski, *Righteousness in Matthew and His World of Thought* (Cambridge: Cambridge University Press, 1980).

43. Stephen C. Barton, *The Spirituality of the Gospels* (Peabody, MA: Hendrickson, 1992), 28.

people. He intends for judgment to be carried out swiftly (18:8a). But what will the Son of Man find when he comes? Will he find faith on earth (ἄρα εὑρήσει τὴν πίστιν ἐπὶ τῆς γῆς)? What exactly is this πίστις? David Catchpole outlines four options that scholars consider: assent to orthodox Christianity,[44] faithful confession in times of persecution, trust in eschatological intervention, and ongoing adherence to Jesus's message.[45] Catchpole warns, though, against interpretations that are too narrow or anachronistic. Could not one simply assume πίστις refers here to a "total relationship to Jesus"? This makes good sense, but contextually, Catchpole also sensibly links Jesus's rhetorical question back to the widow and the matter of prayer. The widow's persistence in petition, a model for believing prayer, demonstrates, as John Donahue notes, an "active quest for justice" before God rather than mere "passive waiting."[46] In this case, the Son of Man will find πίστις in disciples who show trust in God through continual prayer or a prayerful devotion. Dorothy Jean Weaver draws out Luke's πίστις theology aptly: "Prayer is no sedentary, cerebral, or even safe activity in the eyes of Jesus or the mind of Luke. *Rather prayer is those sturdy, audacious, perhaps even outrageous acts that go by the name of faith.*"[47]

Furthermore, Weaver deftly links Luke's theology of faith, discipleship, and prayer in 18:8 to the rest of the Gospel:

> Prayer is the gut-wrenching desperation that digs through roof tiles or claws through the crowds to reach the healer on the other side (5:17–26). It is the unimaginable trust to believe in a miracle sight unseen (7:1–20). It is the sheer audacity to throw all caution to the wind and break every rule on the books in a scandalous and highly public display of love and repentance

---

44. Some argue that because πίστις is articular here, it appears to refer to *the faith*, as in Christian doctrine. This is a flawed understanding of the breadth of use of the Greek definite article. Joseph Fitzmyer offers the more convincing argument that this is the anaphoric function of the article, where it refers *back* to ideas already stated, in this case the πίστις of the widow; see *The Gospel according to Luke*, Anchor Bible 28 (Garden City: Doubleday, 1985), 2:1181.

45. David Catchpole, "The Son of Man's Search for Faith (Luke 18:8)," *Novum Testamentum* 19 (1973): 81–104 at 87.

46. John R. Donahue, *The Gospel in Parable: Metaphor, Narrative, and Theology in the Synoptic Gospels* (Minneapolis: Fortress, 1988), 185.

47. Dorothy J. Weaver, "Luke 18:1–8," *Interpretation* 56 (2002): 317–19; similarly Luke Timothy Johnson: "For Luke, prayer is faith in action. Prayer is not an optional exercise in piety, carried out to demonstrate one's relationship with God. It *is* that relationship with God"; *The Gospel of Luke*, Sacra Pagina 3 (Collegeville: Liturgical, 1991), 274.

(7:36–50). It is the utter impertinence to cry out loudly and persistently for healing (18:35–43) and justice (18:1–8) until those cries are heard. This is the prayer to which Jesus calls his disciples. And this is the prayer that Luke splashes in vivid color across the canvas of his gospel.[48]

Belief in the Gospel of John

The lion's share of attention on the matter of faith and the Gospels goes to the Synoptics, and especially Matthew's story. The Fourth Gospel is peculiar insofar as it does not contain even a single occurrence of πίστις. Nevertheless, the verb πιστεύω appears many dozens of times and serves as one of the most formative theological concepts in John and the Johannine literature.[49]

First, how it is possible that John does not use πίστις? Could it be a mere coincidence (i.e., he was not against using πίστις in theory, but just happened not to employ the word)? Johannine scholars claim that overall John had a preference for *verbs* doing the theological loadbearing rather than nouns. A few propose that by the end of the first century, πίστις perhaps took on a technical meaning ("doctrine") that John did not convey.[50] But one might wonder why this does not seem to be a problem for Luke's Acts or Revelation, and examination of the apostolic fathers' use of πίστις does not bear this out either (see 22–24). Teresa Morgan offers an interesting theory, namely, that John may have been assimilating to the Septuagint's preference for πιστεύω over πίστις.[51] Morgan admits, however, that this accounts for the frequency of πιστεύω but not the absence of πίστις.

It is a consensus in Johannine scholarship that the primary reason for this preference for πιστεύω involves John's interest in "the dynamic nature of the Johannine concept of belief."[52] This almost certainly is true, but there is probably more to it.

---

48. Weaver, "Luke 18:1–8," 319.

49. Raymond Brown puts the count of occurrences of πιστεύω at ninety-eight compared to thirty-four times in the Synoptics; *The Gospel according to John I–XII*, Anchor Bible 29 (Garden City, NY: Doubleday, 1966), 1:512.

50. See David Rensberger, *1 John, 2 John, 3 John*, Abingdon New Testament Commentary (Nashville: Abingdon, 1997), 130.

51. Morgan, *Roman Faith and Christian Faith*, 397.

52. Brown, *John*, 1:513. For a more extreme approach to this view, see Yung Suk Kim, *Truth, Testimony, and Transformation* (Eugene OR: Wipf & Stock, 2014), 6–7.

It is common for scholars to observe that for John πιστεύω is a highly *relational* verb, indicating in the Fourth Gospel a posture of trust and reliance.[53] Some uses of πιστεύω seem to bear this out (11:26; 12:11; 14:1; 16:27). This social aspect of πιστεύω is present in John's use, but it does not encompass the totality of how and why John employed this language.[54] Belief is often characterized in John as "in Jesus." This tends to imply believing in a specific claim about his identity, for example, that he is the Messiah (11:27, 48; 13:19) or that he was sent by the Father (10:38; 17:21; cf. 14:10–11). But sometimes John can use belief language in an absolute sense: true followers of Jesus are simply referred to as "believers" (6:47). This includes not just assenting to a particular set of claims but also involves epistemological insight into the true ways of God. One way to make sense of this is to relate John's belief language to those who argue that the Fourth Gospel presents the story of Jesus within the framework of a criminal trial, with Jesus in the dock.[55] Far more than the other evangelists, John refers to witnesses and the power of testimony for the sake of belief. Humans testify to Jesus (1:7; 4:39; 17:20), Jesus's signs testify (1:50; 2:11, 23; 11:45; 12:37; 20:8), as do his works (10:25, 37), his words (2:22; 4:41; 5:24; 8:30; 11:42), and the Jewish scriptures (5:46). Those who encounter Jesus are called to see rightly and hear this testimony—hence believing in Jesus can be synonymous with believing *in the light* (12:36, 46). The so-called trial motif also helps to explain why John often ties together belief and truth (4:42; 8:45; 19:35).

Another crucial factor in the interpretation of John's belief language is his interpretation of the rejection of Jesus in 12:38–41. Explaining why some disbelieved Jesus in spite of witnessing his miraculous signs, John 12:38 quotes Isa 53:1: "Lord, who has believed our message, and to whom has the arm of the Lord been revealed?" (NRSV). Belief is not merely a matter of sensory reaction, cause and effect. Divine *revelation* leads to true belief, and it takes such a heavenly *push* to believe what seems unbelievable. John immediately quotes another Isaianic text (Isa 6:10): "He has blinded their eyes and hardened their heart, so that they might not look with their eyes, and understand with their heart and turn—and I would heal them" (John

---

53. See Craig Koester, *The Word of Life: A Theology of John's Gospel* (Grand Rapids: Eerdmans, 2008), 162.

54. For a well-nuanced discussion of belief in John, see Paul A. Rainbow, *Johannine Theology* (Downers Grove, IL: InterVarsity, 2014), 286–308.

55. See Andrew T. Lincoln, *Truth on Trial: The Lawsuit Motif in the Fourth Gospel* (Peabody, MA: Hendrickson, 2000).

12:40 NRSV). John relates this to belief in Jesus (12:41), where true belief requires a transformed imagination.[56]

Clearly it is difficult to boil John's use of faith language down to a simple definition, but it appears that the epistemological aspect of πιστεύω is prominent, which helps to account for his clear preference for the verb over the noun. For John, accepting Jesus requires acceptance of his claims to truly reveal God in his life, words, and signs.

Conclusion

This relatively brief examination of faith language in the Gospels easily demonstrates the breath of meanings and nuances of πίστις (and πιστεύω) in these texts, covering such ideas as *seeking, believing, trusting, and obeying*. The apostle Paul himself never quotes Jesus himself on the matter of faith. And it is worth noting the many differences between Paul's faith language and the Gospels: the specific emphasis on believing in the death and resurrection of Jesus ("the Proclaimer has become the proclaimed"),[57] the focus on Abraham as model of faith, and faith/works juxtaposition. But the similarities between the Gospels and Paul on the theology of Christian faith should not be underestimated. We can start with Paul's brief mention of a kind of faith that can "remove mountains" (1 Cor 13:2), a statement that appears to echo a teaching of Jesus in Matt 17:20 (cf. Mark 11:23).[58] Beyond

---

56. Dru Johnson refers to the Fourth Gospel as "the most conspicuously epistemological of the Gospels"; *Biblical Knowing* (Eugene OR: Wipf & Stock, 2013), 118; cf. John Ashton, *Understanding the Fourth Gospel* (Oxford: Oxford University Press, 1991), 515: "Every major motif in the Gospel of John is linked to the concept of revelation."

57. Famously stated by Rudolf Bultmann and paraphrased by many after him; *Theology of the New Testament*, 2 vols., trans. K. Grobel (New York: Scribner, 1951, 1955, 1.33.

58. As Yeung points out, most scholars believe Paul was influenced here by a Jesus saying; *Faith in Jesus and Paul*, 30–33. A few scholars argue that Paul may have simply been repeating a popular cultural proverb (and not something passed on from early Christian tradition), but no evidence is ever given for the existence of such a proverb. Frans Neirynck appeals to Isa 54:10, but there only mountains are mentioned; see "The Sayings of Jesus in 1 Corinthians," in *The Corinthian Correspondence*, ed. Riemund Bieringer (Leuven: Peeters, 1996), 141–76 at 152.

that, many of the broader ways Paul used faith language resonates with what we find in the Gospels:

- emphasis on believing in and trusting in God (1 Thess 1:8; Rom 4:5; 1 Cor 16:13)
- faith as a distinctive quality of followers of Jesus (Rom 1:8)
- the association of belief and salvation (1 Cor 1:21)
- the divine origin of saving wisdom and faith (1 Cor 2:5; 2 Cor 5:7; 1 Thess 2:13)
- the extraordinary faith of gentiles (Rom 9:30; cf. Gal 3:22)
- shared interest in Isa 53:1 (Rom 10:6)[59]

This does not mean Paul read anything like a "gospel" in his time. He certainly came to know teachings of Jesus one way or another,[60] not least the Lord's Supper tradition (1 Cor 11:23-25; cf. Mark 14:22-24; Matt 26:26-28; Luke 22:19-20). Paul's faith language may have been influenced from the Jesus tradition, but it must be remembered that decades of intervening influence of primitive Christianity may have produced its own religious language, and Paul was undoubtedly nurtured in the Christian faith through that wider agency.

---

59. We may include as well here Paul's and John's mutual interest in Isa 53:1 (cf. Rom 10:6).

60. See Victor P. Furnish, *Jesus according to Paul* (Cambridge: Cambridge University Press, 1993), 40-65; and Craig L. Blomberg, "Quotations, Allusions, and Echoes of Jesus in Paul," in *Studies in Pauline Epistles*, ed. Dane C. Ortlund and Matthew S. Harmon (Grand Rapids: Zondervan, 2014), 129-43.

5 Faithfulness Is Better

Πίστις in 1 Thessalonians and Philippians

> Love your friends to the death. For faithfulness is better.
>
> —Pseudo-Phocylides (1.218)

> Man cannot live without faith because the prime requisite in life's adventure is courage, and the sustenance of courage is faith.
>
> —Harry Emerson Fosdick, *The Meaning of Faith*

Plutarch and Odysseus's Silent Friends

Plutarch was a prolific writer, penning many dozens of works in his lifetime—a rather long lifetime of more than seventy years. He is famous for his biographies, such as *Parallel Lives*, but he obviously had a special interest in moral philosophy. He gave counsel in his writings on attaining wisdom and navigating life prudently (e.g., *How to Distinguish a Flatterer from a Friend*). One of my favorite works of Plutarch is *De garrulitate* (*On Talkativeness*). The topic itself is quite humorous, but as W. C. Helmbold points out, Plutarch takes the matter very seriously.[1] Plutarch laments that the garrulous need instruction on this matter, but they simply won't stop talking long enough to listen! Plutarch tells a story about Aristotle the philosopher finding him-

---

1. "Though Plutarch again and again, by his narrative skill and naïve or unconscious humour, will delight even those who have hardened hearts against him (I mean his editors), he cannot at last resist the temptation to indulge in what he considered scientific analysis and enlightened exhortation"; *Plutarch*, vol. 6: *Moralia*, trans. W. C. Helmbold, LCL 337 (Cambridge: Harvard University Press, 1939), 394–95.

self trapped in a conversation with a chatty fellow. After Aristotle stopped responding, the man said, "Poor philosopher, I've wearied you with my talk!" Aristotle retorted, "Heavens, no! I wasn't listening" (*Moralia* 503B, trans. Helmbold in LCL).

At one point Plutarch promotes the power of silence and the virtue of keeping secrets with sealed lips. Zeno, he explains, once bit off his own tongue and spat it out to defy a tyrant trying to cajole him. Plutarch carves out extra space in his essay to extol the virtues of Odysseus and his comrades on this matter. In particular, he observes the defiance they showed to the cyclops Polyphemus, even under severe duress:

> Even when they were dragged about and dashed upon the ground by the Cyclops, they would not denounce Odysseus nor show that fire-sharpened instrument prepared against the monster's eye, but preferred to be eaten raw rather than to tell a single word of the secret—an example of self-control and loyalty which cannot be surpassed [ὑπερβολὴν ἐγκρατείας καὶ πίστεως οὐκ ἀπολέλοιπεν]. (*Moralia* 506C, trans. Helmbold in LCL)

Πίστις is here sensibly translated "loyalty," implying fidelity and commitment to Odysseus, even at the prospect of torture and death. The pairing with ἐγκρατεία ("self-control") demonstrates that sense of commitment and composure that holds to the value of friendship over and against relief of pain or shame. This use of πίστις (as loyalty or faithfulness) is not the *only* way that Plutarch uses this word. In fact *De garrulitate* showcases a remarkable breadth of how this word can be employed. Still, Plutarch's illustration about the companions of Odysseus represents a very common use of πίστις in Greek literature, one that relates to a relational bond that goes beyond belief or even trust to a kind of ruthless or no-limits commitment (see 40–46). It is interesting and instructive to note that of the more than one thousand appearances of πίστις in the Greek literature of antiquity, the vast majority of these are in political or conflict-oriented histories, and the obvious connotations involve allegiance and pledges of loyalty.[2] It is important to keep in mind this pervasive use of πίστις in Greek literature as we turn

---

2. See Arrian, *Anabasis*; Dionysius of Halicarnassus, *Roman Antiquities*; Diodorus Siculus, *Bibliotheca Historica*; Appian, *Civil Wars*; Appian, *Foreign Wars*; Herodotus, *Histories*; and Polybius, *Histories*. Notable exceptions to this would be the more than three dozen appearances of πίστις in Strabo's *Geography* and the many references to πίστις ("proof") in Aristotle's *Rhetoric*.

to Paul, because when Paul does use πίστις in this way, it goes far beyond what we think of today as faith or belief.³

The work of Douglas Campbell on πίστις attempts to make a similar case. In his *Quest for Paul's Gospel*, he explains that an openness to translating πίστις as "faithfulness" should be quite natural when we look at Paul's usage, because this is the dominant meaning in wider Hellenistic employment including the Septuagint and Josephus:

> This dominance is probably because faithfulness is such a ubiquitous feature of human relationships, and especially in the context of a hierarchical and highly status-conscious society like the one Paul inhabited. Ideally, patrons and clients act faithfully towards one another, as should ideal families, marriages, political associations, religious and covenantal associations, and so on. The partners in these relationships should be reliable, trustworthy, and faithful to one another.⁴

Campbell also argues that πίστις's semantic domain can include notions of obedience as well as endurance, loyalty, and trustworthiness:

> A faithful servant is also an obedient servant. And hence we find *pistis*, when used in this basic sense, sometimes placed alongside notions of submission and obedience in Paul, which were often denoted in Greek by *hupakoê*, or the verbs *hupakouô* and *hupotassô*. Obedience as a theme *per se* is of course readily apparent in Paul. And even Christ is explicitly described as obedient to God in certain important texts.⁵

I could note all manner of relevant texts in Paul, and Campbell offers several in his discussion,⁶ but I will narrow the field of view to 1 Thessalo-

---

3. It is remarkable how resistant modern English translations are to rendering πίστις as "faithfulness" in Paul. My impression is that there is an ideological concern to preserve the nonworks, "passive-righteousness" theology that can be read into Paul's anthropological use of πίστις. Leon Morris argues, matter-of-factly and without evidence, that πίστις *never* means "faithfulness" when it is used in reference to humans in the New Testament; see *1 and 2 Thessalonians*, Tyndale New Testament Commentary (Grand Rapids: Eerdmans, 1984), 101n5 (also 51).

4. Douglas A. Campbell, *The Quest for Paul's Gospel: A Suggested Strategy* (London: T&T Clark, 2015), 186.

5. Campbell, *Quest for Paul's Gospel*, 187.

6. In passing Campbell offers these: Rom 1:5, 8, 12; 16:26; 2 Cor 5:7; arguably

nians and Philippians. Why these epistles? Besides having a similar region in common (ancient Macedonia), they both happen to be occasions where Paul was writing to encourage beleaguered believers who were feeling and experiencing the weight of local persecution. Furthermore, and not unrelated to this, Paul employs military metaphors in both 1 Thessalonians and Philippians to give these believing communities some perspective on their role and mission as they faced affliction and suffering with resilience and forbearance. He calls the Thessalonian believers to be "day" people who stand at the ready and don the "breastplate of *faith* and *love*, and for a helmet the hope of salvation" (1 Thess 5:8 NRSV). In his letter to the Philippians, Paul refers to Epaphroditus (a Philippian himself) as a "fellow soldier" (2:25); and given the context of this commendation of Epaphroditus, he represents for Paul the model of a committed and unwavering believer, one who was willing to risk everything for the sake of his ministry and mission (2:27), something demonstrated in the Roman image of "the good soldier."[7] With these features in mind, it makes sense to translate and interpret πίστις as "loyalty" or "faithfulness" in most instances in these letters, as Paul showed concern for their wholehearted and steadfast commitment to the gospel, even and especially in the face of adversity. The best English translation of πίστις is primarily determined by its use in an individual discourse, not a whole book, but these letters as a whole seem to prefer "faithfulness" because of the wider social context of the texts and their rhetorical aims.

First Thessalonians

First Thessalonians is Paul's letter of encouragement and consolation for a troubled church.[8] Early in the letter he makes mention of their suffering and

---

Gal 5:5, 6, 22; Phil 1:25, 27; also 2:17; Phlm 5, 6; cf. Eph 1:15; 6:16, 23; Col 1:4, 23; 2:5, 7, 12; 2 Thess 1:3, 4, 11.

7. See Jon E. Lendon, *Empire of Honour* (Oxford: Oxford University Press, 1997), 237–66; Nijay K. Gupta, "Paul and the *Militia Spiritualis* Topos in 1 Thessalonians," in *Paul and the Greco-Roman Philosophical Tradition*, ed. Joseph R. Dodson and Andrew W. Pitts (London: T&T Clark, 2017), 13–32; and Gupta, "Fighting the Good Fight: The Good Life in Paul and the Giants of Philosophy," in *Paul and the Giants of Philosophy*, ed. David Briones and Joseph R. Dodson (Downers Grove, IL: InterVarsity, 2019).

8. For my interpretation of this letter's situation and background, see Nijay K. Gupta, *1–2 Thessalonians* (Eugene, OR: Wipf & Stock, 2015); and *1–2 Thessalonians*,

Πίστις in 1 Thessalonians and Philippians

how they managed to maintain a sense of joy that inspired both the apostles and fellow believers throughout Macedonia and also Achaia (1:6–8).[9] In particular, Paul commends their πίστις (1:8). Paul cheers the Thessalonians on as if they are like a boat trying to stay in one piece in a storm, or a runner struggling to finish a marathon going uphill in wearying heat. In 1:3 he points to their incredible and inspiring "work of faith and labor of love and steadfastness of hope in our Lord Jesus Christ" (NRSV). The faith-hope-love triad present here (repeated again in 1 Cor 13) has generated much theological reflection over the years (e.g., Augustine, *Enchiridion*), but in 1 Thessalonians in particular it would be dangerous to unhinge it from its historical moorings. Paul addresses their *work, labor,* and *endurance* and their *faith, love,* and *hope* to affirm the onward march of their walk with Christ in spite of resistance and much cultural friction.[10]

Paul uses πίστις language several times in this letter, apparently to reassure the Thessalonians in their commitment to Christ and to encourage them to press on with vigilance and hope.[11] Within this context, it makes sense to interpret πίστις as relating to Paul's encouragement toward *faithfulness* and *loyalty* as the Thessalonians persevere through adversity.

To take another example of πίστις, we might jump to the end of 1 Thessalonians where, in a section that includes extensive parenesis, Paul exhorts the Thessalonians to live as day-people and to "put on the breastplate

---

Zondervan Critical Introductions to the New Testament (Grand Rapids: Zondervan, 2019).

9. For detailed treatments of the Thessalonian situation, see Todd D. Still, *Conflict in Thessalonica*, Journal for the Study of the New Testament Supplement 183 (Sheffield: JSOT Press, 1999); cf. also Mikael Tellbe, *Between Synagogue and State: Christians, Jews, and Civic Authorities in 1 Thessalonians, Romans, and Philippians* (Stockholm: Almqvist & Wiksell, 2001); and James Harrison, *Paul and the Imperial Authorities at Thessalonica and Rome*, Wissenschaftliche Untersuchungen zum Neuen Testament 273 (Tübingen: Mohr Siebeck, 2011).

10. See Elizabeth Johnson, "Paul's Reliance on Scripture in 1 Thessalonians," in *Paul and Scripture: Extending the Conversation*, ed. Christopher D. Stanley (Atlanta: Society of Biblical Literature, 2011), 143–61 at 155; B. J. Oropeza, "1 and 2 Thessalonians: Persecution, *Porniea*, and Parousia in a New Congregation," in *Jews, Gentiles, and the Opponents of Paul* (Eugene OR: Wipf & Stock, 2012), 36–65; and Andy Johnson, "Response to Witherington," *Ex Auditu* 24 (2008): 176–80 at 178.

11. See Zeba Crook, *Reconceptualising Conversion: Patronage, Loyalty, and Conversion in the Religions of the Ancient Mediterranean*, Beihefte zur Zeitschrift für die neutestamentliche Wissenschaft 130 (Berlin: de Gruyter, 2004), 213.

πίστεως καὶ ἀγάπης, and for a helmet the hope of salvation" (5:8). The phrase πίστεως καὶ ἀγάπης is almost always rendered in English as "faith and love." The reason for this is presumably because 5:8 bookends what Paul mentioned in 1:3 (faith, hope, and love). Insofar as these appear to be theological and spiritual concepts, translating πίστις as "faith" reflects Pauline theological language of faith in Christ. But a number of factors challenge this translation in preference of something like *loyalty* or *faithfulness*.[12] First, Paul employs here military language (e.g., armor, helmet), setting up a scene where πίστις would naturally be taken as fidelity to the sovereign (in this case the Lord Jesus). Second, πίστις does not stand on its own, but appears in a pair linked with ἀγάπη. As scholars often note, the study of the diachronic usage of ἀγάπη is difficult.[13] The noun form does not appear before the first century CE in extant Greek literature. Its etymology is uncertain, and even the verb ἀγαπάω was used much less commonly in nonbiblical Greek than in the New Testament itself on scale.[14] As Ceslas Spicq observes, Greek had four words for love: στοργή for familial love, ἔρως for sexual love, φιλία for friendship—but what about ἀγάπη? Spicq argues that its usage points to "the most rational kind of love," a love that is not driven by impulse, but implies care and intention in showing generosity and kindness.[15] In practice Spicq admits, though, that nonbiblical usage of ἀγάπη overlaps semantically with the use of φιλία.[16]

---

12. Ernest Best expresses the nature of πίστις: "For Paul, faith is the total response of man to the goodness of God seen in the death and resurrection of Christ through which man is redeemed. Such a total response includes man's obedience to God and must therefore result in activity (achievement) on the part of man"; *A Commentary on the First and Second Epistles to the Thessalonians* (Peabody, MA: Hendrickson, 1972), 68. Best explicitly states: "Faith sometimes passes into the sense of 'faithfulness' as 1:6 refers to the tribulations the Thessalonians have experienced on becoming Christians" (68).

13. For a helpful lexicographic discussion, see Anthony Thiselton, *Thiselton on Hermeneutics* (Grand Rapids: Eerdmans, 2006), especially the chapter titled "Exegesis, Lexicography and Theology: 'Love, the Essential and Lasting Criterion,' 1 Corinthians 13:1–7" (305–34).

14. E. Stauffer, "ἀγαπάω, ἀγάπη, ἀγαπητός," in *Theological Dictionary of the New Testament*, ed. Gerhard Kittel and Gerhard Friedrich, trans. Geoffrey W. Bromiley (Grand Rapids: Eerdmans, 1964–76), 1:36.

15. C. Spicq, "ἀγάπη," in *Theological Lexicon of the New Testament*, ed. and trans. J. D. Ernest (Peabody, MA: Hendrickson, 1994), 1.8.

16. Spicq, "ἀγάπη," 1:9–11.

As a case in point, Josephus never uses the noun ἀγάπη but rather frequently uses the verb ἀγαπάω and occasionally links ἀγαπάω to πίστις in the context of sociopolitical alliances (*Jewish Antiquities* 14.186; cf. 7.43; *Jewish War* 4.418). In the Psalms of Solomon, we see a similar coordination of this language, but pairing cognate πιστός with ἀγαπάω: "The Lord is faithful [πιστός] to those who love [τοῖς ἀγαπῶσίν] him in truth, to those who endure his discipline" (Psalms of Solomon 14.1). Love, as should be obvious here, is not primarily about emotional affection in the first place but about commitment and covenantal orientation. We ought to place this concept within the covenantal framework of Israel; note how the Shema itself communicates covenantal obligation as love: "You shall love the LORD your God with all your heart, and with all your soul, and with all your might" (Deut 6:5 NRSV). As Moshe Weinfeld explains: "Although love between God and Israel involves also affection and emotion, the practical meaning of the command of love is loyalty and obedience."[17] So it is with the Shema and Psalms of Solomon 14.1, and this is a rather natural meaning of ἀγαπάω in sociopolitical contexts in general in Hellenistic literature.

Greek historian Appian of Alexandria (ca. 95–165 CE) provides another example regarding this use of ἀγαπάω. His *Mithridatic Wars* recounts a letter sent from King Mithridates of Pontus to the Chians:

> You favour the Romans even now, and many of your citizens are still sojourning with them. You are reaping the fruits of the Roman lands in Chios, on which you pay us no percentage. Your trireme ran against and shook my ship in the battle before Rhodes. I willingly imputed that fault to the pilots alone, hoping that you would consult the interests of your safety and rest content [εἰ᾽ δύναισθε σῴζεσθαι καὶ ἀγαπᾶν]. (12.7.47, trans. White in LCL)[18]

Horace White renders ἀγαπᾶν as "rest content" here, which is a very loose way of referring to the Chians' commitment to him. In another translation, White renders ἀγαπᾶν as "remain my submissive subjects."[19] Obviously Mithridates is not concerned with the Chians' love in any emotional or af-

---

17. Moshe Weinfeld, *Deuteronomy 1–11*, Anchor Bible 5 (New York: Doubleday, 1991), 351; cf. Jon D. Levenson, *The Love of God: Divine Gift, Human Gratitude, and Mutual Faithfulness in Judaism* (Princeton: Princeton University Press, 2015).

18. Later he threatens them with a fine of two thousand talents!

19. See Horace White, *The Roman History of Appian of Alexandria* (London: Macmillan, 1899), 1:355.

fectionate way. More precisely he expects *devotion* that is tangible in sociopolitical allegiance, and given his relationship with them, this amounts to their submission and obeisance.

How does this shed light on the Pauline phrase πίστεως καὶ ἀγάπης in 1 Thess 5:8? It is likely that Paul was offering a hendiadys here, "utter devotion," to represent a firm commitment to the Lord in the face of resistance. This would not completely obviate seeing πίστις and ἀγάπη as separable Christian cardinal virtues. Still, we tend to draw sharp distinctions between these words—faith is what you *believe*, and love is what you *feel* or *do*. When we place these words in their ancient context, though, many people would not isolate their meanings so rigidly.[20] James Dunn makes a similar case in relation to the use of πίστις and ἀγάπη in Gal 5:6 (πίστις δι' ἀγάπης ἐνεργουμένη). Dunn resists the temptation to separate these words as if faith were the beginning and love the outcome: "The phrase is more like a single concept—faith-through-love, love-energized-faith."[21]

While we do not have instances outside of the Septuagint/New Testament where πίστις and ἀγάπη come together, we *do* have situations in Hellenistic Jewish literature where πίστις and φιλία appear together. For instance, Josephus uses the phrase φιλίᾳ καὶ πίστει in relation to the King of Hamath wanting to form an alliance with David (*Jewish Antiquities* 7.107). Later Josephus refers to those cities that honor the Roman emperor as demonstrating πίστιν καὶ φιλίαν (*Jewish Antiquities* 19:289). All of this is to underscore the point that faith and love are commonly brought together to talk about loyalty and devotion; in a place like 1 Thess 5:8 Paul's call to don the armor πίστεως καὶ ἀγάπης probably resonated with the Thessalonians as a *Christianized* call to arms, so to speak, a pep talk from a general encouraging his troops to persevere in the battle in spite of an intimidating enemy or foul circumstances.

The concentration of faith language in 1 Thessalonians comes in chapter three, where Paul refers to his concern for the stability of their πίστις. In 3:2 he notes how he dispatched Timothy to check in on them and to strengthen and encourage them ὑπὲρ τῆς πίστεως ὑμῶν. His fear was that they would be shaken up by persecution and their πίστις would waver. Out of fear that

---

20. David Konstan, "Trusting in Jesus," *Journal for the Study of the New Testament* 40 (2018): 247–54 at 251.

21. James D. G. Dunn, *The Theology of Paul the Apostle* (Grand Rapids: Eerdmans, 1998), 638, where he cites as relevant 1 Thess 1:3 and 5:8; for a similar perspective, see Beverly R. Gaventa, *First and Second Thessalonians*, Interpretation (Louisville: Westminster John Knox, 1998), 44; Campbell, *Quest for Paul's Gospel*, 186.

the tempter would stoke fear, panic, and hopelessness, Timothy was sent εἰς τὸ γνῶναι τὴν πίστιν ὑμῶν (3:5). Paul was utterly overjoyed to learn from Timothy of their τὴν πίστιν καὶ τὴν ἀγάπην (3:6), news that brought reassurance and relief to Paul (3:7). It is rather obvious that by πίστις in this passage, Paul is *not* referring simply to beliefs.[22]

We are best helped in our interpretation of πίστις here by Paul's next statement that he was relieved to know that they "stand firm in the Lord" (3:8 NRSV).[23] As James Thompson explains, this use of πίστις resembles the language of faithfulness, courage, and resilience modeled in the Septuagint and Hellenistic Jewish literature in relation to the unrelenting commitments of the great heroes of Israel (Sir 45:4; 46:15; 1 Macc 2:59).[24] Thompson explicitly mentions the reference to the faithful mother of 4 Maccabees who is praised as demonstrating nobility in her πίστις (4 Macc 17:2; cf. 1:8). In the face of torture and inducements to apostasy, the intrepid matriarch encouraged her sons to die courageously for the sake of εὐσεβεία (15:12). As the narrator comments, "This mother, who saw them tortured and burned one by one, because of εὐσεβεία did not change her attitude" (15:14 NRSV). This appears to be thematically similar to Paul's use of πίστις in 1 Thess 3. His employment of πίστις has much more to do with courage and less with doctrine qua doctrine, or something particular about Christian *beliefs*.[25] Overall, L. Ann Jervis cogently captures the overall purpose of 1 Thessalonians and how Paul's use of πίστις is related: "This letter addresses the suffering that results from living a life of faithfulness to Christ."[26]

---

22. So Eugene Boring observes, "Timothy had not been sent to determine whether the new converts were orthodox, but whether the cultural pressures, which had probably already taken a violent turn, have caused them to withdraw from the church or at least keep a low profile"; *1 and 2 Thessalonians*, New Testament Library (Louisville: Westminster John Knox, 2015), 117.

23. Jouette Bassler comments: "They were (or should have been) characterized by love, righteousness, hope, peace, and endurance. But when Paul reported what was proclaimed abroad about them, what he most feared their losing, what he most celebrated their having, it was to their *pistis*, their faith, that he referred to. In a fundamental way *pistis* defined them in their relationship with God"; *Navigating Paul* (Louisville: Westminster John Knox, 2007), 23.

24. James W. Thompson, *Moral Formation according to Paul: The Context and Coherence of Pauline Ethics* (Grand Rapids: Baker, 2011), 69; cf. also David deSilva, *Honor, Patronage, Kinship, and Purity: Unlocking New Testament Culture* (Downers Grove, IL: InterVarsity, 2012), 98.

25. See Gaventa, *Thessalonians*, 44.

26. L. Ann Jervis, *At the Heart of the Gospel* (Grand Rapids: Eerdmans, 2007), 31.

Philippians

Like 1 Thessalonians, Philippians is also a letter in which Paul offers a suffering church consolation.[27] After expressing his gratitude to God for their friendship and partnership in the work of the gospel in the early part of chapter 1, Paul addresses the challenges he has faced in his situation "in chains." Despite the uncertainty of his fate, he remains confident that he would eventually be able to visit them and minister to them in their time of need. We can sense some turmoil in the church in Philippi as Paul encourages them to come together and represent well the gospel of Christ. What could have stirred up this community in Philippi? In 1:28, Paul explicitly mentions "opponents" who apparently posed a threat to the church. Paul used this occasion to show how this situation is not a curse but perhaps even a blessing: "For he has graciously granted you the privilege not only of believing in Christ, but of suffering for him as well" (1:29). Paul also goes on to explain that their *struggle* (ἀγών) is the same as his, a fight for the sake of the gospel.

The identity of these opponents remains elusive—the scholarship on the subject is voluminous and convoluted.[28] For our purposes, determining their exact profile and concerns is not necessary. Rather, I am more interested in what Paul has to say to the Philippians about how to process and respond to this persecution and suffering.

Alongside Paul's reassurance to the Philippians in light of opposition, he also exhorts them to learn to live as one. We ought not to exaggerate the problem of disunity in the Philippian church; after all, Paul is rather pleased overall with the health of their community.[29] He gushes over their steady

---

27. See L. Gregory Bloomquist, "Subverted by Joy: Suffering and Joy in Paul's Letter to the Philippians," *Interpretation* 61 (2007): 270–82; Jervis, *At the Heart of the Gospel*, 37–76. For an up-to-date commentary that focuses on the consolation-driven purpose of Philippians, see Paul Holloway, *Philippians*, Hermeneia (Minneapolis: Fortress, 2017).

28. See the cautionary words of Morna Hooker, "Phantom Opponents and the Real Source of Conflict," in *Fair Play: Diversity and Conflict in Early Christianity*, ed. Ismo Dunderberg et al., Novum Testamentum Supplement 103 (Leiden: Brill, 2002), 377–95; cf. also Chris Mearns, "The Identity of Paul's Opponents at Philippi," *New Testament Studies* 33 (1987): 194–204; and Joseph B. Tyson, "Paul's Opponents at Philippi," *Perspectives in Religious Studies* 3 (1976): 83–96.

29. Davorin Peterlin may go too far in his monograph *Paul's Letter to the Philippians in the Light of Disunity in the Church*, Novum Testamentum Supplement 79

commitment to the gospel. Still, the kind of counsel that he offers seems to imply, if not breaches of the integrity of their community, then perhaps small cracks and fissures.[30] He prays for mutual love among the Philippians that overflows (1:9). He inspires cooperation (2:1-2) and avoidance of any hint of competitiveness (3:3-4) and grumbling (2:14). And of course Paul mentions the disagreement between Euodia and Syntyche, a problem of enough importance that it had to be publicly addressed in his letter (4:2). Some consider the possibility that Paul was giving general counsel about the importance of unity in Philippians, but it is not hard to imagine how a community under pressure can show signs of wear and tear, so to speak, and forbearance and patience can be in short supply. It is in this context that Paul addresses, among other things of course, the matter of πίστις.

In chapter 1, Paul offers assurance and encouragement to the Philippians that his imprisonment is neither an unfortunate accident nor a sign of the defeat of the gospel. On the contrary, it has become a remarkable means of *propelling* the gospel's witness and work (1:13-14). While Paul knows that he is in a vulnerable and uncertain situation, he boldly expresses his resolve that he will "continue with all of you for your progress and joy τῆς πίστεως" (1:25 NRSV). The assumption here is that recent events and present circumstances have had the effect of suppressing their πίστις. In 1:27 he offers the Philippians a rather sobering charge: "Only, live your lives as citizens worthy of the gospel of Christ, so that, whether I come and see you or am absent and hear about you, I will know that you are standing firm in one spirit, striving side by side with one mind τῇ πίστει τοῦ εὐαγγελίου" (NRSV modified).

It is a mistake to interpret πίστις here in relation to belief alone, though Paul does show interest in their (right) understanding of the gospel. John Reumann glosses πίστις in 1:27 as "religion," an unusual choice, but perhaps it comes closer to Paul's concerns and serves as a better conceptual domain than "belief."[31] Ben Witherington defines Paul's faith language here as "the Christian way of life, since this letter is all about behavior and orthopraxy."[32]

(Leiden: Brill, 1995); for an overview of criticism against Peterlin's argument see, Nijay K. Gupta, "Mirror-Reading Moral Issues in Paul's Letters," *Journal for the Study of the New Testament* 34 (2012): 361-81.

30. See Gordon D. Fee, *Paul's Letter to the Philippians*, New International Commentary on the New Testament (Grand Rapids: Eerdmans, 1995), 32-34.

31. John Reumann, *Philippians*, Anchor Yale Bible 33B (New Haven: Yale University Press, 2008), 228-29.

32. Ben Witherington III, *Paul's Letter to the Philippians* (Grand Rapids: Eerd-

FAITHFULNESS IS BETTER

Gordon Fee is right to ground Paul's statements about πίστις in 1:25 and 1:27 in the concern raised in 1:26, namely the desire for them to overflow in their boast in Christ Jesus.[33] Thus, their slow progress of πίστις has something to do with how they analyze Christ and the way they perceive how his people are faring in the world. Fee connects πίστις to the totality of a Christian vision that includes commitment to the gospel even within the fog of affliction. This large-as-life interpretation of πίστις goes beyond creed or conceptualization and includes will and action. In 1:25 it makes good sense to translate πίστις as "loyalty" or "commitment" (*joyous progress of your commitment*). In 1:27 we might go even further, especially as the text carries the tone of a unified militaristic march, to understand πίστις as something like "mission" or "campaign." *How committed are you, Philippians, true citizens of Christ's empire, to keep up the fight for this community, believing in its mission and progress?* Here in Philippians, then, we are not far off from the kind of counsel and encouragement that Paul sought to offer to the Thessalonians—concern for their πίστις was a concern for their commitment and loyalty to the gospel of Jesus Christ, especially in view of oppressive pressures and obstacles.

As Dieter Georgi explains, πίστις would have been a loaded term to the church in *Roman* Philippi (even if not all the people in the city or the church were themselves ethnically Roman or Roman citizens).[34] The Philippians would have naturally heard πίστις as expressing faithfulness and loyalty.[35] Beginning in the Augustan age, *fides* (and πίστις) took on deeper, more central political meaning in the Roman world. For Paul to make reference to the "πίστις of the gospel," as it were, would conjure up images of allegiance to a particular community and leader and its master ideology. Another text

---

mans, 2011), 104. As Witherington goes on to explain, there is no evidence that the Philippians needed doctrinal correction.

33. Gordon D. Fee, *Paul's Letter to the Philippians*, New International Commentary on the New Testament (Grand Rapids: Eerdmans, 1995), 153–55.

34. See too the sociohistorical perspective of Joseph Hellermann regarding the romanized nature of Philippi; *Reconstructing Honor in Roman Philippi* (Cambridge: Cambridge University Press, 2005), 1–109. On the question of whether the church in Philippi was Roman or had citizenship status, see Eduard Verhoef, *Philippi: How Christianity Began in Europe* (London: Bloomsbury, 2013), 1–52; cf. Peter Oakes, *Philippians: From People to Letters*, Society for New Testament Studies Monograph 86 (Cambridge: Cambridge University Press, 2001), 66–68.

35. Dieter Georgi, "God Upside Down," in *Paul and Empire: Religion and Power in Roman Imperial Society*, ed. Richard A. Horsley (Harrisburg, PA: Trinity, 1997), 148–57 at 149.

Πίστις in 1 Thessalonians and Philippians

in Philippians (2:17) illustrates this well, but before turning to the second chapter of Paul's letter to the Philippians, a detour into Xenophon's *Anabasis* illustrates what it looked like elsewhere in the Greco-Roman world to see a cohort of people struggling with the progress of a mission and with concerns of πίστις (and ἀπιστία).

The *Anabasis* is a tale of bravery, devotion, and perseverance as the Greek army under Xenophon struggled to find their way home after a series of unfortunate events (to put it mildly). In book 3, as a weary and exhausted army falters under leadership disputes, Cleanor (the Orchomenian) stands before the troops with words of inspiration. He begins by acknowledging many disappointments: "Come, fellow soldiers, you see the perjury and impiety of the King; you see likewise the faithlessness [ἀπιστίαν] of Tissaphernes" (3.2.4, trans. Brownson/Dillery in LCL).[36] Cleanor also observes the deception of Arieus (Cyrus's righthand man), whom the Greek troops trusted. The sting of betrayal is especially bitter to Cleanor because Arieus exchanged with these Greeks pledges of loyalty (καὶ ἐδώκαμεν καὶ ἐλάβομεν πιστὰ μὴ προδώσειν ἀλλήλους; 3.2.5), but then turned over to oppose his allies.[37] In reference to Arieus, Cleanor wishes upon them due punishment from the gods. Offering a final exhortation though, he says that when they observe the deeds of the traitors: "We must never again be deceived by them, but must fight as stoutly as we can and meet whatever fortune the gods may please to send" (3.2.6).

Next Xenophon himself, dressed in his finest, most noble battle gear, rises to address the army. Xenophon too begins with the "perjury and faithlessness of the barbarians" (τὴν μὲν τῶν βαρβάρων ἐπιορκίαν τε καὶ ἀπιστίαν; 3.2.7). He observes how the generals (who were betrayed and killed as they were entangled in this duplicity) experienced a failure of *trust* (διὰ πίστεως; 3.2.8). He affirms that the gods always side with honest, brave, and just men (3.2.11). After offering a series of strategies for how to survive their dangerous journey home, the group makes a plan for the next day.

---

36. On the theme of loyalty and infidelity in the *Anabasis*, see John Marincola, "Xenophon's Anabasis and Hellenica," in *The Cambridge Companion to Xenophon*, ed. Michael A. Flower (Cambridge: Cambridge University Press, 2016), 103–18 at 110–11. See too Anton-Hermann Chroust, "Treason and Patriotism in Ancient Greece," *Journal of the History of Ideas* 15 (1954): 280–88; on Xenophon's *Anabasis* in particular, see 285–86.

37. See Joseph Jansen, "Greek Oath Breakers?" *Mnemosyne* 67 (2014): 122–30.

Mithridates approaches their camp and says, "I was faithful to Cyrus" (Κύρῳ πιστὸς ἦν). He claims to come on "friendly" terms (φίλος)[38] and asks if he might join them in their travels (καὶ βουλόμενον κοινῇ σὺν ὑμῖν τὸν στόλον ποιεῖσθαι; 3.3.2). The Greeks see through the ploy of Mithridates and regard his intentions as dastardly (3.3.4). In fact, Mithridates was in league with the enemy Tissaphernes, and one of Tissaphernes's relations was sent secretly to spy on Mithridates to make sure he maintained loyalty (πίστις; 3.3.4). On this occasion, Mithridates was sent away and Xenophon's army agreed to disregard any alliances while in enemy territory. Later, though, Mithridates gets revenge. And so the Greek army's difficulties carry on for the rest of the story.

It is rather remarkable how much of the language found in just this short section of the *Anabasis* resembles the language in Philippians—language of loyalty (πίστις), friendship (φίλος), giving and receiving/reciprocity (ἐδώκαμεν καὶ ἐλάβομεν), and open sharing in community (κοινός). I am not implying that Paul had the *Anabasis* in mind when he wrote Philippians. Rather, the language found in Philippians is common to social-, political-, and military-alliance discourses in general, where loyalty and commitment to a group's leadership, ideology, and mission were considered paramount. The journey, survival, and salvation motif of the *Anabasis* is parallel to the way Paul calls the Philippians to remain strong on their journey, finding a way to "work out your salvation" in a manner not dissimilar to how Mithridates wished to secure his own survival by tethering his fate to theirs (σωτήριος in 3.2.2; σῴζω in 3.3.4).

Turning back to Phil 2:17, Paul gives a speech to the Philippians that, again, approximates that of a commander trying to inspire his troops: "Do not grumble and complain, but instead shine like stars, set an example, represent the lord and the mission with maturity, or else what I have done and stand for will be meaningless" (2:14–16). Then Paul entertains the possibility of his own demise: "What if my life is being poured out?" But instead of turning to despair, he says with hope and resilience, "My life is like a drink offering poured onto the sacrifice and service of your πίστις." Paul is saying here, even if he were to die, it was for the right reasons and still serves the gospel's mission and service. And he paints *their* lives into that story; their suffering and affliction for the gospel is of a piece with Paul's imprisonment, their fates intertwined. It would be a mistake, in just such a context, to re-

---

38. On the subject of friendship, see Gabriel Herman, *Ritualised Friendship and the Greek City* (Cambridge: Cambridge University Press, 2002), 4–5.

duce their πίστις to beliefs or a creed. He calls their lifestyle *sacrificial* and identifies their energies involved in the work of the gospel (see 1:3–7). This activity is part of their holistic commitment (πίστις) to Jesus Christ.

First Thessalonians and Philippians are two Pauline letters where Paul was especially concerned to strengthen the resolve of churches experiencing persecution. In both epistles, he shows direct concern with believers' πίστις. Is it best to interpret this as belief/faith, as if Paul's concern were with primarily doctrinal matters? Given that Paul employs militaristic metaphors in both letters to help these believers build up a resilient attitude toward their afflictions, it would seem responsible to fit his use of πίστις within the setting of ancient conflict or military texts that align the same constellation of terms in view of the reinforcement of loyalty and commitment to the central leadership, ethos, and mission of the community.[39] We will find, of course, as we study the full range of Paul's use of faith language in his letters that things are not always neat and tidy, and finding the right English words to translate πίστις is difficult (*traduttore, traditore!*). For heuristic reasons I have isolated here certain trends in 1 Thessalonians and Philippians—especially in light of their historical and literary contexts—that lead one to prefer those semantic values and resonances that relate to fidelity and bold commitment.

Revelation

Before leaving this chapter and moving on to other nuances and values of Paul's faith language, it benefits us to briefly look at how faith language is used in Revelation, a text that bears some contextual similarities to 1 Thessalonians and Philippians, especially the reinforcement of faithful witness and hope in a situation of social hostility and persecution. One of the reasons why it is helpful to bring Revelation into the conversation for comparison is because we often flatten out how Paul can use faith language and impose on his usage the notions of faith versus works or faith as doctrine. But given the affinities between 1 Thessalonians, Philippians, and Revelation from a social-contextual standpoint, we will easily see that Paul's use of πίστις

---

39. See Timothy Geoffrion, *The Rhetorical Purpose and the Political and Military Character of Philippians: A Call to Stand Firm* (Lewiston, NY: Mellen, 1993); and Edgar Krentz, "Military Language and Metaphors in Philippians," in *Origins and Method: Towards a New Understanding of Judaism and Christianity*, ed. B. H. McLean (Sheffield: JSOT Press, 1993), 105–27.

FAITHFULNESS IS BETTER

looks quite similar to how πίστις is used in Revelation—and it will become clear that πίστις in Revelation regularly involves loyalty, faithfulness, and sacrificial witness.

In the seven letters to the seven churches, Revelation addresses a variety of communities that interacted with the wider culture. Some are commended for their testimony and integrity. Others are condemned for their weak resolve and haughty attitude. To the church in Smyrna, for example, the Seer acknowledges their affliction and material deprivation (θλῖψιν καὶ τὴν πτωχείαν; 2:9). Indeed, more suffering is predicted (2:10), temptations and trials will come from the hands of the devil: "You will suffer hardship for ten days. Be faithful even to the point of death [πιστὸς ἄχρι θανάτου], and I will give you the crown of life" (2:10 CEB).[40]

The church in Pergamum is caught in the realm of Satan. Yet, they are clinging to Christ's name, "and you did not deny your faith in me [τὴν πίστιν μου] even in the days of Antipas my witness, my faithful one, who was killed among you, where Satan lives" (2:13 NRSV). The persecution potentially threatened their πίστις, but they remained loyal, demonstrated by the martyrdom of the respected witness Antipas who is called ὁ πιστός μου. Revelation brings together here πίστις and πιστός as sibling terms, perhaps not with identical meaning, but close enough that one is led to interpret πίστις as loyalty.[41]

The church in Thyatira is given both commendation and rebuke. It is castigated for putting up with "that woman Jezebel," a false teacher (2:20). She and those who follow her (2:23-24) will be judged. Thyatira is warned to "hold fast to what you have until I come" (2:25 NRSV). The words of encouragement come at the beginning of the letter to Thyatira:

> I know your works—your love, πίστιν, service, and patient endurance. I know that your last works are greater than the first [οἶδά σου τὰ ἔργα καὶ τὴν ἀγάπην καὶ τὴν πίστιν καὶ τὴν διακονίαν καὶ τὴν ὑπομονήν σου, καὶ τὰ ἔργα σου τὰ ἔσχατα πλείονα τῶν πρώτων]. (2:19 NRSV)

---

40. Observe the remarkable similarity with this chapter's epigraph from Pseudo-Phocylides: στέργε φίλους ἄχρις θανάτου· πίστις γὰρ ἀμείνων.

41. See David E. Aune, *Revelation*, 3 vols., World Biblical Commentary 52A–C (Grand Rapids: Zondervan, 1997), 1:184. Crook also prefers the translation "loyalty" for πίστις in this context: "It is loyalty to Christ that resulted in the persecution of Christians at the hands of the Romans. Like many Jews before them, some Christians were unwilling to divide their loyalties between Roman leaders and God"; *Reconceptualizing Conversion*, 213.

The constellation of terms that appear here laud their loyalty: at least three of these are also reinforced in 1 Thessalonians (love, faith, perseverance), and Phil 2:17 uses λειτουργία in a similar way to διακονία here. According to traditional Pauline categories, one might find it odd that Revelation ties together works and faith in 2:19, but this is remarkably similar to "work of faith" in 1 Thess 1:3.[42]

By now it should be rather obvious that translating πίστις as faith in this context can be misleading, as Revelation uses these letters to reaffirm the importance of steadfast trust in the gospel and in Jesus Christ in a context of stark opposition. For just this reason, Greg Beale argues that the cluster of terms used in 2:19 points to "persevering witness," something that goes far beyond what we think of as doctrine or cognitive belief.[43] In Rev 13:10, John uses πίστις to give counsel that true witnesses must demonstrate the "faithful endurance of the saints" (ἡ ὑπομονὴ καὶ ἡ πίστις τῶν ἁγίων; my translation).[44]

---

42. Eugene Boring, *Revelation*, Interpretation (Louisville: Westminster John Knox, 2011), 95, writes: "John is not thinking in the Pauline terms of 'faith versus works,' of how the guilty sinner becomes acceptable before God or how God can incorporate gentiles into the saved community without failing in his promises to Israel. 'Believe' as a verb does not occur in Revelation at all; 'faith' as a noun means 'faithfulness' (2:13, 19; 13:10) or *the* faith, the content of faith (14:12); 'faithful' as an adjective means not 'believing' but 'loyal, enduring, having integrity. . . . In Revelation the whole word group for faith and believing is thus never used in contrast to works, as in Paul, and never has the Pauline meaning of 'obedience in personal trust that mediates our relationship to God." The thrust of what Boring is saying about Revelation is correct but his comments about Paul are too rigid, especially given the affinities between Revelation and 1 Thessalonians already identified in terms of how they use πίστις.

43. Gregory K. Beale, *The Book of Revelation*, New International Greek Testament Commentary (Grand Rapids: Eerdmans, 1999), 260; see Aune, *Revelation*, 1:202; cf. Michael J. Gorman, *The Death of the Messiah and the Birth of the Covenant* (Eugene. OR: Wipf & Stock, 2014), 73.

44. See also Craig Koester, *Revelation and the End of All Things*, 2nd ed. (Grand Rapids: Eerdmans, 2018), 182; Greg Carey, "Revelation as Counter-Imperial Script," in *In the Shadow of Empire: Reclaiming the Bible as a History of Faithful Resistance*, ed. Richard A. Horsley (Louisville: Westminster John Knox, 2008), 157–76 at 173.

Conclusion

Paul sometimes uses πίστις with the meaning "faithfulness" or "loyalty," in line with the great many times it carries this meaning in wider Hellenistic literature of the time. Even more specifically, one can expect its employment when a hellenophone author has the intention of reinforcing in-group values and esprit de corps for a community under pressure. This is identifiably the case in 1 Thessalonians and Philippians, where both church communities were experiencing societal pressure and rejection. Paul shows concern, not just that they maintain some kind of mental commitment to certain beliefs (though this matter should not be taken out of the equation altogether), but rather with a whole-package πίστις that involves the will and an active sense of allegiance. My goal in this book is to move *beyond* overly simplistic, rigidly cognitive, and spiritualized definitions of πίστις in Paul. Thus, I isolated, however heuristically as is necessary at this stage, particular instances where he was addressing loyalty or what we might call "obeying faith." But it is equally mistaken to *always* presume that Paul implies allegiance when he used πίστις. As I will demonstrate in the next chapter (1 Corinthians), Paul could use πίστις in ways that place it semantically more in the realm of the mind and in association with words like wisdom/folly and thought/belief. Paul was well aware of the polyvalent nature of πίστις and leveraged this dynamic feature to give a kind of fullness to how he communicated the way of Jesus.

6 Strange Wisdom

The Cross's Wisdom and the Humble Foolishness of Faith in 1 Corinthians

> Faith is recognition of and a living into a poverty of self-generated, self-reliant knowledge and wisdom. It is clinging to the "strange wisdom" of God in Jesus Christ.
>
> —Nijay K. Gupta

In Martin Luther's tract called *Freedom of a Christian*, he makes the case for his emphasis on faith and freedom from works of the law through Jesus Christ. Luther recognizes that he is running against the grain of so much Christian thought before and around him; thus, at the end of the text, he urges that if his position is to be taken seriously, the readers will need to think anew—Luther says they would need to be *theodidacti*, taught by God. Dependence on natural wisdom and reason would not lead someone *toward* Luther's gospel of faith and freedom in Christ but rather *away from* it.

David H. Hopper explains that this perspective runs consistently throughout Luther's works, the idea that "God's revelation in Christ [is] to be a confounding of the world's wisdom in line with 1 Corinthians 1:18–25."[1] Hopper goes into more detail regarding Luther's theological epistemology:

> God's unique transforming wisdom is strange to the world—and the world declares its judgment upon it in the death of Jesus on the cross. But the transcendent God reverses and overrules that judgment, making it the very basis of faith, hope, and love. Faith understands God's strange wisdom and its proffered righteousness to be liberation, to be nothing less than God's promised salvation.[2]

---

1. D. H. Hopper, *Divine Transcendence and the Culture of Change* (Grand Rapids: Eerdmans, 2010), 104.

2. Hopper, *Divine Transcendence*, 104. One notes obvious connections here to

This chapter teases out this notion of the relationship between "strange wisdom" and "faith" in 1 Corinthians (not thoroughly in line with Luther's hermeneutics, but capturing the core of his thought). Paying attention to Paul's faith language in 1 Corinthians helps us to understand his main argument in the letter regarding the wisdom of the cross. After a brief tour of the faith language in 1 Corinthians as a whole, we examine the use of πίστις in 2:5, Paul's discussion of faith as a gift (12:9), and the use of πίστις (faith-hope-love) in the famous Pauline discourse on ἀγάπη in 1 Cor 13.

Faith Language in 1 Corinthians

Faith language appears in nearly every chapter of 1 Corinthians.

Πιστεύω

Often Paul uses πιστεύω as a Christian convention to refer to those who have embraced ("believe in") the gospel of Jesus Christ; we see it used this way in 3:5 and 14:22, as well as 15:2 and 15:11 in relation to belief in the resurrection. The appearance of πιστεύω in 1:21 is more calculated and serves his wider argument more intentionally (see comments on 1:18–2:5 below). Another instance where Paul's use of πιστεύω merits closer attention is 13:7: love *believes* all things (see below).

Πιστός

The adjective πιστός occurs five times in this epistle. On two occasions it is attributed to God—straight away in 1 Corinthians Paul notes how God is *faithful* in his calling of them (1:9). Toward the end of the letter he underscores how God faithfully delivers his people through trials (10:13). These

---

Luther's famous comparison of the "theologian of glory" and the "theologian of the cross" in the Heidelberg Disputation. Luther turns to 1 Cor 1:25 to explicate his perspective that the nature of the true theologian who "comprehends the visible and the manifest things of God seen through suffering and the cross"; see "Heidelberg Disputation," in *Luther's Works*, ed. Jaroslav Pelikan and Helmut T. Lehmann (Philadelphia: Fortress, 1957), 31.40.

occurrences appear to be a kind of bookend; God is faithful from the first day until the last.

Paul also uses πιστός in reference to apostolic trustworthiness and loyalty. The apostles are faithful stewards (4:2). Timothy is a model of this trustworthiness (4:17) and so is Paul himself (7:25).

Πίστις

Πίστις appears seven times in this letter. Paul refers to the gospel teaching on which their πίστις relies in 2:5 (see below). Later he uses πίστις in regard to a particular gift the Spirit can bestow on believers (12:9; cf. 13:2). It is mentioned again as part of the famous triad πίστις-ἐλπίς-ἀγάπη (13:13).

In Paul's discourse on the resurrection, he has occasion to mention that without Jesus's bodily resurrection their πίστις is empty (15:14, 17). Finally, in his concluding words, he calls the Corinthians to stand firm "in the faith" (ἐν τῇ πίστει; 16:13; see below).

Strange Wisdom, Humble Faith (2:5)

The use of πίστις in 1 Cor 2:5 is largely overlooked by scholars and offers an important glimpse into Paul's understanding of faith's relationship to knowledge and wisdom. Before engaging directly with the text, though, I offer a brief overview of the problems in Corinth, the reasons why Paul wrote 1 Corinthians, and what he was trying to communicate in the wider unit of the letter (1:18–2:16).

Anthony Thiselton argues that Paul was wrestling with a church that tried to embrace Christ while also holding onto their pre-Christian Corinthian social and cultural values. Thiselton notes three traits that occluded their Christian growth:[3]

- agonism: the Corinthian believers had a "drive toward competitiveness, self-achievement, and self-promotion"
- autonomy: they had "an attitude of self-sufficiency, self-congratulations, and autonomy and entitlement to indulge freedoms"

---

3. Anthony Thiselton, *1 Corinthians: A Shorter Exegetical and Pastoral Commentary* (Grand Rapids: Eerdmans, 2011), 9; cf. James D. G. Dunn, *1 Corinthians* (Sheffield: Sheffield Academic Press, 1995), 18.

- transcendence: they demonstrated the "tendency to *over-value gifts of 'knowledge,' 'wisdom,' and 'freedom'* over and above more basic gifts in everyday life such as *love and respect for others*"

In regard especially to Paul's early discourse on "persuasive words of wisdom" (2:4 NET), Thiselton singles out the Corinthians' obsession with status and self-promotion being associated with their expectations of the use of a certain kind of rhetoric.[4] Thiselton argues that Paul was clever enough that he *could have* played their game of "rhetorical self-glory" but made it a point *not* to.[5] When it comes to making sense of 1:18–2:16, it is helpful to note the following pieces of background and context.

Philotimia *("Love of Honor")*

Mark Finney wrote an important monograph on 1 Corinthians, pointing to *philotimia* as a foundational Greco-Roman value. Undoubtedly, this contributed to the agonistic nature of the divisions and disagreements in Corinth and also played a role in the Corinthians' ongoing criticisms and concerns regarding Paul's apostolic leadership. Paul must convince the Corinthians to think in new ways about the nature of honor, what the proper "court of reputation" should be, and how to interpret the cross of Christ vis-à-vis glory and shame. Paul must break through their honor-assumptions and values to shape a new pattern of communal existence—and he does so not by minimizing the cross, but by magnifying it. Finney comments:

> There, in the cross, the believer discovers that wisdom and power consist not in what the world values but in something quite different: it is found not in the lusting for honour but in selflessly laying status aside; not in taking advantage of others for the sake of appropriating more honour, but in giving up one's own advantage for the sake of the disadvantaged.... For Paul, the paradox of Christ crucified becomes the sole model for an ensuing paradoxical relation between the Jesus-movement and the honour-bound structures around them.[6]

---

4. Thiselton, *1 Corinthians*, 10.
5. Thiselton, *1 Corinthians*, 19.
6. Mark T. Finney, *Honour and Conflict in the Ancient World: 1 Corinthians in Its Greco-Roman Setting* (London: T&T Clark, 2012), 220.

The Cross's Wisdom and the Humble Foolishness of Faith in 1 Corinthians

The cross of Christ expected and inspired a kind of humility and meekness alien to the aspirations of many Greeks and Romans. As Victor Furnish reminds us, Greco-Roman religions tended to dwell on images of power in worship, "like a stalk of grain, a basket of fruit, or an erect phallus"—images of *life, power*, and *abundance*.[7] How disappointing it would have been, then, for Paul to fixate on the cross (1 Cor 2:2).

Rhetoric and Wisdom

Paul made it a point *not* to fulfill their desires for ear-tickling oration. An important monograph by Adam White gives extensive background to the matter of the expectations placed on, and approval given to, orators. White argues that Paul was being measured against the standards of popular orators of his day. Paul did not match up to their hopes, but Apollos apparently fared far better.[8]

The broader Greco-Roman concern for clever rhetoric notwithstanding, Richard Horsley rightly emphasizes that what we are probably dealing with in Corinth is a *Jewish* version of a value system that placed a strong weight on eloquent speech (cf. Philo; Wisdom of Solomon).[9]

In 1 Cor 1:8–2:16, Paul criticizes the Corinthians for their trivial divisions (1:10–17). Instead of refereeing their petty and divisive rallying, he brings the matter back to ground zero by reckoning with the cross (1:18). God seeks a "wiser wisdom" than the world can muster (1:18–20). The world's wisdom simply could not recognize the news of the gospel as good. Thus, the divine plan involved foolish proclamation "to save those who believe" (1:21 NRSV). The apostles focused neither on signs for Jews nor wisdom for Greeks but simply the crucified Christ, Jesus the criminal and fool (1:22–23).

Those who reject this crucified Jesus prove to be deaf and blind, but those who are called—both Jews and Greeks—see power in the message of the cross, and they hear divine wisdom (1:24)—that is, power and wisdom of a whole different category and order than mortals can produce (1:25).

---

7. Victor Furnish, *The Theology of the First Letter to the Corinthians* (Cambridge: Cambridge University Press, 1999), 39.

8. See Adam White, *Where Is the Wise Man? Graeco-Roman Education as a Background to the Divisions in 1 Corinthians 1–4* (London: T&T Clark, 2015).

9. Richard A. Horsley argues that Apollos would have been the historical link between the Corinthian situation and the Hellenistic-Jewish wisdom tradition; see *Wisdom and Spiritual Transcendence in Corinth* (Eugene, OR: Wipf & Stock, 2008).

In 1:26–31, Paul appeals to their reception of the gospel. God sought out the have-nots to prove that the world's values needed to be overturned (1:26–28).[10] Otherwise, the gospel would become another context for status, boasting, pride, and power, just as it has come to pass in Corinth (1:29). The message of the cross offers the chance, not for shame, but for new life, new wisdom, new righteousness, new consecration, and new redemption (1:30). To open oneself up to these things, though, one can no longer lay claim to any self-inflating boast; the glory belongs to God alone (1:31).

In chapter 2, Paul turns to his perspective on his ministry in Corinth. He went to Corinth "in weakness and in fear and in much trembling" (NRSV) when he came to preach the cross (2:1–3). His speeches had impact by the Spirit's power, not his impressive orations, otherwise the medium would drown out the message (2:4–5).

Paul does not deny that he came to impart wisdom—indeed he did offer wisdom—but it was God's "secret and hidden" wisdom, nonsense to the naked ear, eye, and brain (2:6–7). The Spirit alone sheds light on the wisdom that leaves everyone without aid in the dark (2:8–15). By the Spirit (and by πίστις), having the "mind of Christ," the believer could find wisdom in the "foolish" gospel of God and the message of the cross (2:16).

In 1 Cor 1–4, Paul connects these concepts together into one web: factionalism, wisdom, cross, boasting, Spirit, building, and apostleship.[11] In 1 Cor 1–2, the persistent emphasis is placed on divine wisdom.[12] Interestingly enough, despite the Corinthians being obsessed with wisdom, Paul was not shy about using the word σοφία in positive ways. Peter Lampe explains the matter in this way: "Paul wrests from the Greeks one of their most cherished terms. Taking over the term *sophia* as a vessel, he empties it of the associations that the Greeks have with 'wisdom.'"[13] The question before us presently relates to 2:5: how does Paul use πίστις to explicate this secret wisdom revealed in the cruciform gospel of Jesus Christ?

He writes: "My speech and my proclamation were not with plausible words of wisdom, but with a demonstration of the Spirit and of power, so that your πίστις might rest not on human wisdom but on the power of God"

---

10. See White, *Where Is the Wise Man?*, 76.

11. See Harm-Jan Inkelaar, *Conflict over Wisdom: The Theme of 1 Corinthians 1–4 Rooted in Scripture* (Leuven: Peeters, 2011), 105.

12. See Inkelaar, *Conflict over Wisdom*, 105–6.

13. Peter Lampe, "Theological Wisdom and the 'Word about the Cross': The Rhetorical Scheme in 1 Corinthians 1–4," *Interpretation* 44 (1990): 117–31 at 122.

(2:4-5 NRSV). Obviously most translations render πίστις here as faith, and commentators pay little attention to its occurrence in 2:5. Most scholars reckon this as a conventional use of πίστις, offering very little direct contribution to Paul's wisdom discourse. But Paul's careful wording actually bears much more weight than recognized on first glance.

First, 1 Cor 2:4-5 has an important role in Paul's early teaching in this letter, forming a bookend with 1:18.[14] In terms of how πίστις might relate to the particular controversies in Corinth, it should be pointed out that a few scholars identify πίστις as a kind of technical Hellenistic rhetorical term, in similar contexts encouraging the translation "conviction." In 2:4 Paul employed the word ἀπόδειξις, which is also standard Hellenistic rhetorical terminology; R. F. Collins is correct that πίστις (in such rhetorical contexts) means "proof" and ἀπόδειξις means "demonstrative proof."[15] Pheme Perkins, along these lines, translates πίστις in 2:5 as "conviction."[16] Scott Nash explains that when πίστις is used as a rhetorical term, "the focus is on how the hearers become convinced of the truth of the message."[17]

These observations are on the right track. That is, Paul purposefully used conventional rhetorical language here, but he was doing more, perhaps even alluding to a rhetoric term with a bit of irony. Paul may have tried to catch their ear with the word "conviction" (πίστις) but intended πίστις to be understood in light of a more Jewish prophetic use of faith language.

Πίστις here, then, becomes a catchword for a special way the mind embraces the foolish, "strange wisdom" of the cross message. The reason why πίστις serves the right role for this meaning relates to the kind of invisible nature of faith. Believing can sometimes be a sort of grasping in the dark, a leap into the abyss. This line of interpretation of πίστις in 2:5 may be demonstrated and defended by discussing three matters: (1) Paul's later

---

14. Richard B. Hays, *First Corinthians*, Interpretation (Louisville: Westminster John Knox, 1997), 36; cf. Gordon D. Fee, *The First Epistle to the Corinthians*, 2nd ed., New International Commentary on the New Testament (Grand Rapids: Eerdmans, 2014), 101.

15. Raymond F. Collins, *First Corinthians*, Sacra Pagina 7 (Collegeville, MN: Liturgical Press, 1999), 117.

16. Pheme Perkins, *First Corinthians*, Paideia (Grand Rapids: Baker, 2012), 57.

17. R. Scott Nash, *First Corinthians* (Macon, GA: Smyth & Helwys, 2009), 93; cf. Craig S. Keener, *1-2 Corinthians* (Cambridge: Cambridge University Press, 2005), 35. Interestingly, Inkelaar *does* give attention to how ἀπόδειξις (2:4) can function as a rhetorical term but does not address the rhetorical use of πίστις; *Conflict over Wisdom*, 46.

link between πίστις and the resurrection (15:12–34), (2) his use of πιστεύω in 1:21, and (3) the important role that πιστεύω plays in Septuagint Isaiah, especially in view of Paul's use of Septuagint Isaiah in 1 Cor 1–4.[18]

In 15:12 Paul responds to those who deny the resurrection of the dead. As many scholars argue, the underlying problem seems to be the distaste among pagans of the idea of the raised and eternal *body*. Nash explains: "The prospect of reinvigorated corpses was alien to most Gentiles."[19] Paul works backward from this disbelief. If there will be no raising of the dead bodies of Christ followers, then this denies the resurrection of Jesus's body. And the reclaiming and renewal of Jesus's body from the sentence of death is so central to the gospel that the whole structure of the gospel would collapse. As many scholars affirm, resurrection is not just about the reanimation of the body, but the nature of discipleship and the Christian life itself—the claims of the gospel promise ultimate justice and vindication from the suffering of the body: "If there is no resurrection, this self-denying style of life makes no sense; those who follow the example of Jesus and Paul are chumps missing out on their fair share of life's rewards."[20]

Believers anticipating the bodily resurrection, then, must live by *faith* because the restoration they bank on is almost inconceivable. But if it proves a lie, that πίστις was indeed misplaced and hollow (15:14, 17). Almost certainly with intention (in view of 13:13), Paul links faith (πίστις) and *hoping* (ἐλπίζω): "If for this life only we have hoped in Christ, we are of all people most to be pitied" (15:19 NRSV). Paul could have virtually said: "If for this life only we *had faith in* Christ" or "*believed in* Christ." What faith and hope have in common in this context is a kind of *wager*, the *risk* of faith. It is a gamble. But that does not mean Paul did not see evidence or reason. Rather, the evidence must be recognized by the eyes of faith, seeing what many do not see, recognizing what is virtually imperceptible.

---

18. Teresa Morgan's approach to Paul's use of πίστις in 1 Corinthians, even 2:5, is decisively nonepistemological; that is, she views Paul's use of πίστις here as part of the relational dynamic between God, Christ, and humanity, and in particular to the "divine power which the faithful human channels." This does not seem to capture Paul's own clear focus in this section on foolish belief through divine wisdom; see *Roman Faith and Christian Faith: Pistis and Fides in the Early Roman Empire and the Early Churches* (Oxford: Oxford University Press, 2015), 248–52 at 252.

19. Nash, *First Corinthians*, 402.

20. Hays, *First Corinthians*, 262; cf. C. K. Barrett, *The First Epistle to the Corinthians* (Peabody, MA: Hendrickson, 1968), 350.

The Cross's Wisdom and the Humble Foolishness of Faith in 1 Corinthians

In 1:18 Paul dropped the bomb of his cross hermeneutic. That is, the cross establishes the true dividing line between those who think with the wisdom of God and those who remain in the stupor of carnal folly. It is almost as if the cross is portrayed as a test. I think of the old nickel and dime trick. One child may say to an unsuspecting friend, "If you give me all of your dimes, I will give you all of my *larger* nickels." The trick is that, even though—to the eager eye—the nickels are larger, they are *actually* of lesser value. One must be "in the know" to recognize that the thinner and smaller dimes are more valuable.

That kind of *seeing-with-something-other-than-eyes* is what Paul means by faith and how he identifies those who believe: "For since, in the wisdom of God, the world did not know God through wisdom, God decided, through the foolishness of our proclamation, to save those who believe" (1:21 NRSV). It is clear that Paul is establishing a link between foolishness and those who believe. "Believing" is not a neutral term here. Almost certainly it is meant to carry a negative value from the standpoint of the wider world. *Believers are fools*. In that sense, then, believers are treated by the world as blind, hence they do indeed have a sense of "blind faith." They see the (hidden) value in the dull, small dimes, but the world is transfixed on the shiny, large nickels.

Paul could have used other language for Christians in 1:21 (e.g., those who are "called"; cf. 1:24). But using πιστεύω in 1:21 makes perfect sense as an anticipation of 1:28. God intentionally chose "what is low and despised"— *the nothings*—to devalue what seems to be precious on worldly standards. For Paul, this transvaluation, difficult to explain, impossible to prove, requires the eyes and wisdom of faith. The section ends with the repudiation of boasting (1:29) and the elevation of Christ (1:30). Paul underscores that boasting in what is leads to self-inflation. But the word of the cross leads to humble faith.

This view of belief and faith in 1:18–30 relates to Alexandra Brown's work on Pauline apocalyptic epistemology. In her important monograph *The Cross and Human Transformation*, Brown argues that Paul sets his sight in 1 Corinthians on transforming the Corinthians' imagination via his "Word of the Cross." She writes: "His battleground is the realm of human perception; wielding the Word of the Cross, he invades the perceptual landscape of his hearers, cutting across their accustomed (and, he believes, false) ways of knowing with the sharp expression of a new reality."[21]

---

21. Alexandra Brown, *The Cross and Human Transformation: Paul's Apocalyptic Word in 1 Corinthians* (Minneapolis: Fortress, 1995), xvii.

While Brown does not discuss πιστεύω directly, she taps into the kind of meanings that Paul associates with this word group in 1 Corinthians. Brown notes how Paul referred to the Corinthians as believers insofar as they were tuned into the gospel he preached, which aimed to alter their perception and interpretation of the world around them. Certainly his letter is corrective, but he was simply desiring to further build on the gospel message that they had already accepted. They had embraced Christ, but their minds had not fully integrated the gospel regarding wisdom and power.[22]

Brown offers a long list of "perception" terms in 1 Cor 1–2 to strengthen her case that Paul dwells on this wisdom-cross-perception nexus, but I am surprised that she left πιστεύω/πίστις off the list.[23] Later on, she offers a chart of asymmetrical terms/phrases in 2:5 and excludes πίστις there as well. Her juxtaposition of "human wisdom" with "power of God" offers a sensible contrast, but πίστις here is shaped or formed by that source (human wisdom or divine power) and also is what accepts Paul's message (see 2:4).[24] Another two dozen pages or so later, she returns to 2:5 and briefly mentions faith, but her comments are closely aligned with Paul's use of πίστις and πιστεύω in 1 Cor 1–2: "The 'power of God' on which faith rests in 2:5 is none other than the power manifested in the cross of Christ. The human wisdom in which faith must *not* rest is the wisdom that perceives the cross as folly and thus 'empties' it."[25]

Paul's use of πιστεύω (1:21) and πίστις (2:5) are not merely conventional or traditional but instead contribute to his argument on cross wisdom and the transvaluation of values. According to Paul, Christian faith requires a

---

22. See Brown, *Cross and Human Transformation*, 163. Brown sees Paul's corrective teaching as epistemologically oriented: "The Word he offers can move his hearers into the transfigured wisdom and power of the cruciform existence only if it *both* creates cognitive dissonance (dislocation) *and* provides the positive impetus to *re*-locate in the new world it prescribes" (163).

23. See Brown, *Cross and Human Transformation*, 24–25; cf. 97, where πιστεύω/πίστις is absent as well. She includes ἀπόδειξις in this list, which is particularly surprising given that these words appear together commonly within discussions of rhetoric. Furthermore, and perhaps more important, of the more than twenty-five words in 1 Cor 1–2 that Brown finds to be related to "perceptual terminology," according to Johannes Louw and Eugene Nida, several of these (such as κρίνω, φρονέω, πείθω, and γινώσκω) fit into the same semantic family as πιστεύω/πίστις; see "Hold a View, Believe, Trust," in *Greek-English Lexicon of the New Testament: Based on Semantic Domains* (New York: United Bible Societies, 1996), §31.1–107.

24. See Brown, *Cross and Human Transformation*, 76.

25. Brown, *Cross and Human Transformation*, 101.

The Cross's Wisdom and the Humble Foolishness of Faith in 1 Corinthians

transfigured perception that sees wisdom and power in the cross, accepting the truth of the way of Jesus humbly. This access to truth requires careful thought, patience, and lowliness to gain the right perspective on the matter. Paul acknowledges in 1 Corinthians that this kind of wisdom from God is strange—unusual and even repulsive, just as the cross was offensive. In light of this nonsensical nature of the cross of Christ, faith must learn to see with new sight the reality of God *sub contrario*.

Let us examine 1 Cor 1–2 once more with a view toward this epistemological dimension of his faith language in mind, but this time pay attention to echoes of Septuagint Isaiah in these chapters. Many scholars observe the close integration of word and thought from Septuagint Isaiah in the early chapters of 1 Corinthians:

1 Corinthians (NRSV)	Septuagint Isaiah (NETS)	Isaianic Context
"For it is written, 'I will destroy the wisdom of the wise, and the discernment of the discerning I will thwart.'" (1:19)	"Therefore look, I will proceed to remove this people. I will remove them and destroy the wisdom of the wise, and the discernment of the discerning I will hide." (29:14)	Isaiah describes the mysterious way of God working out his plan. He will crush Jerusalem, then its enemies. God will shut off the sources of knowledge and wisdom (29:11–13).
"Where is the one who is wise? Where is the scribe? Where is the debater of this age? Has not God made foolish the wisdom of the world?" (1:20)	"Where are the scholars? Where are the counselors? Where is the one who counts those gathering together?" (33:18)	This is a prophecy of eschatological judgment on the wicked. When the king comes, he will shatter the old systems.
"God decided, through the foolishness of our proclamation, to save those who believe." (1:21b)	"See, I will lay for the foundations of Sion a precious, choice stone, a highly valued cornerstone for its foundations, and the one who believes in him will not be put to shame." (28:16)	The people have set up their own safety nets via deals with the devil (28:15), but God wants to give them a stable place if they put their trust in him (28:16).

1 Corinthians (NRSV)	Septuagint Isaiah (NETS)	Isaianic Context
"But, as it is written, 'What no eye has seen, nor ear heard, nor the human heart conceived, what God has prepared for those who love him.'" (2:9)	"From ages past we have not heard, nor have our eyes seen any God besides you, and your works, which you will do to those who wait for mercy." (64:4)	Israel is called to trust in the faithfulness of its God.
"'For who has known the mind of the Lord so as to instruct him?' But we have the mind of Christ." (2:16)	"Who has known the mind of the Lord, and who has been his counselor to instruct him?" (40:13)	YHWH the Creator knows all things and will make good on his promises of deliverance. He needs no counsel or help.

From the texts Paul quoted (or alluded to), we see that he was picking up on themes in Septuagint Isaiah that contrast the folly of human assumptions and carnal decisions with the often imperceptible wisdom and ways of God. Particularly in the allusion to Isa 28:16 (cf. 1 Cor 1:21b), there is that strong emphasis on *belief* (πιστεύω). The Hebrew verb אמן could be translated "the one who trusts" (NRSV) or "the one who relies" (NIV). The verb πιστεύω draws out especially the aspect of *believing with the mind*. The world can be divided, so Septuagint Isaiah underscores, into those with believing eyes and those without.[26] Interestingly, even beyond the texts used formally in 1 Corinthians, there is a connection between believing and understanding:

> And if you do not believe, neither shall you stand [ἐὰν μὴ πιστεύσητε, οὐδὲ μὴ συνῆτε]. (Isa 7:9 NETS)

> Be my witnesses; I too am a witness, says the Lord God, and the servant whom I have chosen so that you may know and believe and understand [ἵνα γνῶτε καὶ πιστεύσητε καὶ συνῆτε] that I am. Before me there was no other god, nor shall there be any after me. (Isa 43:10 NETS)

---

26. See H. H. Drake Williams, *The Wisdom of the Wise: The Presence and Function of Scripture within 1 Corinthians 1:18–3:23* (Boston: Brill, 2001), 52, 98, 342.

The Cross's Wisdom and the Humble Foolishness of Faith in 1 Corinthians

In both of these passages we see the same two words used in tandem: believe (πιστεύω) and understand (συνίημι). Clearly, for Isaiah, God was calling for trust, but these texts seem to go even further to understand the kind of shift in thinking and perspective that can *see* and *perceive* the work of God where others cannot.[27] This comes to a head in the fourth Servant Song (52:13–53:12), starting with 53:1: "Who has believed our report? And to whom has the arm of the Lord been revealed?" (NETS). The idea is that what God is up to is *unbelievable*. How can it be trusted if it seems so outlandish? So ridiculous? In order for it to be accepted, the Lord will have to *reveal* to them (hence ἀποκαλύπτω; Isa 53:1b).

This undercurrent of Septuagint Isaiah fits rather well Paul's overall agenda in 1 Cor 1–4. One cannot simply glance over at God and see what he is up to. Or, one cannot look at success and wisdom in the world and glibly conclude that God has been at work. However things may have been intended to work, sin has distorted and frustrated such earthly reflections of divine wisdom. Thus, human wisdom and human senses cannot be trusted; they are not foolproof. Charles Cousar captures rather poignantly Paul's key points in these chapters, particularly 1:18–25:

> The problem with "the language of worldly wisdom" is that it cannot enable the world to know God; it cannot bring God to speech. Instead, Paul argues that the preaching of the crucified Messiah, understandably foolish to the eyes of the world, becomes the instrument whereby God confounds the wisdom of the wise and thwarts the cleverness of the clever; and irony of ironies, the crucified Messiah turns out to be the very wisdom of God.[28]

Paul's language of *faith* and *believing* in 1 Corinthians contributes to these points on wisdom and knowing God and his ways. Faith is the mode of perception and reception that can see light in the darkness of God's foolish wisdom. Belief is the hand that can reach into the knot of the divine mystery and pull at the loosest thread. This faith is strange because it is the mind and heart working and thinking and interacting in an unnatural way, a way uncomfortable in the world. It is a humble faith because it cannot rest on dominant cultural securities, nor natural senses per se, but especially on the ways and promises of God. That is why I call this kind of πίστις "believing

---

27. See Inkelaar, *Conflict over Wisdom*, 268–69.
28. Charles B. Cousar, "1 Corinthians 2:1–13," *Interpretation* 44 (1990): 169–73 at 170.

the unbelievable." It is unbelievable to embrace the cross. As Cousar notes, "In the cross God does not look and act like a respectable God ought to look and act. God's ways are simply not our ways."[29] So the mind and heart are stretched. They are not bypassed but trained to operate differently: *"This revelation of God remains imperceptible to human criteria and canons of knowing."*[30] Faith is needed to make sense of God beyond the noise of the world's idols: "To know God is to be refashioned as knowers, to abandon the illusion that we are self-made and self-taught."[31]

Paul and the Gift of Πίστις (12:9; 13:2)

One of the issues about which the Corinthians inquired to Paul involves spiritual gifts (περὶ δὲ τῶν πνευματικῶν; 12:1). As Richard Hays interprets this, "Some of the Corinthians have placed inordinate emphasis on showy displays of spirituality, especially the gift of speaking in tongues; it seems that some of them are disrupting or dominating the church's meetings by disorderly spirit-inspired utterance that is unintelligible to other members of the community."[32] No doubt this sort of attitude toward spiritual power, exclusivism, and superiority is self-centered. Paul pushes the discussion toward building up the community with these spiritual gifts.[33]

Paul lists numerous gifts in the early part of chapter 12 (12:7-11): utterances of wisdom and knowledge,[34] prophecy, "discernment of spirits,"

---

29. Cousar, "1 Corinthians 2:1-13," 172.

30. Cousar, "1 Corinthians 2:1-13," 172.

31. Cousar, "1 Corinthians 2:1-13," 173; cf. similarly Richard B. Hays, "Wisdom according to Paul," in *Where Shall Wisdom Be Found?* ed. Stephen C. Barton (Edinburgh: T&T Clark, 1998), 111-23.

32. Hays, *First Corinthians*, 206.

33. See Gail R. O'Day, "The Ethical Shape of Pauline Spirituality," *Brethren Life and Thought* 32 (1987): 81-92 at 82: "The move Paul makes is to locate the Corinthians' concerns about spirituality and spiritual gifts in the context of the worship of the assembled community.... The worship of the [community] is the strongest demonstration of the community empowered and gifted by the Spirit, and the clearest demonstration of the purpose and function of this spiritual empowerment."

34. Marion Soards rightly associates wisdom here with "God-given insight into the mysterious purposes and workings of God in and through Jesus Christ"; see *1 Corinthians*, New International Biblical Commentary (Peabody, MA: Hendrickson,

The Cross's Wisdom and the Humble Foolishness of Faith in 1 Corinthians

various kinds of tongues (and interpretation of tongues), and so forth. In 12:9 Paul mentions a gift of faith (πίστις) along with a (separate) gift of "healing by the one Spirit." What is this "gift of faith"? One line of reasoning, especially supported by Paul Sampley, is that this is simply a reference to Christian faith.[35] That is, this is a kind of egalitarian move, whereby Paul is undercutting any sense of gift-enabled superiority. Thus, Paul would be saying, everyone has a gift, in some cases that gift is their faith, and "accordingly, no one can view himself or herself as being bereft of Spirit-endowed *charismata*."[36] The major drawback of this view is that Paul is imagining a group of people and hypothetically saying *one has the wisdom gift, another has the tongues gift, and yet another (ἑτέρῳ) has a gift of faith*. That would imply that *some* have this πίστις gift, but others do not.[37]

A more likely interpretation treats the reference to πίστις as relating to miracle working.[38] This view goes back at least to Chrysostom, who defines this πίστις as not "the faith of doctrines, but the faith of miracles" (*Homilies on 1 Corinthians* §29.5). The use of πίστις implies that the focus is not simply on the *act* of healing, but on the personal *faith* that trusts God and acts accordingly, from a "supernatural conviction that God will reveal divine power or mercy in a special way in a specific instance," as Gordon Fee explains.[39]

James Dunn's view overlaps somewhat with the above, but his emphasis is more on inexplicable trust and reliance on God to do something extraordinary; he describes the πίστις gift as "a mysterious surge of confidence which sometimes arises within a man in a particular situation of need or challenge and which gives him an otherly certainty and assurance that God is about to act through word or through an action (such as laying hands on someone sick)."[40] For Dunn, this certainly could include the gifted

---

1999), 258; cf. David E. Garland, *First Corinthians*, Baker Exegetical Commentary on the New Testament (Grand Rapids: Baker, 2003), 581.

35. Paul Sampley, "The First Letter to the Corinthians," in *The New Interpreter's Bible*, ed. Leander E. Keck (Nashville: Abingdon, 2002), 10:944.

36. Sampley, "First Letter to the Corinthians," 944; similarly see Roy A. Harrisville, *1 Corinthians* (Minneapolis: Augsburg, 1987), 208.

37. Ben Witherington III, *Conflict and Community in Corinth* (Grand Rapids: Eerdmans, 1995), 257.

38. See Brian Rosner and Roy Ciampa, *The First Letter to the Corinthians*, Pillar New Testament Commentary (Grand Rapids: Eerdmans, 2010), 577.

39. Fee, *First Corinthians*, 581.

40. See James D. G. Dunn, *Unity and Diversity in the New Testament* (Philadelphia: Westminster, 1977), 211, as cited in Garland, *First Corinthians*, 581.

person performing a healing act, but it could also be the faith that he or she is going to *be* healed.[41]

It is appropriate to heed Hays's word of warning about reading too much into this list of gifts—it is meant to be illustrative, not encyclopedic.[42] Nevertheless, I still find Dunn's argument compelling. As noted above, in the early chapters of 1 Corinthians Paul used πίστις and πιστεύω as the way one relies on the foolish wisdom of God, "strange wisdom" that requires sometimes upside-down thinking, patience, and humility to be perceiving and judging rightly in the way of Jesus in the face of accusations of weakness and ignominy. To rely on that kind of faith (πίστις) involves, again, stepping into the dark to grasp the hand of God, to walk by the wisdom of God in the twilight of the cross. This sort of meaning or nuance of the word "faith" depends on the sometimes inscrutable will of God. One might even dare to translate this "gift of foolish faith," a strangely confident sprint into the abyss when you are the only one who can hear God's voice.[43]

Despite the great value of *this* sort of faith, Paul almost immediately makes a caveat: "If I have prophetic powers, and understand all mysteries and all knowledge, and if I have all faith, so as to remove mountains, but do not have love, I am nothing" (13:2 NRSV). Paul used πίστις in 12:9 precisely to subvert boasting (faith is the foolish risk of trusting the invisible God), but even *that* gift can be distorted and ruined by selfish ambition. The usage of the Spirit's gifts is ultimately for the blessing, goodness, and welfare of the other; even God-given, miracle-working (or miracle-believing) πίστις can become empty without that motivation and enactment of love. On that note, I turn to πίστις in 1 Cor 13, where Paul dwells on the virtues of faith, hope, and love (13:13).

Faith, Hope, Love: Is Faith Eternal? (13:13)

In 1 Cor 13, he transitions from his discourse on spiritual gifts (12:1–11) to an affirmation of the interdependence of the members of the body (12:12–31). Only thirteen verses long, 1 Cor 13 presents Paul's argument that the show-stopping gifts given and empowered by the Spirit are ultimately meaningless

---

41. Dunn, *Unity and Diversity*, 211.
42. Hays, *First Corinthians*, 211.
43. For a similar expression of this idea, see Thiselton, *1 Corinthians*, 945.

and vapid without the motivation and action of love.[44] The exercise of gifts can do more damage than good if love is not present.

Obviously the focus of 1 Cor 13 is on ἀγάπη, but faith language does figure into the equation as well. Paul refers to the possibility of having "all faith" (πᾶσαν τὴν πίστιν), and yet the believer languishes without love (13:2). Starting in 13:4, Paul waxes on the many virtues of ἀγάπη—it is patient, kind, generous, humble, and gentle (13:4–5). It dwells on truth and justice (13:6). It bears all things, and it *hopes* (ἐλπίζει) and *believes* (πιστεύει; 13:7). It is not necessary to unpack exactly what Paul means here, but as the discussion of 13:13 will show, πιστεύω here foreshadows Paul's climactic, triadic statement.[45] Paul is at pains to argue that real love is tough as nails. It is resilient, tenacious, waterproof, fireproof, indestructible, impenetrable, and indefatigable.

Starting in 13:8b, Paul transitions to the passing of eras or stages. Prophecies, tongues, and even knowledge will fade away. They are not permanent, eternal things. As Hays explains:

> The Corinthians . . . seem to have lost hold of the future temporal orientation of Paul's preaching. They have moved into a frame of reference that thinks only in spatial categories of "above" and "below." They believe that their spiritual gifts give them immediate access to the divine world, and they are not thinking at all about the future event of God's judgment and transformation of the world. In their frame of reference, revelatory spiritual gifts have assumed ultimate significance, because they provide the open, "hot line" links to heavenly reality. Paul wants to relativize these gifts by situating them within the unfolding epic narrative of God's redemption of the world: they have a role to play for now, but the time of their usefulness will pass.[46]

---

44. See Steven L. Cox, "1 Corinthians 13—An Antidote to Violence: Love," *Review and Expositor* 93 (1996): 529–36. Cox sums up the thrust of this chapter particularly well in his conclusion: "Spiritual gifts are not a sign of spiritual maturity in themselves. . . . Spiritual maturity is demonstrated in how we uses [*sic*] the spiritual gifts with which we have been endowed. Every Christian is commissioned to use these gifts, with the motive of love as the antidote to evil and violence in the world" (535).

45. See Hays, *First Corinthians*, 228.

46. Hays, *First Corinthians*, 229. Similarly, Garland writes: "In contrast to love, the spiritual gifts have a built-in obsolescence. They are not permanent and do not get perfected"; *First Corinthians*, 621.

STRANGE WISDOM

What lasts then, are not the boast-worthy products of these gifts, but rather those things that remain: faith, hope, and love. Given that the emphasis in this chapter is on love, why does Paul include faith and hope? We ought to note the distinct way these are introduced. He very well could have written: Νυνὶ δὲ μένει πίστις, ἐλπίς, ἀγάπη and stopped there, but he adds τὰ τρία ταῦτα ("these three"), which means something like *the big three*. There is probably some sense of formality with Paul including faith and hope in this chapter on love. That is, this family of three virtues ought not to be separated; where love is found, so its siblings are not far away. Undoubtedly, this points to the triad operating even by this time as a common teaching or tradition in earliest Christianity (cf. 1 Thess 1:3).[47]

There is some question in scholarship on 1 Cor 13:13, though, about how Paul views faith and hope in relation to love. He writes: Νυνὶ δὲ μένει πίστις, ἐλπίς, ἀγάπη, τὰ τρία ταῦτα· μείζων δὲ τούτων ἡ ἀγάπη. Most scholars interpret this verse to mean that the spiritual gifts are passing, but these "big three" virtues are permanent. Myron Houghton challenges this reading. First, what does Paul mean by "now"? Is it temporal or logical? Second, what does it mean for these to "remain"? Finally, does not Paul imply in 13:12 that partial knowing (assumingly involve faith) will give way to full knowledge. Thus, how can faith be permanent when it ought to be replaced by sight (cf. 2 Cor 5:7)?[48] So, Houghton reads 1 Cor 13:8–13 in this way: faith and hope are not permanent (they will cease at Christ's return; Rom 8:24), but they will outlast prophecy, tongues, and knowledge. Love is greater than faith and hope because love alone is truly eternal.[49]

---

47. See Wolfgang Weiss, "Glaube-Liebe-Hoffnung: Zu der Trias bei Paulus," *Zeitschrift für die neutestamentliche Wissenschaft* 84 (1993): 197–217. Weiss resists the idea that the tradition is pre-Pauline. Rather he considers it a Pauline formulation. After considering the scholarly options for its origins and main influences, Ceslas Spicq argues that neither Greek thought nor Judaism inspired this triad per se, but it seems to derive from "the teaching and the life of the Lord, especially in the Sermon on the Mount, and the fruit of the Holy Spirit in the soul of the converts" (214); *Agape in the New Testament* (St. Louis: Herder, 1963), 205–14; cf. A. M. Hunter, *Paul and His Predecessors* (London: SCM, 1961), 33–35.

48. Myron J. Houghton, "A Reexamination of 1 Corinthians 13:8–13," *Bibliotheca Sacra* 153 (1996): 344–56.

49. See especially Houghton's concluding statement in "1 Corinthians 13:8–13," 356.

The Cross's Wisdom and the Humble Foolishness of Faith in 1 Corinthians

Houghton raises important questions about 1 Cor 13:8–13, but he downgrades the significance of faith and hope for Paul.⁵⁰ Paul treats them as equals in the triad elsewhere (1 Thess 1:3). And, even in 1 Corinthians, he emphasizes the absolute significance of faith *and* hope (1 Cor 15). Richard Morgan addressed this matter about a decade earlier than Houghten and argued for a reading that supports the *permanence* of faith alongside hope and love.⁵¹ Instead of reading πίστις as a temporary, perhaps even inferior, form of knowledge, Morgan interprets it in 13:13 as *trust*: "Faith is *trust* in God, *reliance* on God, it is a personal relationship with God. Faith says that God grasps, holds and supports us, and not vice-versa.... Knowledge or ... sight cannot replace this, to all eternity."⁵²

Morgan adds a second point about Paul's use of πίστις here. Faith is also associated for Paul with *humility*, and this virtue too is eternal. Humble faith "places the centre of [the believer's] being in the one in whom he has faith."⁵³ Morgan admits that in the present time πίστις does carry a sense of uncertainty, but in the age to come, though the uncertainty will give way to full knowledge, the *trust* will persist as "gratitude in love's response to Love."⁵⁴ Hays defines it as "the trust that we direct toward the God of Israel, who has kept faith with his covenant promises by putting forward Jesus for our sake and raising him to new life."⁵⁵

To sum up the interpretation of πίστις in 13:13, then, Paul's invocation of the virtue triad of faith-hope-love was not incidental. It was not a piece of tradition wedged into his love teaching. Almost certainly his desire to write about love may have *called to mind* the virtue's siblings faith and hope, but

---

50. On the interpretation of νυνὶ, I concur with Hays that the eschatological orientation of 13:8–12 points to a temporal reading; *First Corinthians*, 230.

51. Richard Morgan, "Faith, Hope, and Love Abide," *Churchman* 101 (1987): 128–39.

52. Morgan, "Faith, Hope, and Love Abide," 128.

53. Morgan, "Faith, Hope, and Love Abide," 130.

54. Morgan, "Faith, Hope, and Love Abide," 130. Somewhat similar sentiments are expressed in John W. Bowman, "Three Imperishables: A Meditation on 1 Corinthians 13," *Interpretation* 13 (1959): 433–43. Thiselton argues that faith, hope, and love all eternally abide, but only love does not go through a transformation; see *1 Corinthians*, 1074.

55. Hays explains hope as "our fervent desire to see a broken world restored by God to its rightful wholeness." Love, then, is "the foretaste of our ultimate union with God, graciously given to us now and shared with our brothers and sisters"; *First Corinthians*, 230.

they too brought something important to his point in 1 Cor 13. They help to explain and define the nature of love. And here is where we can glance back toward 13:7: love *believes* all things. What would it mean for love to *believe*? Almost certainly Paul is not talking about believing "beliefs" per se. He is not focused on *what* love believes but on the *weight* and *strength* of that believing. Just as love *bears* and *endures*, so it *believes* and *hopes*. That is, it is intimately invested without hesitation, just as we might say today, *I believe in you*! That means that we trust and have full confidence in the other; we rely on the other. We put something at risk, we wager something in our dependence on and trust of the other. For love to believe all means that it never loses faith and hope.[56]

This reading of πίστις for 13:13 (with consideration of πιστεύω in 13:7) probably fits the "believing allegiance" or "trusting faith" nuance of πίστις. That would make sense only in light of the comprehensive quality of the faith-hope-love triad. Still, one must read 1 Cor 13 in light of the important formative teaching on wisdom and faith in 1 Cor 1–4. The Corinthians' pride in spirituality and wisdom demonstrates their attitude of autonomy, self-sufficiency, and superiority. The Corinthians wanted to revel in pride and (vain)glory. For Paul to underscore πίστις was theologically calculated to pull the Corinthians toward humble faith in the strange wisdom of God. This is not oriented around particular ear-tickling ideas, nor stupefying tricks or electrifying sophistry. It is utterly dependent on the revelation and work of the *deus absconditus* hidden under the sign of the cross.

Conclusion

Paul could use faith language to point to the importance of a cruciform epistemology. To have faith in Christ is necessarily counterintuitive and requires a conversion or transformation of the imagination—hence, "strange wisdom." In Paul's second canonical letter to the Corinthians, this same concept is reinforced in an even more overt and extreme manner. It is almost as if Paul speaks with the voice of a prophet to the Corinthians, inquiring, *Who has believed our message? And to whom has the arm of the Lord been revealed?*

---

56. See Thiselton, *1 Corinthians*, 1059.

7   On Faith and Forms

Πίστις and True Ministry in 2 Corinthians

> Cleave ever to the sunnier side of doubt,
> And cling to Faith beyond the forms of Faith!
> She reels not in the storm of warring words,
> She brightens at the clash of "Yes" and "No,"
> She sees the Best that glimmers thro' the Worst,
> She feels the Sun is hid but for a night,
> She spies the summer thro' the winter bud,
> She tastes the fruit before the blossom falls,
> She hears the lark within the songless egg,
> She finds the fountain where they wail'd "Mirage"!
>
> —Alfred Tennyson, "The Ancient Sage"

When one thinks of Paul's faith language, his "justification by faith" statements perhaps come most readily to mind. But a close second would perhaps be the pithy line "we walk by faith, not by sight." One sometimes hears this quoted when something unfathomable happens, a tragedy perhaps, and all that can be said is "we walk by faith." That is, we don't know the *why*, but we trust that God has things under control. Sometimes this is equated with the notion of *blind faith*. Is that what Paul was encouraging? The kind of faith that has no rhyme or reason? Paul's lengthy Corinthian epistles themselves should show us that he was a skilled thinker and writer who invested heavily in evidence-based argumentation and reasoning from logic. He never encouraged the Corinthians, or anyone else for that matter, to "just believe."

And yet. How should we understand this notion of living *by faith* as opposed to *sight*? When we read 2 Cor 5:7 in light of the wider context of 4:1–5:10, the overaching message has directly to do with Paul's understanding of the framework for how a believer ought to view *reality*, especially in light of how one knows and relates to *Christ*. He presses a counterperspective to the way that some have taught the Corinthians to think. One perspective—namely that of Paul's opponents in Corinth—promotes the diagnostics of glory and external power as indicators of leadership and success in ministry and life. *When searching for signs of life, be on the lookout for radiance, beauty, majesty, and strength, they urged. Why would it be otherwise?* Paul, probably to the chagrin of a status-concerned Corinthian community, points to signs of life in rather the opposite—weakness, meekness, what is not, and what is often unseen. That is, what is absent to the eye but visible to the spirit; what lacks in resplendent form but is priceless in the economy of faith.

Paul engages with this clash of worldviews via the ideology of idolatry. Jews famously repudiated idols and the crafting of divine forms for a number of reasons, not least because idol construction and idol worship seek to domesticate the divine and shape it into a creaturely image. Jews entrusted themselves to an invisible God, a God who desires the kind of attention that goes beyond making requests before a statue. First I overview 2 Corinthians with an interest in its context. Then I focus more directly on 4:1–5:10. In tandem I note how Paul connects the theology of idolatry to this situation and articulates a theology of πίστις that stands against a form-centered and glory-centered perspective.

Second Corinthians and the Corinthian Situation

Second Corinthians is called the "sleeping giant" among Paul's letters because it is one of the most theologically rich texts, but too often overshadowed by Romans, Galatians, and of course its older sibling 1 Corinthians. Furthermore, the interpretation of 2 Corinthians is fraught with technical debates concerning the Corinthian situation, the identity of troublemakers in Corinth, and the nature of the text of the letter itself (especially its literary integrity).

When it comes to the unity of the letter, it is common for scholars to presume two separate documents, 2 Cor 1–9 and 2 Cor 10–13. Furthermore, some divide it up into smaller pieces; a common assertion, for example, is that 6:14–7:1 is an interpolation. John Barclay probably captures the current attitude toward the whole letter: "Reading 2 Corinthians as a whole, one is impressed both by its thematic coherence and by its sometimes disjointed progression of thought."¹ While it was not long ago that most scholars presumed that 2 Corinthians was originally more than one Pauline letter, the tide is turning such that either the majority of scholars find arguments for textual integrity convincing or else they at least take an agnostic perspective, unwilling to read letter portions on the basis of hypothetical origins and reconstructed chronology. Here I presume the unity of the letter.²

Again, taking for granted the literary integrity of 2 Corinthians, we can assume the presence of certain superapostles in Corinth who questioned Paul's authority in, and effectiveness of, his ministry (11:5, 13; 12:11). While these troublemakers are not explicitly mentioned until the final chapters of the letter, a case can be made that Paul builds the letters *toward* explicitly naming their presence and influence.³

Who were these rivals? George Guthrie, working from hints and clues in 2 Corinthians itself, describes them as "Jewish-Christian ministers working under strong influences of the Sophistic tradition."⁴ Guthrie notes how Paul addresses before the Corinthians problems related to "public appearance, social status, powerful oratory, words of worldly 'wisdom,' style over content, pay for speaking, boasting about achievements, public applause," that is, elements that can be linked to the Sophistic movement.⁵

---

1. John M. G. Barclay, "2 Corinthians," in *Eerdmans Commentary on the Bible*, ed. James D. G. Dunn (Grand Rapids: Eerdmans, 2003), 1353–73 at 1353.

2. Defenders of letter unity include David A. deSilva, "Measuring Penultimate against Ultimate: An Investigation of the Integrity and Argumentation of 2 Corinthians," *Journal for the Study of the New Testament* 52 (1993): 41–70; Murray J. Harris, *The Second Epistle to the Corinthians*, New International Greek Testament Commentary (Grand Rapids: Eerdmans, 2005); George Guthrie, *2 Corinthians*, Baker Exegetical Commentary on the New Testament (Grand Rapids: Baker, 2015); David Garland, *2 Corinthians*, New American Commentary (Nashville: Broadman & Holman, 1999), 40. On 6:14–7:1 in particular see Jan Lambrecht, "The Fragment 2 Cor 6:14–7:1: A Plea for Its Authenticity," *Miscellanea neotestamentica* 2 (1978): 143–61; more recently, Christopher Land, *The Integrity of 2 Corinthians and Paul's Aggravating Absence* (Sheffield: Sheffield Phoenix Press, 2015), esp. 238–81.

3. See Jerome Murphy-O'Connor, *The Theology of the Second Letter to the Corinthians* (Cambridge: Cambridge University Press, 1991), 12.

4. Guthrie, *2 Corinthians*, 45. See similarly, Craig S. Keener, "Paul and the Corinthian Believers," in *The Blackwell Companion to Paul*, ed. Stephen Westerholm (Oxford: Blackwell, 2011), 46–62 at 58.

5. Guthrie, *2 Corinthians*, 45.

These superapostles not only focused on their own impressive speeches and ministries but apparently criticized Paul directly. J. C. Beker imagines that they posed to the Corinthians this kind of probing inquiry: "How can a man whose life is so unspectacular and whose actions are so inconspicuous claim to be an apostle of 'the gospel of the glory of Christ' (2 Cor 4:4)?"[6] Ironically, as David deSilva points out, "In many respects they reinforced precisely that ethos (competition, comparing one person against another, boasting in gifts and achievements as a means of asserting precedence) that Paul had sought to overturn in 1 Corinthians."[7]

What makes 2 Corinthians that "giant" in the New Testament is the masterful way that Paul responds to this theology of glory, not by puffing up his own status and splendor—he only entertains this tactic to mock them (11:16)—but by painting elegant pictures of "the life-giving grace of God amid weakness and death."[8]

In the first portion of the letter (1:8-10), Paul recounts a life-threatening incident in Asia that opened up a fresh perspective on life and ministry—mortal death cannot be ignored, and it cannot be escaped.[9] One could live out the rest of one's days playing make believe, or one could embrace death and embrace the cross with the powerful hope of finding life to give for others (4:12). Paul knew that this sounded ridiculous (5:13), but he believed the Lord was teaching him to let his mortification become an altar for the worship of God. The heart of ministry is found in service, not supremacy. Barclay writes: "Wounded and shamed as he was, Paul finds cause to reflect on the grace of God, which is sufficient precisely in his weakness; and, in reestablishing his standing as the Corinthians' apostle, he transmutes self-justification into renewed commitment both to the church at Corinth and to the cause of the gospel."[10]

Put another way, these superapostles, and apparently also many of the Corinthian believers, were evaluating spirituality and ministry based on ex-

---

6. J. Christiaan Beker, *Paul the Apostle: The Triumph of God in Light and Thought* (Philadelphia: Fortress, 1994), 295.

7. David A. deSilva, *An Introduction to the New Testament* (Downers Grove, IL: InterVarsity, 2004), 58; deSilva notes one ancient orator who claimed that "the greatest defect in a person is to show his or her humanness, for then a person ceases to be held divine" (586).

8. Barclay, "2 Corinthians," 1353.

9. See Michael P. Knowles, "Paul's 'Affliction' in Second Corinthians: Reflection, Integration, and a Pastoral Theology of the Cross," *Journal of Pastoral Theology* 15 (2005): 64-77 at 65.

10. Barclay, "2 Corinthians," 1356.

ternal dimensions, the wrappings and the cover. When they looked at Paul and his way of ministry, it was not ostentatious. It did not have the polish and gleam that was expected of popular oratory. Paul was concerned that the Corinthians would have been quite content with a ministry that was resplendent on the outside but hollow inside. This plays rather nicely into allusions associated with idolatry. Famously, early Jews and early Christians rejected idols and argued that one ought not to honor a mortal-fashioned object that may look impressive but lacks efficacy. So too Paul is pointing out in 2 Corinthians that these superapostles are obsessed with the *outside* and take too little care for what is *inside*. That brings us to a short, but necessary, reflection on Jewish thought relating to idolatry; Paul regularly appeals to an inside-versus-outside juxtaposition about the Christian life that bears influence from how Jews (and, later, Christians) thought about the *absconditus* nature of God. This opens up one of the central rhetorical strategies that Paul deploys in this letter to combat the Corinthians' misguided glory theology.

The Theology of Idolatry

Jews in the ancient world were often mocked and criticized for not worshiping via cult statues (or, in their parlance, "idols"). Psalm 115 reflects the challenge this posed to Israel ("Where is their God?"; 115:2 NRSV), but they came to understand that the ostensible absence of their God and his invisibility was distinctive to their identity. That is, idols are not gods; they are manufactured objects, but YHWH alone is Creator (115:4). While idols *appear* to be alive, they are fake and inefficacious. They shine and impose, but inside they are hollow and dead (115:5–7). Furthermore, Israel followed a certain theological principle, *you become what you worship*: "Those who make them are like them; so are all who trust in them" (115:8 NRSV). For heuristic reasons, we can isolate three distinctives of Israel's (anti-)idol theology. First, idols are *made*, they are not makers. Second, Israel's God chose to reveal himself primarily or especially through *word* (and Torah), rather than by what can be seen. Third, the idol-crafting enterprise is all about the impressiveness of what can be seen on the *outside* (hence idols gilded and decked with jewels and rubies), but YHWH cares about what is *inside* (e.g., Jer 20:12). Ultimately, a Jewish theology of idolatry has much to do with epistemology, recognizing the invisibility of God and learning to see reality beyond the dazzling outside and instead discerning the heart of the matter.

What does this have to do with 2 Corinthians? Paul draws from this theology of idolatry (common to Jewish thought in this period) to point the Corinthians toward a deeper understanding of God, the Pauline apostolic mission and ministry, and the folly of focusing on external splendor to see the work of God. At times Paul seems to be engaging with this (anti-)idolatry conceptual platform more directly or overtly, and in 2 Cor 4:1–5:10 his faith language plays off of these themes and epistemological convictions.

Paul mentions idols explicitly in 6:16: "What agreement has the temple of God with idols? For we are the temple of the living God; as God said, 'I will live in them and walk among them, and I will be their God, and they shall be my people'" (NRSV). In the series of contrasts starting with 6:14, Paul calls the Corinthians to break any partnerships they have with unrighteous and anti-God people. Just as light cannot work together with darkness, just like righteousness cannot partner with wickedness, so too the true temple cannot be polluted by idols. The temple symbolically stands for the pure, holy, and true *locus* of God's presence, the hospitable home for his Spirit and glory. Idols, on the other hand, represent darkness, vapidity, wickedness, and the absence of life. Most scholars simply assume 6:14–7:1 is a statement about believers separating from *pagans* but there is good support for the view that Paul is referring to his enemies (the so-called superapostles) as the ἄπιστοι, perhaps better translated "the unfaithful" or "the infidels" rather than "unbelievers."[11] The reference to Jewish Christians (or even Jews) as akin to idols is harsh language indeed, but keep in mind this is the same Paul who elsewhere said that he wished other Jewish-Christian opponents would castrate themselves (Gal 5:12).

---

11. See J. F. Collange, *Énigmes de la deuxième épitre aux Corinthiens: Étude exegetique de 2 Cor.* (Cambridge: Cambridge University Press, 1972), 305–6; David Rensberger, "2 Corinthians 6:14–7:1—A Fresh Examination," *Studia Biblica et Theologica* 8 (1978): 25–49; Michael Goulder, "2 Cor. 6:14–7:1 as an Integral Part of 2 Corinthians," *Novum Testamentum* 36 (1994): 49–57 at 53–57; and Gregory K. Beale, "The Old Testament Background of Reconciliation in 2 Corinthians 5–7 and Its Bearing on the Literary Problem of 2 Corinthians 6:14–7:1," *New Testament Studies* 35 (1989): 550–81, 573; cf. also Jerome Murphy-O'Connor, "Relating 2 Corinthians to Its Context," *New Testament Studies* 33 (1987): 272–75 at 272–73; and more recently Volker Rabens, "Paul's Rhetoric of Demarcation: Separating from 'Unbelievers' (2 Cor 6:14–7:1) in the Corinthian Conflict," in *Theologizing in the Corinthian Conflict: Studies in the Exegesis and Theology of 2 Corinthians*, ed. Reimund Bieringer et al. (Leuven: Peeters, 2013), 229–53, who advocates for a kind of double reading, first as unbelievers, but second "as a reference to Paul's opponents" (232; cf. 244).

Πίστις and True Ministry in 2 Corinthians

Another text of interest in relation to (anti-)idol theology is 2 Cor 5:1, where Paul makes this affirmation: "For we know that if the earthly tent we live in is destroyed, we have a building from God, a house not made with hands [οἰκίαν ἀχειροποίητον], eternal in the heavens" (NRSV). As with 6:16, Paul associates the Corinthians with the dwelling place of the divine, but here his focus is not on the wider community, but more particularly on the body. The "earthly tent" is the weak body, able to be scarred, torn, and even destroyed (in biological death). But in hope Paul anticipates the receiving and indwelling of a "building from God," an eternal and heavenly domicile. No doubt this sounds a lot like a temple, and he describes this building as οἰκίαν ἀχειροποίητον.

There are a few places in the New Testament where we see this same kind of language used. In Mark 14:58 false witnesses testify at Jesus's trial that he claimed to destroy the temple "made with hands" and erect another "not made with hands." Hebrews 9:11 makes reference to a greater and perfect tent "not made with hands," and an explanatory note is added: "not of this creation." This language of "(not) made with hands" differentiates what is directly made by God from what is a human fabrication. Obviously this can apply to the construction of temples, but the same terminology was also commonly used by ancient Jews and Christians in relation to idols:

> You also see and hear that not only in Ephesus but in almost the whole of Asia this Paul has persuaded and drawn away a considerable number of people by saying that gods **made with hands** are not gods [οὐκ εἰσὶν θεοὶ οἱ διὰ χειρῶν γινόμενοι]. (Acts 19:26 NRSV)

> For never in our generation, nor in these present days, has there been any tribe or family or people or town of ours that worships **gods made with hands** [θεοῖς χειροποιήτοις], as was done in days gone by. (Jdt 8:18 NRSV)

> But the idol **made with hands** [τὸ χειροποίητον] is accursed, and so is the one who made it—he for having made it, and the perishable things because it was named a god. (Wis 14:8 NRSV)

> [The Babylonian] king said to [Daniel], "Why do you not worship Bel?" He answered, "Because I do not revere idols **made with hands** [εἴδωλα χειροποίητα], but the living God, who created the heaven and earth and has dominion over all living creatures." (Bel 4b–5 NRSV)

The Septuagint also refers to idols simply as τὰ χειροποίητα (the "handmades"; Isa 2:18; 10:11; 16:12; 19:1; 21:9; 31:7; 46:6; Dan 5:4, 23; 6:28). When Paul refers to a new body that is indestructible, the building language he uses carries the sense of *temple body*, but the phrase "made without hands" also overlaps with (anti-)idol theology. What temples and idols have in common is that they serve as vessels, portals, and pathways to the divine. Idols go further in creating a particular shape to match the idols' form or image; a temple is more of a *place* for the divine to appear or dwell. In Jewish thought, a true temple is filled with the glory of God; idols are notoriously void.[12] Idols have an appearance of glory on the *outside*, but contain no substance, nothing sacred, holy, divine, glorious, or powerful within.

Second Corinthians 4:1–5:10

Paul could use this inside-outside dynamic to shed light on his ministry and the nature of Christian faith, and indeed to communicate something about seeing reality tuned into divine wisdom. This works in 2 Cor 4:1–5:10 and is more focused in 5:7, where Paul juxtaposes πίστις (faith) and εἶδος (sight or form).

The Light and Glory of the Christoform Gospel (4:1–6)

In 2 Cor 4 Paul opens with a bold apostolic manifesto regarding his open and irreproachable ministry. He defies any notion that he operated in the shadows or carried out furtive deeds. Beginning in 4:3, he plays on the notion of "veiled." Perhaps some accused Paul of having hidden motives or a secret agenda.[13] Paul argues, on the contrary, that he acted publicly and

---

12. The conceptual relationship between idols and temples in the ancient world is closer than one may think; in Acts 19:24 Luke refers to a certain Demetrius, a silversmith, who made "silver shrines of Artemis [ποιῶν ναοὺς ἀργυροῦς]." Lynn A. Kauppi describes these as "portable niches" that would have contained small statues of the goddess Artemis. Such objects consisted of features of both idol and temple, but here the focus is on the presence of the deity via mortal-made objects. See *Foreign but Familiar Gods: Greco-Romans Read Religion in Acts* (London: T&T Clark, 2006), 94–95; cf. also Gregory K. Beale, *The Temple and the Church's Mission* (Downers Grove, IL: InterVarsity, 2005), 225.

13. As argued by Ralph P. Martin, *2 Corinthians*, Word Biblical Commentary 40 (Grand Rapids: Zondervan, 2014), 225: "Admittedly Paul's writing is polemi-

transparently—if his message is hidden or veiled, it is so only "to those who are perishing" (4:3b NRSV). They cannot see "the light of the gospel of the glory of Christ, who is the image of God" (4:4 NRSV). With his use of light and darkness imagery, Paul is obviously drawing from creation language, as he goes on to quote: "For it is the God who said, 'Let light shine out of darkness,' who has shown in our hearts to give the light of the knowledge of the glory of God in the face of Jesus Christ" (4:6 NRSV).

Paul's message here is thoroughly christoform. That is, one cannot conceive of the glory of God without seeing the face of Jesus Christ. By drawing attention to Christ, Paul defies any sense of a theology of glory that tries to define power according to worldly metrics. The contours of glory must be traced in relation to the person of Jesus and the strange wisdom of the cross.

The Gospel of Life, a Deathly Sight (4:7–12)

Paul expounds further the nature of his apostolic ministry using the now famous image of the earthen vessel: "We have this treasure in clay jars, so that it may be made clear that this extraordinary power belongs to God and does not come from us" (4:7). The overall point is straightforward: in the present age, as James Dunn explains, "divine power [is contained] in human transience and corruptibility—not divine power obliterating or leaving behind human weakness, but *in* human weakness."[14] What is less clear is why Paul talks about "earthen vessels." Is there a dominant metaphor in mind? Victor Furnish offers a few possibilities.[15] It could refer to cultic vessels (Lev 11:33; 15:12) or perhaps artisan imagery that relates to divine creation, the potter shaping the clay (Isa 29:15; 45:9; 64:8). Furnish also mentions an interesting statement from Cicero, describing the body as container: "For

---

cally charged throughout as he continues his running debate with his detractors at Corinth. They charged him with all manner of unworthy motives and the discrediting liabilities of physical weakness and theological perversity"; see too Jan Lambrecht, "Reconcile Yourselves . . . : A Reading of 2 Corinthians 5:11–21," in *Studies in 2 Corinthians*, ed. Reimund Bieringer and Jan Lambrecht (Leuven: Leuven University Press, 1994), 363–412 at 363.

14. James D. G. Dunn, *The Theology of Paul the Apostle* (Grand Rapids: Eerdmans, 1998), 482.

15. Victor P. Furnish, *II Corinthians*, Anchor Bible 34A (Garden City, NY: Doubleday, 1984), 253–54.

the body is as it were a vessel of or a sort of shelter for the soul" (*Tusculan Disputations* 1.22.52).[16]

Jerome Murphy-O'Connor adds to the options by presenting the ingenious idea of the muddy wrestler: "Before a bout wrestlers oiled their bodies. When they got to grips sweat mixed with the oil, and so after a number of falls on the soft floor of the ring their bodies became encrusted with clay to the point where they looked like clay statues, men made out of the same material as cheap household vessels."[17]

Linda McKinnish Bridges proposes yet another possibility. She associates Paul's language with a common ancient practice of hiding personal valuables in inconspicuous containers. She mentions how among the Nag Hammadi findings were discovered valuables concealed in plain sight in humble earthenware to protect them from thieves.[18] Bridge's suggestion makes good sense of Paul's metaphor. In terms of interpreting 2 Cor 4:7, one could leave it as that and follow Paul's train of thought easily. But I cannot help but wonder if there might be the hint or whisper of a kind of anti-idol image here. Idols were famously criticized by Jews for having an impressive exterior but lacking anything worthwhile inside (as extensively parodied in the Epistle of Jeremiah). Paul's point would be the opposite about his humble ministry—no shiny exterior, no gold plating, but what is inside emanates with the glory and power of God for those with eyes to see.

Some Jewish texts actually describe idols as vessels made of earth. Wisdom of Solomon, for instance, carefully paints a picture of the artisan kneading the "soft earth" to mold the idol vessel (15:7, 13). He forms from the same lump of clay useful tools (like dishware) but also a "futile god." What foolishness, the author exclaims, because the artist is himself made of earth and will return to earth (15:8). Their idols cannot see, breathe, hear, feel, or move (15:15). They have no animating spirit (15:16). Humans have the life of God in them; idols are dead (15:17).

Similarly, in Bel and the Dragon, Daniel remarks to the Babylonian king that the idol before them is "only clay inside and bronze outside," and it never eats or drinks offerings (7). If Paul were playing on this idol imagery

---

16. See Furnish, *II Corinthians*, 253.

17. Murphy-O'Connor, *Second Letter to the Corinthians*, 45; cf. Ceslas Spicq, "L'Image sportive de 2 Cor 4:7–9," *Ephemerides Theologicae Lovanienses* 13 (1937): 209–29.

18. Linda M. Bridges, "2 Corinthians 4:7–15," *Interpretation* 86 (1989): 391–96 at 392.

in 2 Cor 4:7, his point would be that he is not a false teacher, a sham, a counterfeit apostle with a hidden agenda. He is like a simple clay pot concealing a glorious treasure. He is like an anti-idol. The idol is covered in bronze, but its shell is mostly clay. His ministry may *look* like brittle clay, but its value is hidden within.

So Paul boldly proclaims that he carries around the body of Jesus's death in him, so that he might display the life of Jesus (4:10). His life and work looks like death, it smells like death (2:12–17), but one cannot deny that paradoxically this is how the gospel gives life, life from which the Corinthians are benefiting (4:12). This hiddenness of glory as Paul describes it is captured well by Beker:

> The dialectic of cross and resurrection seems to displace any obvious marks of the resurrection in this world by the power of the Spirit. God's power in Christ is primarily viewed in this context as "weakness" and as "the sufferings of Christ" (2 Cor 1:3–7), which conforms to the cruciform signature of apostolic experience. And yet apostolic experience in the world is not defeatist but victorious, because it lives by the promise of the final resurrection of the body and the glory of the dawning kingdom, which is even operative in the midst of suffering.[19]

Gospel-Participation and Faith—Believing the Unbelievable (4:13–15)

Next, Paul relates this humble ministry to the nature of faith itself and quotes Ps 116:

> But just as we have the same spirit of faith that is in accordance with scripture—"I believed, and so I spoke"—we also believe, and so we speak, because we know that the one who raised the Lord Jesus will raise us also with Jesus, and will bring with you into his presence. Yes, everything is for your sake, so that grace, as it extends to more and more people, may increase thanksgiving, to the glory of God. (2 Cor 4:13–15 NRSV)

Ultimately, Paul explains, the boldness to carry out this deathly apostolic ministry derives from *faith*, πίστις. And it relies on hope, the hope of resurrection, believing that following the way of Jesus leads to life and the

---

19. Beker, *Paul the Apostle*, 301.

ultimate honoring of God in obedience and self-offering. Paul explains this via a quotation of Ps 116. Why this psalm?[20] To begin with, Ps 116 dwells on the subject of suffering and death.[21] The psalmist exclaims that "the snares of death encompassed me" and "I suffered distress and anguish" (116:3 NRSV). He talks about being "brought low" (116:6) and being vulnerable to grief, doubt, and ultimate oblivion (116:8). Throughout the psalm, though, the tone is one of trust and hope: "I love the LORD, because he has heard my voice and my supplications," he cries (116:1 NRSV). The Lord hears the anguish, and he is declared gracious, righteous, and merciful (116:5). Thus, one might title this hymn, "Ode to YHWH, Redeemer of the Suffering Faithful."

The small portion from which Paul quotes is Ps 116:10 (= 115:1 LXX). The respective English translations of the Hebrew and Greek text versions are as follows:

> I kept my faith, even when I said, "I am greatly afflicted." (NRSV)

> I believed; therefore I spoke, but I, I was brought very low. (NETS)

Paul was obviously quoting the Septuagint (ἐπίστευσα, διὸ ἐλάλησα) in 2 Cor 4:13. Instead of shrinking from criticism, Paul stood boldly in solidarity with the vocal faith of the resilient psalmist. Note how the psalmist declares, "Precious in the sight of the LORD is the death of his faithful ones" (Ps 116:15 NRSV = 115:6 LXX). Just as the psalmist refuses to let his shameful and weak situation be the defining word, so too Paul is forced to believe in a glory that is not so easily seen by the naked eye. Jerome Murphy-O'Connor captures this idea:

> The interpretation which Paul has just given of the relation of his sufferings to his ministry is based on faith. He believes, as did the writer of Psalms (LXX), that his perseverance, despite deprivations and setbacks, is due to God's grace, and that his dedication shows forth "the life of Jesus." He cannot produce any rational proof of the truth of such statements. He empha-

---

20. Roy Harrisville believes that Paul takes little interest in the original context of the psalm. Rather, in this case "the original sense is absorbed in an *absolute interpretation*, and the retrospection is consequently altered to prospect"; "Paul and the Psalms: A Formal Study," *Word and World* 5 (1985): 168–79 at 174. This is, of course, possible, but it seems to be a reductionistic perspective.

21. Barclay, "2 Corinthians," 1361.

sizes the faith element (4:13), however, not in order to stress the obvious, but to insinuate that the Spirit-people should have "the spirit which is faith." They prided themselves on such gifts of the Spirit as speaking in tongues. They should rather cultivate the gift of faith that would permit them to penetrate beyond externals to the reality of God's plan (cf. 4:18; 5:12; 11:18). Since Paul's comportment is based on faith they can understand him only if they too have faith.[22]

What links Paul to his psalmist counterpart is this "spirit of faith" that they share (τὸ αὐτὸ πνεῦμα τῆς πίστεως; 2 Cor 4:13). Some, like Douglas Campbell, take Paul's use of Ps 116 here to be christological. That is, the psalm is read as a "prefiguration of Christ" and, thus, the Spirit of faith involves coparticipation with Christ "as Christ speaking prophetically through that text of his own suffering and resurrection."[23] This theory is unnecessarily complex. Jan Lambrecht provides a straightforward reading that is more compelling. Paul is simply stating that he shares an attitude of trust and hope in God despite the bleak circumstances.[24] As far as Paul is concerned (and his rhetorical aims in this letter), his use of πιστεύω corresponds to the notion of believing faith I have been describing, the ability or will to "believe the unbelievable," to see with the eyes of faith rather than with fleshy eyes. It is not about leaping blindly on a whim; rather, it is the will to live boldly because one is able to see things the way God sees them. And this drives his vocal, apostolic ministry. Just as YHWH, when he wished to give himself to his people, chose not a form but Word, so too Paul carries out a *theophanic ministry of preaching the Good Word*—to believe and to be emboldened to

---

22. Murphy-O'Connor, *Second Letter to the Corinthians*, 48; see too Paul Han, *Swimming in the Sea of Scripture: Paul's Use of the Old Testament in 2 Corinthians 4:7–13:13* (London: T&T Clark, 2014), 33–35.

23. Douglas A. Campbell, "2 Corinthians 4:13: Evidence in Paul That Christ Believes," *Journal of Biblical Literature* 128 (2009): 337–56 at 347. Thomas Stegman also argues in favor of a christological approach to Ps 116 for Paul here, but Stegman prefers to translate "Spirit of faithfulness" wherein this "refers to what the Spirit empowers, namely, the loving, self-giving mode of existence manifested by Jesus"; see "'Ἐπίστευσα, διὸ ἐλάλησα (2 Corinthians 4:13): Paul's Christological Reading of Psalm 115:1a LXX," *Catholic Biblical Quarterly* 69 (2007): 725–45 at 735.

24. Jan Lambrecht, "A Matter of Method (II): 2 Cor 4,13 and the Recent Studies of Schenck and Campbell," *Ephemerides Theologicae Lovanienses* 86 (2010): 441–48; Han, *Swimming in the Sea of Scripture*, 30–35.

speak. Steven Kraftchick summarizes aptly the conceptual and intertextual link between Ps 116 and Paul's ministry:

> Using the terms "believing" and "speaking" he claims that, like the Psalmist he speaks in adversity. He preaches because it is just that action which demonstrates his faith. Believing in the God who raised Jesus means understanding God to be working now in his life; therefore Paul's preaching stems from faith. Though his outward appearance is that of dying, Paul understands this existence to be part of his faithful witness to the one who raises the dead and who will ultimately raise him together with the Corinthians on the final day.[25]

The Power and Hope of the Invisible Gospel (4:16–18)

At the close of 2 Cor 4, Paul goes into further detail about what this faith perspective entails, why he is bold in his speech and in his belief that Christ speaks through him (cf. 13:3a). Paul lives in hope, not in despair. He is well aware that pain hurts and that repeated rejection leads to worldly shame. He experiences repeated afflictions that cause his appearance to waste away (4:16–17). He puts the focus not on the temporary view, but on what is eternal and unseen (τὰ μὴ βλεπόμενα; 4:18). Parallels to Heb 11:1 are readily apparent: "Now faith is the assurance of things hoped for, the conviction of things not seen [ἔλεγχος οὐ βλεπομένων]" (NRSV).

Paul plays on the contrast between the inner and outer person. Murphy-O'Connor describes the outer person as "the visible dimension of human existence," where others see his "wounds, blows, illness and fatigue" (and the like). Alternatively, for Murphy-O'Connor, Paul's inner man is the "invisible dimension of human existence."[26] Paul is not talking about soul and body. He is referring to the truth of one's character and choices that cannot be seen in a photograph. Again, one can see the resonance this has with an anti-idolatry theology. The idol worshiper assumes the shiny statue must be a powerful god but kneels before a dead object with no power. *What is inside is what counts*, Paul posits. That can be seen only with the eyes of faith.

---

25. Steven J. Kraftchick, "Death in Us, Life in You: The Apostolic Medium," in *Pauline Theology: 1 and 2 Corinthians*, ed. David M. Hay (Atlanta: Society of Biblical Literature, 2002), 2:156–81 at 176.
26. Murphy-O'Connor, *Second Letter to the Corinthians*, 49.

Hoping for Vindication and Glory, as We Struggle in Tent-Bodies (5:1–5)

In 2 Cor 5, Paul turns his attention to the body, particularly the broken body, what he calls in Philippians the "lowly body" (3:21). Some may have said about Paul: *Look at him, how can he be one of God's agents of good news? He is so frail and weak.* Paul did not put oil on his face and say, *No, see how strong I can look!* Instead, he dwells at length on the matter of the earthly body. Truth be told, it is weak indeed; it is even liable to destruction. But "if the earthly tent we live in is destroyed, we have a building from God, a house not made with hands, eternal in the heavens" (2 Cor 5:1 NRSV). Paul is talking about death and resurrection. Again, glancing at the parallel Phil 3:21 he had a similar message for that community: "He will transform the body of our humiliation that it may be conformed to the body of his glory, by the power that also enables him to make all things subject to himself" (NRSV).

Paul does not pretend the present body is a perfect, solid, indestructible temple. It is a dilapidated tent, a biodegradable tabernacle. It is a dwelling, but it shows wear and tear. And, yes, the fragility of this tent causes believers to groan and long for something sturdier (2 Cor 5:4). But Paul's point is that he dares to live in hope, that this body and its scars and limitations are not the end, that these things do not define Christian identity forever. Believers have a beautiful permanent home (a glory-body) in waiting, a brilliant temple (5:5). But wait they must because the time has not yet come.

Walking in Faith and Hope (5:6–10)

Finally we arrive at Paul's climactic statements about the apostolic persona in 2 Cor 5:6–10, the way that Paul wants the Corinthians—indeed all believers—to view his life and ministry. While he longs to be clothed and not naked, honored and not shamed, still he dares to be confident (5:6). To live in the tent-body is to be a wanderer, a traveler. And itinerants must live with impermanence and the unknown. Thus, διὰ πίστεως ... περιπατοῦμεν, οὐ διὰ εἴδους (5:7). The word εἶδος appears to be the key to understanding Paul's use of the language of πίστις here. Scholars debate whether εἶδος means "seeing/sight" (i.e., an active concept) or "form" (i.e., a passive concept).[27] Louw-

---

27. Furnish argues that εἶδος carries a passive meaning and does not refer to "the act of seeing"; *II Corinthians*, 273.

Nida offers both possibilities: form or sight.[28] The only other occasion where Paul uses εἶδος is 1 Thess 5:22: "Abstain from every form [εἴδους] of evil" (NRSV). Here and elsewhere it seems most sensible to understand εἶδος as "what is seen." The immediate reference in 2 Cor 5:7 is the inability to presently see the form of Christ,[29] as he explains that believers live now in a time of being "away from the Lord" (5:6).[30] But in 2 Corinthians Paul is clearly talking about more than just the current absence and future appearance of the Lord. Put another way, there seems to be a particular epistemological *weight* that Paul puts on the contrast between πίστις and εἶδος.[31]

Εἶδος is not itself an independent noun; it is a nominalized form of ὁράω, and Paul had just finished 2 Cor 4 by talking about what is seen and unseen (though there he used forms of βλέπω). We might, then, woodenly translate 5:7 as "we live by faith, and not by visible form."

In the anti-idolatry Jewish text Wis 15:1–16, the author shows the faith and wisdom of those who are loyal to the one God over and against the idolaters. Wisdom 15 expounds upon the folly of idol creation. Mention is made of the craftsman who decorates a figure (εἶδος) with many beautiful colors (15:4), and its appearance (ὄψις) draws the attention of fools who gravitate toward "the lifeless form of a dead image" (νεκρᾶς εἰκόνος εἶδος ἄπνουν; 15:5). The writer mocks those worshipers who concentrate on the

---

28. Johannes P. Louw and Eugene Albert Nida, *Greek-English Lexicon of the New Testament: Based on Semantic Domains* (New York: United Bible Societies, 1996), §58.14, §24.1.

29. Fredrik Lindgård favors the translation "the shape of the Lord"; see *Paul's Line of Thought in 2 Corinthians 4:16–5:10* (Tübingen: Mohr Siebeck, 2005), 198.

30. Notice the similar statement in 1 Pet 1:8: "Although you have not seen him, you love him; and even though you do not see him now, you believe in him and rejoice with an indescribable and glorious joy" (NRSV).

31. Lindgård argues that 2 Corinthians does carry such an epistemological tension where some are walking with a skewed perspective: "Paul does not conduct himself according to his external shape (which some people do), that is according to his outward appearance, but according to his faith"; *Paul's Line of Thought*, 199. This is where Teresa Morgan's understanding of Paul's faith language falls short. She denies epistemological emphasis in 2 Cor 5:7 and instead prefers a reading where Paul is probably referencing the gift of faith given by God that lights the way for Paul. But Morgan does not take seriously enough the relationship of πίστις to πιστεύω for Paul, especially in 4:13–14; see *Roman Faith and Christian Faith: Pistis and Fides in the Early Roman Empire and the Early Churches* (Oxford: Oxford University Press, 2015), 254–55.

form and its appearance (with dazzling colors), without proper insight into the contents. What they get at the end of the day is devoid of spirit and breath, as good as a corpse.

Paul's point about himself and his apostolic ministry follows this same train of thought. If one focuses on forms, then Paul is little more than a worn-out tent waiting to be discarded. But to live by πίστις means to live in hope and to see with new eyes, to see through the outward appearance of things and to perceive and anticipate what is eternal, the weighty treasure within.

Only a handful of verses later does Paul tell the Corinthians that the boasters obsess over the trappings, they take pride in the glorious form and appearance, but care too little about the heart (2 Cor 5:12). This leads to a climactic statement that in the new era of Christ's reign: believers ought not to see and interpret people κατὰ σάρκα, by "fleshly" standards, that is, by what only the human eye can see (5:16). They must see with the penetrating eye of faith, to see concealed treasure, to perceive the inner renewal, to recognize life instead of death.

For Paul, Jesus Christ makes all the difference in seeing rightly. One can tune into this πίστις perception only because one has now come to see *Christ* in a new way. From a fleshly perspective Jesus was a criminal, a failure, and a scandal. He was weak and frail. But, Paul urges, "we know him no longer in that way" (5:16 NRSV). Those who continue to see only a weak Christ fail to walk by πίστις.

An intriguing connection to the Suffering Servant passage from Isaiah employs εἶδος in the Septuagint text. The Septuagint passage begins with the eventual exaltation of the Servant—he will be elevated and praised (52:13). Immediately after this declaration, though, the reader is brought down to the reality that the Servant must first face utter rejection based on his appearance: "Just as many shall be astonished at you—so shall your appearance [εἶδος] be without glory from men, and your glory be absent from the men" (52:14 NETS).

Later it is said again, "He has no form [εἶδος] or glory, and we saw him, and he had no form or beauty"; and "his form [εἶδος] was without honor, failing beyond all men" (53:2-3 NETS). The whole Servant passage dwells on this tension between the true glory and honor of the servant (recognized in his innocence, magnanimity, and self-sacrifice) and the repulsion and dismissal by mortals due to his appearance or form. And this can be traced back to *faith*: "Lord, who has believed [πιστεύω] our report? And to whom has the arm of the Lord been revealed?" (53:1 NETS; see 105–7). Those who live by *faith* can see the glory of the Suffering Servant, and those who live by *forms* can see only a pariah and a pathetic nobody.

One can detect this epistemological dialectic in 2 Corinthians clearer than any other Pauline letter.[32] For Paul, knowing Christ means learning to see him, and consequently everything else, with the eyes of believing faith. For some, "seeing is believing." Paul was directly undermining this attitude. And for this he turned to the (presently and temporarily) *unseen* Christ. For Paul, this requires not blind faith but a special kind of attunement to this unseen Lord. As C. K. Barrett explains: "Faith does not proceed on the basis of an objectively authenticated Christ; it trusts the absent and undemonstrable Christ, whose history has already vanished into the past and whose coming lies in the unknown future."[33]

Conclusion

With 2 Cor 4:1–5:10 as our focus, Paul's thematic statement that "we walk by faith and not by sight" in 5:5–7 merits close examination of the context and meaning. The significance of Paul's quote from Ps 116:10 in 2 Cor 4:13 links *belief* to the foundational perspective that drives the boldness of Paul's apostolic proclamation of the cross and the transformative death of Jesus and the cruciform way. While Paul could use faith language in a variety of ways, 2 Corinthians focuses concern for how the Corinthian imagination analyzes glory and life. According to Paul, there is a *sarkic perspective* (5:16b)—one where the fleshly eyes place a value only on what it sees. Paul tips his hat to the notion that once *he too* operated with a *sarkic* epistemology, formerly condemning the weak Christ but *now* has been confronted with a new vision of Christ (5:16c), and that has changed the filter for how he sees *all things* (5:16a). The *sarkic* viewpoint cannot see past *forms*. But Paul proclaims the

---

32. For a helpful related discussion see Dominika A. Kurek-Chomycz, "The Scent of (Mediated) Revelation?" in *Theologizing in the Corinthian Conflict: Studies in the Exegesis and Theology of 2 Corinthians*, ed. Reimund Bieringer et al. (Leuven: Peeters, 2013), 69–107.

33. C. K. Barrett, *The Second Epistle to the Corinthians*, Black's New Testament Commentary (Peabody, MA: Hendrickson, 1991), 158; cf. Timothy B. Savage, *Power through Weakness: Paul's Understanding of the Christian Ministry in 2 Corinthians*, Society for New Testament Studies Monograph 86 (Cambridge: Cambridge University Press, 2004), 181.

Πίστις and True Ministry in 2 Corinthians

possibility and necessity of a πίστις lens to view the world. This *faith* lens is not a fancy way for Paul to refer to a guess or an unreflective opinion. Rather, it is like a microscope that can make visible things invisible to the naked eye. This is what we call *believing faith*, faith that can believe the unbelievable and "see" what is unseen because the eyes have been trained to *look* for the right things. Glory is not found in the flamboyant exterior but the density, determination, and weightiness of the soul and will. Honor is not about the absence of scars, but the interpretation of vicarious scars as reflective of a noble heart.

8 Covenantal Pistism

Πίστις and the Agency Question in Galatians

> Faith means openness to and finally participation in the redemptive power of God operative in Christ's death and resurrection. Through faith the believer "dies" to sin and death as Christ died to them and lives in hope of resurrection with him.
>
> —Victor P. Furnish, *Theology and Ethics in Paul*

> Because Paul sees trust/faith as a new mode of existence made possible by Christ and the irruption of the New Age into the present, he regards also its alternatively as a new mode of existence, as a way of life, including a way of relating to God.
>
> —Leander Keck, *Paul and His Letters*

Πίστις and the Quest for Paul's Soteriology

There is, perhaps, nothing more well known about Paul than that he juxtaposed faith and works, a perspective reinforced in Protestant doctrine and placed at the center of Paul's theology. The classic interpretation of Galatians, then, maintains that those Jewish Christian interlopers who disturbed the Galatians attempted to persuade them toward a works-orientation, while Paul championed a faith-orientation. What troubles me about this standard reconstruction of the Galatian situation is precisely the reception and use of the word πίστις in Galatians. Because of a long history of *Christian* appropriation of the word πίστις (assumed to be a distinctly *Christian* term), we have neglected to consider how the Jewish Christian missionaries would have reacted to Paul's use of πίστις to represent *his* approach to the gospel of Jesus Christ. Put another way, we tend to think there are two sides in this theological tug-of-war, the Jewish Christian missionaries advocating for *works of the law* (ἔργα νόμου), and Paul advocating for the opposite, that is, *faith* (πίστις ['Ιησοῦ Χριστοῦ]). However, *would not the Jewish Christian missionaries have also identified with the word πίστις in relation their understanding of commitment and obedience to God?* Surely it would not have been to them νόμος *versus* πίστις but rather πίστις *through* νόμος (Torah).

Jews were comfortable using the term πίστις to represent their relationship with God, even if it was not a popular or preferred term in their religious Greek literature (see chap. 3). That is what makes Galatians such an extraordinary text, especially as one of the earliest extant expressions of his theology. Paul makes a bold move by *separating* πίστις from νόμος precisely so that he can examine them *as* separable concepts. This would be the theological equivalent of splitting an atom for the first time: unprecedented, volatile, and suddenly a new way of thinking emerges.[1] Before we can look forward to why Paul establishes this contrast, it behooves us to look back at how the faith/works pattern was interpreted in the past.

The faith/works juxtaposition of Galatians obviously received a major theoretical construct via Martin Luther (see 24–27). From his time until the middle of the twentieth century, the perspective was passed on with hardly a second thought that faith and works were at opposite ends of a spectrum. Works involved striving, doing, and earning, and faith was about receiving and believing. To offer one example, G. G. Findlay (1849–1919) argues that Paul sets as extreme opposites "evangelical and legal righteousness" or "salvation by faith and [salvation] by law-works."[2] The tendency among interpreters of Galatians with this mindset was to represent faith as if it were basically a *passive* concept. Thus Findlay notes that works reflect the "intrinsic merit in the doer" while "faith has its virtue in Him it trusts."[3] Faith, Findlay explains, entails "the soul's recumbency on Christ ... Christ evokes the faith which shakes off legal bondage" and rests in the "glorious consciousness of its Divine sonship."[4]

---

1. See James D. G Dunn, *The Theology of Paul's Letter to the Galatians* (Cambridge: Cambridge University Press, 1993), 81; also "The Theology of Galatians," in *Pauline Theology*, ed. Jouette M. Bassler (Minneapolis: Fortress, 1991), 1:138–46.

2. George G. Findlay, *The Epistle to the Galatians* (New York: Armstrong, 1902), 140–41.

3. Findlay, *Galatians*, 228.

4. Findlay, *Galatians*, 228–29. John Murray's interpretation of Paul in his commentary on Romans is remarkably similar: "Justification by works always finds its

Obviously, in the middle-to-late twentieth century, the so-called New Perspective on Paul resisted this reading of Paul, rejecting both the assumption that Paul viewed the Judaism of his time as legalistic and also attempting to retrieve the nature of Pauline Christianity. It could easily be demonstrated that Paul was concerned with the life lived in obedience to God, and his emphasis on final judgment according to deeds was brought closer to the forefront of the discussion of Paul's theology.[5]

In the twenty-first century certain tides have resisted the ways that the New Perspective tried to weaken Paul's works/faith juxtaposition. Some defend the notion that works involves doing in Paul and faith involves trusting in God. Douglas Moo, for example, makes this statement in view of Gal 3:7-14:

---

ground in that which the person is and does; it is always oriented to that consideration of virtue attaching to the person justified. The specific quality of faith is trust and commitment to another; it is essentially extraspective and in that respect is diametrically opposite of works. Faith is *self*-renouncing; works are *self*-congratulatory. Faith looks to what God does; works have respect to what we are. It is this antithesis of principle that enables the apostle to base the complete exclusion of works upon the principle of faith"; see *The Epistle to the Romans* (Grand Rapids: Eerdmans, 1997 [originally 1968]), 123. Cf. Rudolf Bultmann, "*Pisteuō*," in *Theological Dictionary of the New Testament: Abridged Edition*, ed. Gerhard Kittel and Gerhard Friedrich, trans. Geoffrey W. Bromiley (Grand Rapids: Eerdmans, 1985), 849–57 at 855: "As a negation of self-will, faith is the supreme act, and as such it is the opposite of works in every sense. It is correlative to grace, which stands in antithesis to works that merit payment."

5. For a helpful summary of the development of the New Perspective on Paul, see N. T. Wright, *Paul and His Recent Interpreters* (Minneapolis: Fortress, 2015); James D. G. Dunn, *The New Perspective on Paul* (Grand Rapids: Eerdmans, 2008), 1–98; and Magnus Zetterholm, *Approaches to Paul* (Minneapolis: Fortress, 2009). On the subject of the nature of early Judaism, helpful analysis can be found in John M. G. Barclay, *Paul and the Gift* (Grand Rapids: Eerdmans, 2015), 194–330. For an insightful "beyond the New Perspective" approach to the question of Judaism and legalism, see the mature reflections of Charles H. Talbert and Jason A. Whitlark, "Paul, Judaism, and the Revisionists," in *Getting "Saved": The Whole Story of Salvation in the New Testament* (Grand Rapids: Eerdmans, 2011), 11–34; cf. Francis Watson, "Constructing an Antithesis: Pauline and Other Jewish Perspectives on Divine and Human Agency," in *Divine and Human Agency in Paul*, ed. John M. G. Barclay and Simon J. Gathercole (London: T&T Clark, 2006), 99–116. On the New Perspective emphasis on final judgment, see Kent L. Yinger, *Paul, Judaism, and Judgment according to Deeds*, Society for New Testament Studies Monograph 105 (Cambridge: Cambridge University Press, 1999); and N. T. Wright, *Paul and the Faithfulness of God* (Minneapolis: Fortress, 2013), 2:1084–28.

Paul's argument in these verses transcends the particular circumstances of his situation. For his polemic is not only directed to the law but also to "doing"; indeed, one of the reasons (although not the only one) why Paul denies that the law can lead to justification is precisely because it is, by its nature, something to be "done." The Reformers, therefore, were entirely justified to find in Paul's argument here a fundamental and universally valid principle about the exclusive value of believing versus doing.[6]

As I reread Galatians in light of Paul's faith language in ancient context, my response to this kind of juxtaposition is this: *how did Jews use the language of faith (πίστις), and how would they have received or responded to Paul's juxtaposing of πίστις and νόμος?*[7] Fellow Jews could hardly make sense of anyone (even the maverick Paul!) referring to πίστις as if it were something that does not inherently involve active operation—Jews would have simply taken for granted that πίστις is not only central to life with God but also that it is something that you *do* (see 46–56).

Lively conversations are happening related to Pauline soteriology under the label "divine and human agency."[8] An interesting case study in this discussion is Preston Sprinkle's *Paul and Judaism Revisited*.[9] Sprinkle argues that the Old Testament contains two approaches to salvation and covenantal

---

6. Douglas J. Moo, *Galatians*, Baker Exegetical Commentary on the New Testament (Grand Rapids: Baker, 2013), 210; see again 324–25. The following essay spells out more how Moo arrives at this position: "Genesis 15:6 in the New Testament," in *From Creation to New Creation: Biblical Theology and Exegesis*, ed. Daniel M. Gurtner and Benjamin L. Gladd (Peabody, MA: Hendrickson, 2013), 147–62.

7. Note Krister Stendahl's classic criticism: "We should venture to suggest that the West for centuries has wrongly surmised that the biblical writers were grappling with problems which no doubt are ours, but which never entered their consciousness"; see "Paul and the Introspective Conscience of the West," in *Paul among Jews and Gentiles* (Philadelphia: Fortress, 1976), 95; cf. 86.

8. Again see John M. G. Barclay and Simon J. Gathercole, *Divine and Human Agency in Paul* (London: T&T Clark, 2006); cf. Jason Maston, *Divine and Human Agency in Second Temple Judaism and Paul: A Comparative Study*, Wissenschaftliche Untersuchungen zum Neuen Testament 297 (Tübingen: Mohr Siebeck, 2010); and Kyle Wells, *Grace and Agency in Paul and Second Temple Judaism: Interpreting the Transformation of the Heart*, Novum Testamentum Supplement 157 (Leiden: Brill, 2014).

9. Preston Sprinkle, *Paul and Judaism Revisited: A Study of Divine and Human Agency in Salvation* (Downers Grove, IL: InterVarsity, 2013).

participation. The Deuteronomic one expected human agency to influence covenantal restoration. The prophetic approach emphasized "God's unilateral acts of restoration." Comparing in particular the Dead Sea scrolls and Paul's letters, Sprinkle argues that the scrolls demonstrate a mixture of both types, while Paul exclusively follows the prophetic model. No doubt, if Sprinkle is correct, it would reinforce the works/faith dichotomy, where Paul would have been placing the emphasis on *divine agency* (where God does the doing, and humans have faith in that divine work) rather than on *human agency* (a Deuteronomic program that, in such a case, Paul would have discarded).

Sprinkle's reading of Paul *and* the nature of Old Testament religion is overly simplistic. After all, the prophets undoubtedly relied on Deuteronomy itself as the basis for the covenant.[10] Second, how do we know one pattern is superior to the other, or meant to be final (and thus best)? Kent Yinger raises an important question on this matter: Sprinkle seems to contrast Paul with James on these soteriological patterns, so where would Sprinkle put Jesus?[11] The new conversations around divine and human agency have not moved the discussion forward beyond a traditional works/faith dichotomy.[12]

A basic affirmation of the works/faith dichotomy appears in another context, namely the apocalyptic reading of Paul.[13] One of the key figureheads of this approach is J. Louis Martyn, and it is instructive how he interprets Gal 2:16 in his respected Anchor Yale Bible commentary. Martyn does not frame Paul's νόμος/πίστις dichotomy in terms of a generic opposition of works and faith. Rather, he offers a penetrating discussion of the development of a

---

10. Don Garlington makes the crucial point that the prophets did not have an unconditional perspective on restoration; Garlington notes many passages from Isaiah and Ezekiel that place a strong emphasis on obedience to the covenant (i.e., an important assumption of human agency); see Review of *Paul and Judaism Revisited*, *Journal of the Evangelical Theological Society* 57 (2014): 442–46 at 443.

11. See Kent L. Yinger, Review of *Paul and Judaism Revisited*, *Bulletin for Biblical Research* 25 (2015): 580–82 at 582. Scot McKnight offers some important critical comments about Sprinkle's book, and Sprinkle offers some responses, to both McKnight and other commenters at patheos.com/blogs/jesuscreed/2013/09/26/challenging-the-new-perspective-on-paul.

12. See Kent L. Yinger, "*Reformation Redivivus*: Syngerism and the New Perspective," *Journal of Theological Interpretation* 3 (2009): 89–106.

13. To get a sense for the state of the discussion of the "apocalyptic Paul," see Ben Blackwell, John Goodrich, and Jason Maston, eds., *Paul and the Apocalyptic Imagination* (Minneapolis: Fortress, 2016).

theological tradition among Jewish Christians, a tradition that Paul agrees with on points and deviates from on others.¹⁴ In particular, Martyn argues, Paul's position on "rectification" depends on getting the πίστις Χριστοῦ formulation correct (see chap. 11 below).

Martyn is insistent that Paul sets up the ἔργα/πίστις dichotomy to underscore the apocalyptic, liberative work of God through the "faithful death" of Christ; hence his preference for the reading "faithfulness of Christ" for πίστις Χριστοῦ.¹⁵ Martyn's approach underscores the hegemony of anti-God forces over humanity and how Christ delivers from their tyranny.¹⁶ He does not deny that *sometimes* Paul refers to the importance of human πίστις as trust in God (i.e., human agency), as often occurs with the verb πιστεύω (2:16; 3:6; cf. 3:22). Nevertheless, Pauline rectification and redemption are viewed by Martyn as purely the result of God's invasion of the human realm, leading to the "mysterious genesis of faith in Christ."¹⁷

Martin de Boer, another proponent of the apocalyptic Paul, presses for an even *more* unilateral interpretation of divine agency, and this deeply affects his interpretation of πίστις in Galatians overall. In de Boer's Galatians commentary, he is reluctant to *ever* read πίστις in Galatians as something related to what humans have or do. To take one important example, de Boer does not interpret the phrase ἐκ πίστεως in Gal 3 (3:7, 8, 9, 11, 12, 22; cf. 2:16) as a reference to "faith in Christ." Rather, he argues that οἱ ἐκ πίστεως means "the people who live on the basis of (Christ's) faith(ful death)."¹⁸

What is similar about Martyn's and de Boer's approaches to Gal 2:16 and the ἔργα νόμου/πίστις Χριστοῦ dichotomy is how both have a tendency to transfer πίστις away from the anthropological realm and into the christological realm. That is, what justifies is not human faith, but rather the "faithfulness of Christ."¹⁹ At the risk of oversimplification, the tendency for both Lutheran interpreters and apocalyptic-Paul interpreters is to diminish the

---

14. See J. Louis Martyn, *Galatians*, Anchor Yale Bible 33A (New Haven: Yale University Press, 1997), 263–75 ("Comment #28: God's Making Things Right by the Faith of Christ").

15. Martyn, *Galatians*, 271.

16. Martyn, *Galatians*, 273.

17. Martyn, *Galatians*, 276.

18. See Martinus de Boer, *Galatians* (Louisville: Westminster John Knox, 2011), 192–97.

19. See J. Louis Martyn, "The Gospel Invades Philosophy," in *Paul, Philosophy, and the Theopolitical Vision*, ed. Douglas Harink (Eugene, OR: Wipf & Stock, 2010), 13–36.

COVENANTAL PISTISM

significance of human faith as a form of human agency.[20] Again, this is a rather flat and modernistic reading of the word πίστις. And treating πίστις as the *opposite* of work, doing, or human agency makes little sense to Paul, the Galatians, or the Jewish Christian missionaries for that matter.[21] As many interpreters of Galatians point out, Galatians carries a strong appeal to *doing* (see Gal 5-6), not least πίστις itself being "worked out" (5:6).[22]

For these reasons, the language of divine agency and human agency is not beneficial for interpreting Paul's use of πίστις, especially when they are placed in some kind of zero-sum formula. No serious Pauline scholars would deny that Paul underscores the prior and superlative salvific work of God.[23] Unfortunately, once any feature of human agency enters the equation, this is often interpreted as a *decrease* in divine contribution. A mathematic approach (*what percentages of divine and human work add up to Pauline soteriology?*) is wrongheaded from the start. I will return to this matter later, but for now suffice it to say that the New Perspective comes *closer* to understanding the nature of the Christian life with God according to Paul than other proposals. The New Perspective tends to focus on the language of "covenantal nomism," with respect to Sanders for this formulation.[24] Forty years after the introduction of this approach, most scholars find it to be in

---

20. See Beverly R. Gaventa, "Galatians," in *Eerdmans Commentary on the Bible*, ed. John W. Rogerson and James D. G. Dunn (Grand Rapids: Eerdmans, 2003), 1374-84 at 1377 (on 2:16): "The fundamental contrast here . . . is not between works (of whatever sort) and faith (either that of humans or of Christ) but between law and Christ."

21. See the problematic interpretation of Richard C. H. Lenski on 3:12-13: "The point Paul makes is that faith and doing are opposites. Doing furnishes what is legally and of right *demanded*; faith receives what is gratuitously *bestowed*"; *The Interpretation of St. Paul's Epistle to the Galatians* (Minneapolis: Fortress, 2008; originally 1946), 147.

22. See especially John M. G. Barclay, *Obeying the Truth: The Study of Paul's Ethics in Galatians* (Edinburgh: T&T Clark, 1988); also Volker Rabens, "'Indicative and Imperative' as the Substructure of Paul's Theology-and-Ethics in Galatians? A Discussion of Divine and Human Agency in Paul," in *Galatians and Christian Theology*, ed. Mark W. Eliott et al. (Grand Rapids: Baker, 2014), 285-305.

23. According to Barclay's *Paul and the Gift*, most interpreters of Paul indeed agree on these points of the priority and incongruity of God's grace.

24. Sanders himself does not think Paul's pattern of religion could be described as covenantal nomism; see *Paul and Palestinian Judaism* (Minneapolis: Fortress, 1977), 511-14.

general a helpful corrective to assuming legalistic works righteousness in early Judaism; nevertheless, scholars (including myself) find bones to pick with the details of Sanders's description and application of covenantal nomism as well as well as how others label Paul a "covenantal nomist."

Covenantal Nomism or Covenantal "Pistism"?

Resisting the accusation that the Judaism of Paul's time was oriented toward meritorious works, Sanders, following an extensive study of early Palestinian Jewish texts, arrives at a pattern of religion that could fit the majority of these texts with more accuracy and nuance. Sanders explains it thusly: "Covenantal nomism is the view that one's place in God's plan is established on the basis of the covenant and that the covenant requires as the proper response of man his obedience to its commandments, while providing means of atonement for transgression. . . . Obedience maintains one's position in the covenant, but it does not earn God's grace as such."[25] While Sanders finds this pattern of religion in Judaism, he does not find it in Paul. Yet others see a remarkable resemblance between Sanders's covenantal nomism and the way Paul talked about the Christian life. Morna Hooker, offering an extensive comparison of Paul's letters and Sanders's Judaism pattern, discovers remarkable coherence.[26] Dunn similarly argues that Paul displays the same emphasis on "the interrelationship between divine grace and human response."[27]

---

25. Sanders, *Paul and Palestinian Judaism*, 75. A more robust description is found on 422 with eight components: "(1) God has chosen Israel and (2) given the law. The law implies both (3) God's promise to maintain the election and (4) the requirement to obey. (5) God rewards obedience and punishes transgression. (6) The law provides for means of atonement, and atonement results in (7) maintenance or reestablishment of the covenantal relationship. (8) All those who are maintained in the covenant by obedience, atonement and God's mercy belong to the group which will be saved." Here we cannot engage in all the critical reactions to Sanders's covenantal nomism, but a major concern is the focus Sanders places on "getting in" and "staying in" (i.e., conversionistic language); see Frederick J. Murphy, Review of *Paul and Variegated Nomism*, Catholic Biblical Quarterly 65 (2003): 148-50, esp. 149-50.

26. See Morna D. Hooker, *From Adam to Christ* (Eugene, OR: Wipf & Stock, 1990), 155: "No doubt many will have thought that they recognized Paul in the pages of the first part of Sanders's book, and will have concluded as they turned to part 2: 'So Paul is thoroughly Jewish after all.'"

27. Dunn, *New Perspective on Paul*, 79; cf. 143, 199, 310, 371. See too the more re-

Both Hooker and Dunn underscore the way that covenantal nomism fits Paul's perspective insofar as it includes both gift and demand; where they find Paul peculiar is his criticism of the mediation and centrality of Torah. So Dunn says that Paul chose to talk about obligation in terms of "obedience of faith" rather than Torah obedience.[28]

I propose that we rework Dunn and Hooker's appropriation of covenantal nomism for Paul and orient it around Paul's πίστις language, calling it (for lack of a more elegant phrase) "covenantal *pistism*." The idea behind this formulation for Paul is that his approach to religion resembles his earlier life in some ways (especially in terms of understanding both God's grace and demand), but after meeting Christ was oriented, *not* around Torah, but Christ alone.[29] The term πίστις (hence *pistism*) is the right word to represent Pauline religion in Christ for a number of reasons, not least of which how it became a catchword for Christianity so early on in history (e.g., Gal 1:23).

As Francis Watson rightly identifies, Paul appears to have chosen πίστις to represent the Christian religion over and against Torah religion:

> "Faith" sums up the way of life of a Pauline congregation, marked by the abandonment of certain of the norms and beliefs of the surrounding society and the adoption of new norms and beliefs. "Works" sums up the way of life of the Jewish community, which seeks to live in conformity with the law of Moses. The two are incompatible not because one stresses grace and the other achievement, but because, as a result, the primary orientation toward Jesus in one community and Moses in the other makes the two communities simply incommensurable.[30]

It should go without saying that the contrastive language Paul uses is not mere wordsmithing, an arbitrary choice of alternative language to set

---

cent reflections by Dunn in his epilogue to *Paul and Judaism*, ed. Reimund Bieringer and Didier Pollefeyt (London: T&T Clark, 2012), 208–20, esp. 215.

28. See Dunn, "Epilogue," 215. See similarly how Hooker finds the *pattern* of covenantal nomism apropos for Paul, but certainly *nomism* does not fit Paul's approach; *From Adam to Christ*, 156, 158, 160.

29. Brian Rosner provides important research on Paul's conscious avoidance of traditional Jewish language of Torah obedience; "Paul and the Law: What He Does Not Say," *Journal for the Study of the New Testament* 32 (2010): 405–19; and *Paul and the Law* (Downers Grove, IL: InterVarsity, 2013).

30. Francis Watson, *Paul, Judaism, and the Gentiles: Beyond the New Perspective* (Grand Rapids: Eerdmans, 2007), 346; see also 212.

the Jesus people apart from the Moses people. There is a reason why Paul settled on this word πίστις to encapsulate the Christian identity. Galatians very clearly sets up a way that πίστις can be separated from Torah and can be found meaningful when it is recontextualized in association with Christ (cf. 3:11–12).

An important point here, then, needs to be made. *Some* readings of Paul amount to little more than turning Paul into a social agent who preached a message of gentile inclusion; in these versions Paul really has nothing new to say about God or salvation, let alone a criticism with the law of Moses. Galatians, though, more than any of Paul's other letters, seems bent on convincing Paul's readers that the law's time is over and that there is a valid reason why this must be so. It is not that the law was evil or contrary to God's good purposes, rather it could play only a temporary role in view of the "coming of πίστις" (3:23).[31] It is helpful to examine 3:23 (and 3:25) and the absolute use of πίστις in order to better understand Paul's employment of πίστις overall in Galatians but before that I proffer my theory regarding πίστις in Galatians.

Πίστις in Galatians

Paul does *not* intend for πίστις to refer to nonwork, a kind of passive reliance on Christ. Paul uses πίστις in reference to the core relational dynamic of the covenant, the nature of a covenantal bond that expects fidelity and mutuality with trust at its core. Jews of Paul's time would undoubtedly have accepted that the language of πίστις was apropos for the Jewish way of life with God, though it only made sense to say that covenantal πίστις was mediated via Torah works. Paul is arguing in Galatians that the coming of the Messiah led to a new era, one where the conduit of Torah (works) is no longer valid, and when it is removed, what fills that void is pure πίστις. This word πίστις, for Paul, represents the essential nature of a social bond with God in and through Jesus Christ, and because Jesus stands at the center of this relationship, πίστις can become a summary word for the "Christ-relation."[32] When it is contrasted to Torah, then, Paul's use of πίστις particularly means

---

31. See Richard B. Hays, "Three Dramatic Roles: The Law in Romans 3–4," in *Paul and the Mosaic Law*, ed. James D. G. Dunn (Grand Rapids: Eerdmans, 2000), 151–64 at 155; cf. Rosner, *Paul and the Law*.

32. See similarly Peter Oakes, "Πίστις as Relational Way of Life in Galatians," *Journal for the Study of the New Testament* 40 (2018): 255–75.

something like the "unmediated covenantal relation with God in and through Christ." Thus, to go back to Sander's covenantal nomism, those who drew a connection between covenantal nomism and Pauline Christianity were on the right track, but did not make the appropriate adjustments (at least not in terminology). Yes, the covenantal part is fitting for Paul, but it is better to qualify that covenantal relationship (especially with Galatians in view) not as a newer form of *nomism* (related to Torah or law) but rather *pistism* (πίστις), recognizing the singularity and exclusivity of the Christ-relation as the way of life in God in the new age.

Galatians 3:23 shows how this works in Galatians. Early on in Gal 3, Paul reinforces a πίστις/νόμος dichotomy, which comes to a head in the consecutive citations of Deut 27:26 ("cursed is everyone who does not observe and obey all the things written in the book of the law" [NRSV] in Gal 3:10) and Hab 2:4 ("the one who is righteous will live by faith" [NRSV] in Gal 3:11). Further ossifying this tension, Paul dares to draw out the implications with these hauntingly brief seven words: ὁ δὲ νόμος οὐκ ἔστιν ἐκ πίστεως (3:12a). After some elaboration on the limitations of the law and the priority of the promises to Abraham, Paul returns to the crucial question about the purpose of the law (3:19). It was given "because of transgressions, until the offspring would come to whom the promise had been made" (NRSV). Despite the πίστις/νόμος tension that Paul introduces, he affirms that the law was never in contention with the divine promises to Abraham (3:21). The law served the role of "enclosing all things under sin"[33] until the proper time of the fulfillment of those promises ἐκ πίστεως Ἰησοῦ Χριστοῦ δοθῇ τοῖς πιστεύουσιν (3:22). Next, Paul offers another statement about the law's deference to promise, this time comparing the period of the law (one of being held in confinement) to that of the revelation of the πίστις to come.

As Hooker and others note, one would have expected Paul to compare the period of the law with the coming of *Christ*,[34] but here we have simply πίστις as the summary term of this new era. Why πίστις? Some imagine that this simply refers to the dawning of a new period of salvation history focused on faith in Jesus Christ.[35] However, previous to this, Paul had not only been foreshadowing the coming of Christ but also setting up πίστις and νόμος as

---

33. For this English translation of the phrase ἀλλὰ συνέκλεισεν ἡ γραφὴ τὰ πάντα ὑπὸ ἁμαρτίαν, I acknowledge my dependence on Barclay, *Paul and the Gift*, 407.

34. See Hooker, *From Adam to Christ*, 173.

35. So, e.g., F. F. Bruce, *The Epistle to the Galatians*, New International Greek

two modes of living.³⁶ Furthermore, πίστις in 3:23 could not *simply* be referring to faith in Christ because Abraham was established as this prototype of the πίστις person (obviously from a period before Christ).

A second approach to the absolute use of πίστις in 3:23 argues that it refers, not to *human faith in Christ*, but rather to *Christ's own* πίστις, the so-called faithfulness of Christ (see 171–76). Thus, de Boer posits that Paul was using πίστις as a metonym for Christ and that the coming of πίστις refers to "Christ's faithful death on the cross."³⁷ The problem here is similar to the first interpretation—why use πίστις to represent Christ (especially because this, as a circumlocution, would so easily invite misunderstanding)? Furthermore, all along (in Gal 3) Paul has been talking about the "faith of Abraham" and those who have modeled that same trust in God, those who live ἐκ πίστεως, in distinction to those who live according to the law. As Dunn cogently argues, the earlier part of Gal 3 sets up the contrastive view of "a (way of) life characterized by doing what the law commands rather than by trusting as Abraham trusted."³⁸

While both proposed readings of πίστις in 3:23 (human πίστις in Christ or Christ's πίστις toward God) offer some merit, neither seems to be very satisfying exegetically. Peter Oakes offers a helpful path for moving forward regarding Paul's use of πίστις. While Oakes is more inclined toward the objective genitive reading of πίστις Χριστοῦ, he does not close the door to other options. He argues that πίστις Χριστοῦ operates for Paul as a way of speaking about "life characteristic of those who are in a properly functioning relationship with Christ." But given the generic (or ambiguous) quality of the phrase, perhaps Paul meant more than just *human trust in Christ*. Oakes imagines that this phrase is wide enough to include "Christ's mode of engagement in that relationship" (i.e., more than "human faith in Christ").³⁹ Despite Oakes's hesitancies about mixing objective and subjective, this fits

---

Testament Commentary (Grand Rapids: Eerdmans, 1982), 181; similarly Moo, *Galatians*, 241.

36. See Leander Keck, *Paul and His Letters* (Philadelphia: Fortress, 1979), 82.

37. De Boer, *Galatians*, 239.

38. James D. G. Dunn, "ΕΚ ΠΙΣΤΕΩΣ: A Key to the Meaning of ΠΙΣΤΙΣ ΧΡΙΣΤΟΥ," in *The Word Leaps the Gap*, ed. J. Ross Wagner, C. Kavin Rowe, and A. Katherine Grieb (Grand Rapids: Eerdmans, 2008), 351–66 at 362.

39. See Peter Oakes, *Galatians*, Paideia (Grand Rapids: Baker, 2015), 88. To be fair, while Oakes ponders the possibility that πίστις plays some double duty (what he calls later "reciprocal fidelity"), he lands quite firmly on the objective genitive view of the debate.

the way πίστις could be used in the ancient world in general implying social concord, and it makes good sense of 3:23, where Paul may be using πίστις as a summary word for "the Christ-relation"—that is, the view of an era of a new possibility of relating to God via Jesus Christ.

This Christ-relation interpretation of πίστις in 3:23 may seem overly convoluted (as it implies fidelity, mutuality, and interrelationship between God, Christ, and the believer), but the proof of the pudding is in the eating, and this reading links 3:23 well to 3:22, where Paul associates the fulfillment of the promise in Jesus Christ to the trust in that promise by the believer.

I am not the first to concentrate on the *relational* and participatory dynamics of πίστις in relation to Paul's theology. In James Dunn's most recent expositions of Galatians, he flags this feature of Paul's faith language. In two essays, Dunn gives special attention to the theme of faith at the heart of Galatians.[40] Dunn observes in Galatians that the focus of πίστις is not on the idea of nondoing, but active trust in God in cooperation and relationship with Jesus Christ. The problem of the law is not that it was about doing, but that the gospel of Jesus Christ revealed to Paul that the relationship with God *itself* stood at the center of religion and the law could *not* become something that circumvented or cut short this πίστις dynamic. So Dunn sums up: "The immediacy of relationship with God through Christ which faith in Christ makes effective is not to be qualified and hedged around by commands which had only a limited role in the divine purpose."[41] Cultural practices and ritual acts could indeed serve as expressions of this faith, Dunn adds, but turning such media and outworkings into universal and permanent laws would compromise and obscure "the primary bond of the believer with God through Christ."[42] What Paul identifies in Abraham, as a precursor of

---

40. See James D. G. Dunn, "What's Right about the Old Perspective on Paul?" in *Studies in the Pauline Epistles*, ed. Matthew S. Harmon and Jay E. Smith (Grand Rapids: Zondervan, 2014), 214–29; and "The Christian Life from the Perspective of Paul's Letter to the Galatians," in *The Apostle Paul and the Christian Life*, ed. Scot McKnight and Joseph B. Modica (Grand Rapids: Baker, 2016), 1–18. Dunn defines faith as "simply trust, acknowledging complete dependence on God"; "What's Right about the Old Perspective on Paul?" 220.

41. Dunn, "Christian Life," 9. Similarly, he writes how in Paul's view on overemphasis on law obedience "distracted from and undermined the more fundamental principle of a relationship with God dependent on the human side only on faith, openness to, and acceptance of the grace of God and reliance on his promise"; "What's Right about the Old Perspective on Paul?" 221.

42. Dunn, "Christian Life," 9.

the gospel πίστις, is the patriarch's trust in God, "his reliance on God's promise—nothing more."[43]

Dunn articulates what I am arguing in this chapter, namely that πίστις is underscored in Galatians in such a way as to emphasize the Christ-relation as central, and prime, and by comparison the mediatory role of Torah is superfluous. This does not mean for Paul the law was evil or destructive, but rather served as a limited but necessary covenantal mechanism *until* the coming of the (unmediated) Christ-relation.[44]

The Christ-Relation in Galatians

Key πίστις texts from Galatians show the covenantal-*pistism* theory at work, namely πίστις as unmediated covenantal relation with God in Christ (i.e., πίστις as the Christ-relation).

Galatians 1:23

A common reading of the word πίστις in 1:23 interprets it as the "content of the Gospel message."[45] This is not entirely impossible, but it ought to be accounted for that Paul's statement here has the ring of primitive Christian vocabulary, where it would be unlikely πίστις carried that load of a comprehensive summary of the gospel.[46]

More likely the use of πίστις here represents the way this word became such a prominent feature in the earliest teaching of Jesus followers, such

---

43. Dunn, "What's Right about the Old Perspective on Paul?" 222.

44. On the nature and role of the law in Paul's perspective, see the cogent discussion by Bruce Longenecker, *The Triumph of Abraham's God* (Edinburgh: T&T Clark, 1998), 117–28.

45. A. Andrew Das, *Galatians* (St. Louis: Concordia, 2014), 146; see Thomas R. Schreiner, *Galatians*, Zondervan Exegetical Commentary on the New Testament (Grand Rapids: Zondervan, 2010), 112; similarly Bruce, *Galatians*, 105; cf. for further discussion of this option, de Boer, *Galatians*, 103; and Ben Witherington III, *Grace in Galatia* (Grand Rapids: Eerdmans, 1998), 125.

46. Ernst Bammel identifies this as "one of the oldest theological statements of Christianity"; "Galater i.23," *Zeitschrift für die neutestamentliche Wissenschaft* 59 (1968): 108–12; cf. James D. G. Dunn, *The Epistle to the Galatians*, Black's New Testament Commentary (Peabody, MA: Hendrickson, 1993), 84.

that it stuck as a label for their way of life. As Oakes argues, πίστις was the right word for Paul to use here (on the lips of earliest believers) because it indicated a "way of life characterized by trust in, and loyalty to, Christ."[47]

Galatians 2:16

Obviously this verse is a crux interpretum for the study of Paul's theology, especially his attitude toward the Jewish law. Throughout Galatians Paul repeats the juxtaposition of "works of the law" and "faith in Jesus Christ." Throughout Gal 3, these are represented as exclusive options (3:2, 5, 10, 12; cf. Rom 4:13). In Gal 2:16, Paul relates these two (works of the law/faith in Jesus Christ) not with ἀλλά but with ἐὰν μή. Most translations and commentators opt for the adversative meaning ("but") of ἐὰν μή in 2:16, mostly because Paul does *indeed* represent these as two opposing options (later). However, given that the most common or natural meaning of ἐὰν μή is "except" or "unless," a reading of this verse with that nuance is worth attempting (for why else would Paul use ἐὰν μή and not ἀλλά?).[48]

What if Paul did intend ἐὰν μή to mean "unless"? The verse would read: "Yet we know that a person is justified not by the works of the law *unless* through faith in Jesus Christ." The main reason why this rubs most interpreters the wrong way is because it seems to contradict Paul's position stated later in the epistle, namely that works and faith are mutually exclusive. Yet, Paul is talking to Peter here, particularly on an issue on which they have disagreement. This may have been Paul's way of granting credence *theoretically* to a Torah-way lifestyle for followers of Jesus, especially *Jewish* followers.

---

47. Oakes, *Galatians*, 85; similarly, Dunn: "For Paul at least 'faith' had become so characteristic of the new movement to which he now belonged, that it could function as an identity marker, an identification which was sufficiently distinct to denote and define the movement itself—as equally the talk of 'preaching Christ'"; Dunn, *The Epistle to the Galatians*, Black's New Testament Commentary (Peabody, MA: Hendrickson, 1994), 84.

48. The pair ἐὰν μή occurs only eight times in the undisputed Pauline letters. Four of these (Rom 11:23; 1 Cor 8:8; 9:16; 14:9) involve the phrase initiating a conditional clause, and thus they are a different sort of use of ἐὰν μή than we see in Gal 2:16. In the remaining cases, ἐὰν μή clearly makes best sense translated "unless" (Rom 10:15; 1 Cor 14:6; 15:36) because ἐὰν μή introduces a qualification or limitation. The standard New Testament lexicon offers no meaning for ἐὰν μή other than "if not, unless" (Vulgate Gal 2:16: *nisi*; BDAG, 268).

Πίστις and the Agency Question in Galatians

Paul would be saying, *Let us suppose that, yes, Torah does help to lead one to being right before God—wouldn't it only be on account of reorienting Torah around the Christ-relation (διὰ πίστεως Ἰησοῦ Χριστοῦ)?* As Andrew Das correctly notes, pitting Torah against πίστις would have been perplexing, even offensive, for Jews.[49] Thus, Das reads ἐὰν μή as "unless" here, recognizing that this "would be agreeable to many Jewish Christians including Paul's rivals in Galatia."[50] David deSilva, in his careful analysis of the Greek text of Galatians, offers a nice summary of the rhetorical benefits of this kind of reading: "Paul states here a position with which even the rival teachers would agree so as to lead the Galatians to see the absurdity of the rivals' position that 'works of the Torah' are essential for Gentiles."[51] This aligns with the argument repeated by Dunn that in 2:16 Paul offers a view that would resonate with the Jewish interlopers, but as the letter progresses the antithesis becomes more prominent.[52]

Would not this use of ἐὰν μή in 2:16 ("unless") give hostages to fortune for Paul? It is possible, especially if Paul ended the letter there. But Paul's position is rather transparent in Gal 3 (e.g., 3:12), and 2:16 would not serve as the only time where a particular word is chosen that might seem to contradict his own point (see 3:10). One can imagine that on these occasions Paul is acknowledging the relationship between faith and works of the law, even though his final position is ultimately clear by the end of the epistle.[53]

Addressing the matter of πίστις in 2:16, then, Paul's line of thought seems to be as follows. A person cannot be "right with God" by Torah-works per se. No program of deeds and responsibilities can do that; if this were possible, then Christ would not be needed (so 3:21b). Even those believers who have committed themselves to an ongoing practice of Torah ought to recognize that the Christ-relation, union with God through Christ by faith and by faithfulness, represents the real core of how one is put right with God.

49. Das, *Galatians*, 323 (on 3:12), 253–54 (on ἐὰν μή).

50. Das, *Galatians*, 253.

51. David deSilva, *Galatians: A Handbook on the Greek New Testament* (Waco, TX: Baylor University Press, 2014), 42. DeSilva rightly adds (43) that even if Paul meant ἐὰν μή to be adversative ("but"), how would the readers have not naturally understood it as "unless," since that was its most common meaning and use?

52. See James D. G. Dunn, "The New Perspective on Paul," *Bulletin of the John Rylands University Library of Manchester* 65 (1983): 95–122 at 112–13.

53. Barclay reluctantly acknowledges this possibility but still notes that "the polarity between Torah-practice and faith in Christ is eventually, at least, quite clear"; *Paul and the Gift*, 373n57.

COVENANTAL PISTISM

Again, even if Torah-works served the purposes of righteousness, they must be secondary to the Christian-relation.

Galatians 2:20

Within the context of Gal 2, Paul is explaining how he is advocating for a fundamental break with Torah as the necessary medium of the divine relation. The question is raised, *If seeking to be made right with God through Christ involves a necessary displacement of the role of Torah, won't the Christ people become "sinners" like the gentiles?* (2:17). Paul believes the opposite. This move from Torah to the Christ-relation is, in fact, the only way to "live to God" (2:19a). What happens with the Christ-relation is that the believer—in this case, Paul—*is crucified with Christ*. So then the self enslaved to sin has been mortified, put to death, and Christ assumes the believer. A key word here for Paul is "now" (νῦν); that is, a time when life lived under this new covenant (where the Christ-relation is central and constitutive) operates by πίστις. Πίστις neither implies something that is nonwork[54] nor focuses on particular beliefs as such. The word πίστις in 2:20 carries a *relational* nuance, akin to what some interpreters call union with or participation in Christ. F. F. Bruce explains in this instance that faith means "the bond of union with the risen Christ. To live by faith in this sense is tantamount to 'living by the Spirit' (5:25), which, as in Rom 8:9–11, enables the believer even now to anticipate the life to come."[55]

Galatians 3:8–9

Throughout the early part of Gal 3, Paul makes it a point to recognize that Abraham is the model of one who was put right by πίστις when he believed God (3:6). Thus, those who are ἐκ πίστεως are proven to be true heirs of Abraham. As most Pauline scholars observe, Paul's appeal to Abraham as a model of faith (without Torah works) would have been ironic. Jewish interpreters in Paul's time came to see Abraham as a kind of prototype of Torah obedience, even though Torah did not come into the picture until Moses

54. Contra Moo, *Galatians*, 159, 325.
55. Bruce, *Galatians*, 145.

(see Jubilees 24.11; 2 Baruch 57.2).[56] As William Baird rightly observes, Paul introduces a distinction between faith and works-oriented obedience in a way that had not been articulated before in Jewish tradition. Furthermore, according to Paul, "it is faith—rather than keeping the law or practice of circumcision—which makes identity with Abraham possible."[57] A particular bloodline, or even imitation of Torah fidelity, is not what makes one a "son of Abraham" according to Paul's message in Gal 3:1–9. Rather, those who are identified with the patriarch are οἱ ἐκ πίστεως. By this Paul means those who "believe God" (hence Gen 15:6 in Gal 3:6). Paul links Abrahamic belief *not* to the future of Israel alone, but especially to the blessing of τὰ ἔθνη (3:8). And then he applies this gospel blessing as well directly to the gentile Galatian believers who are accepted by God along with τῷ πιστῷ Abraham. Virtually all modern English translations render πιστός here as some form of belief:

the man of faith (NIV, ESV)

Abraham who believed (NRSV)

Abraham the believer (NET, NASB)

Abraham who had faith (RSV)

The most natural way to take the phrase τῷ πιστῷ Ἀβραάμ, though, is "faithful Abraham" (hence KJV). In the Septuagint and the New Testament, when πιστός is used as an attributive adjective, it refers to a person or people as *faithful* (2 Macc 1:2; Matt 24:45; Luke 12:42; Col 4:9; 1 Pet 5:12). Presumably the reason why translators choose to use the language of *belief* is because this appears to be Paul's overall point in Gal 3:1–9: *Abraham is not our spiritual father because he was faithful, but because he trusted God and was accepted by God on account of his faith (and not his obedient practice of circumcision).* True as this overall idea may be, nevertheless we must follow Paul's own wording carefully. Had Paul wanted to talk about "Abraham the believer," he would not have chosen πιστός, but probably would have used a participle (e.g., τῷ

---

56. See Jon D. Levenson, "The Conversion of Abraham to Judaism, Christianity, and Islam," in *The Idea of Biblical Interpretation*, ed. Hindy Najman and Judith H. Newman (Boston: Brill, 2004), 3–40.

57. William Baird, "Abraham in the New Testament: Tradition and the New Identity," *Interpretation* 42 (1988): 367–79 at 374.

πιστεύοντι Ἀβραάμ; or perhaps Ἀβραάμ ἀνθρώπῳ τῆς πίστεως; Gal 3:22; 1 Cor 14:22; cf. Acts 4:32).

Richard Hays offers an explanation as to why Paul would end this discourse with a potentially misleading statement about the "faithful Abraham." He notes that linking believing Abraham to οἱ ἐκ πίστεως draws out the unique fullness of the word πίστις. Again, πίστις does not simply or always mean belief. It is a kind of Janus word that can coordinate with the more cognitive semantics of the verb πιστεύω or the more social and virtue-oriented nature of πιστός. So Hays writes: "Paul can read the Scriptural statement 'Abraham believed [*episteusen*] God' and conclude that Abraham is rightly to be called faithful (*pistos*). The root idea in both expressions is that Abraham placed his trust in God; that, for Paul, is the meaning of faithfulness."[58] If this reading is correct, Paul reinforces the Jewish notion that Abraham is a model of obedient loyalty to God. For Paul, he is not a model of *Torah* obedience (and, thus, the father of circumcision) but the father of true faith in God—and such deep and committed faith that it is, after all, natural to call him "faithful Abraham." What is crucial for Paul in his Abraham discourse in Gal 3 is the highlighting of the purity of the God relation for Abraham. His word for this relationship is πίστις.

Galatians 3:12

In Gal 3 Paul makes the overall point that one is not put right with God through Torah but through πίστις. He sets up Hab 2:4 and Lev 18:5 as competing systems. When one chooses the law for justification, he or she is bound to that system and its expected obedience. Alternatively, the Abrahamic way is represented by the prophet where it is written: "The righteous [one] will live by ἐκ πίστεως" (Gal 3:11; cf. Hab 2:4). Paul argues that if people choose the law-works route, they are set on that limited path, and it does not lead to the desired end of freedom, life, and justification before God (Gal 3:21b). Paul goes as far as saying "the law is not from faith" (3:12). There are few statements in Paul that are more astonishing than this. Paul claims that the law is not from—that is, based on—faith. Paul does not explicate what exactly this means—is the law then opposed to the promises of God? Certainly not (3:21)! But the law cannot ultimately provide a me-

---

58. Richard B. Hays, "The Letter to the Galatians," in *The New Interpreter's Bible*, ed. Leander E. Keck (Nashville: Abingdon, 2000), 11:256.

dium for uniting God and his people by faith. The Christ-relation offers the possibility of a new way to know God, one that is unmediated such that this way could itself be called πίστις. This seems to explain why Paul talks about mediators and mediation in 3:19–20. Christ is, of course, a mediator, but given his unique status, nature, and relationship with the Father, his mediation is immediate.[59]

Covenantal Pistism and the Agency Debate

Much of the current debate regarding Pauline soteriology revolves around divine and human agency. If one believes that Paul had a theology of pure divine agency, then faith cannot appear to be a self-generated contribution to the equation. This leads some to rely on a reading of πίστις in Paul that focuses on Christ's own faith(fullness). But Paul reworks Jewish covenantal nomism and portrays human engagement in terms of covenantal *pistism* where the believer associates with God via the Christ-relation, specifically through belief in, trust in, and commitment to Christ.

For some, this can seem like too much human agency (and therefore "synergism" or "semi-Pelagianism").[60] Francis Watson reveals the mistake of setting up divine and human agency as an equation. He explains that "the faith elicited by the gospel is a reorientation rather than a renunciation of human agency":[61]

> To say that such faith *earns* or *merits* salvation would be misleading, for faith is a response to the prior divine grace in Christ that aims precisely to elicit and enable such a responsible. Yet for Paul, God's saving agency includes human agency within its scope, establishing it on a wholly new foundation rather than excluding or eliminating it. For that reason, Paul has no difficulty in maintaining both that righteousness is by faith and that those who do good will attain to eschatological glory and honor and peace.[62]

---

59. See N. T. Wright, *The Climax of the Covenant* (Minneapolis: Fortress, 1993), 172.

60. For a recent discussion of how the language of synergism is used and abused in scholarship, see Yinger, "*Reformation Redivivus.*"

61. Watson, *Paul, Judaism, and the Gentiles*, 212.

62. Watson, *Paul, Judaism, and the Gentiles*, 213.

Watson believes that Paul believed in neither salvation by works ("attained by unaided effort") nor a faith that is passive. He describes human and divine agency as on separate planes such that they cannot function as part of a formula. God's prior grace works in the human and yet, paradoxically, that person experiences a sense of free agency in the act of faith.[63]

It is important to look at the whole scope of Paul's use of faith language even in Galatians, and not just the faith/works juxtaposition. Much can and should be made of 5:6, where Paul talks about the relative unimportance of either circumcision or uncircumcision; what *really* matters is πίστις δι' ἀγάπης ἐνεργουμένη. As with 1 Thess 1:3 (cf. 2 Thess 1:11), Paul brings faith and working language into unison. One is hard pressed to argue that πίστις would not involve human agency. Here Paul's use of πίστις moves into the realm of faithfulness and obedience conceptually. Martyn describes this formulation (πίστις δι' ἀγάπης ἐνεργουμένη) as "the concrete pattern of life, established and incited by Christ's faithful dying love for us. Under the sign of the cross, this loving pattern of life is continued in the community in which each member is the servant of the other, bearing the other's burdens."[64] The word πίστις here, then, stands for "gospel-elicited faith express[ing] itself in love of the neighbor."[65]

Conclusion

For many centuries Galatians was central to understanding Paul's soteriology. And it is in this text where we find some of the most incisive comments from the apostle about faith and works in the divine economy. Some scholars claim that his opponents taught the Galatians about the necessity of Torah works, while Paul reinforced justification by faith alone. But Paul's πίστις language in the context of early Jewish use of πίστις, especially his Jewish Christian opponents, *also* affirms that the righteous live by πίστις. The radical step that Paul took was not to emphasize πίστις but to separate it from Torah works. Jews would naturally have believed that their covenantal relationship with God was based on trust and fidelity (πίστις), but all of this was mediated by and through Torah (ἔργα νόμου). Paul argues that the mediation of Torah works conflicts with the relational agency of Christ, what I call the Christ-relation.

---

63. Watson, *Paul, Judaism, and the Gentiles*, 213.
64. Martyn, *Galatians*, 474.
65. Martyn, *Galatians*, 474.

Past attempts compare Paul's pattern of religion as expressed in Galatians with the general pattern of religion of early Judaism called "covenantal nomism," which involves both grace and obligation. There is good reason to maintain that Paul's conception of covenantal religion did not go through a wholesale change. Still, nomism does not represent well his preferred language, and he comes across quite negative about nomism overall; his expression of the covenantal relationship focuses instead on the centrality and unique mediation of Christ, the living organic link, as it were, between God and his people who are now "in Christ." Therefore, though the phrase is inelegant, it is more proper to refer to this as "covenantal *pistism*."

9 And the Righteous Will Live by Trust

Faith Language in Romans 1:16–17

> The Gospel of salvation can only be believed in; it is a matter for faith only. It demands choice. This is its seriousness. To him that is not sufficiently mature to accept a contradiction and to rest in it, it becomes a scandal—to him that is unable to escape the necessity of contradiction, it becomes a matter of faith. Faith is awe in the presence of the divine incognito.
>
> —Karl Barth, *The Epistle to the Romans*

The academic discussion of the reasons for Romans is notoriously controversial, and most scholars accept that Paul wrote this lengthy letter with several concerns in mind, including rivalry within the church and the commendation of Phoebe. Jeffrey Weima is probably correct when he argues that 1:15 offers a major clue as to Paul's overall intentions. The letter to the Romans is foremost an articulation of his gospel proclamation that he feels the responsibility to share with this community.[1] Paul did not share this message with the Romans as a general tract, but he probably anticipated that there were serious questions about the validity of his ministry and mission.

From the very beginning of the letter, Paul sets out to demonstrate how the good news of Jesus Christ is not really a new development in God's plan, but something "promised beforehand through his prophets in the holy scripture" (1:1–2). He goes on to describe his commission whereby he became responsible for "the obedience of faith among all the Gentiles," which includes many in the Roman churches (1:5–6). He divulges to them the sincere desire he has "to proclaim the gospel to you also who are in Rome" (1:15), as he considered himself to be *their* apostle. Most

---

1. Jeffrey A. D. Weima, "The Reason for Romans: The Evidence of Its Epistolary Framework (1:1–15; 15:14–16:27)," *Review and Expositor* 100 (2003): 17–33.

scholars agree that we find the thesis of the letter (or a key agenda-setting comment) in 1:16–17: "For I am not ashamed of the gospel; it is the power of God for salvation to everyone who has faith, to the Jew first and also to the Greek. For in it the righteousness of God is revealed through faith for faith; as it is written, 'The one who is righteous will live by faith'" (all quotations from NRSV).[2]

Whether or not one considers this to be the main idea or argument of the letter, clearly these two verses contain several key words and concepts central to Romans overall: gospel (εὐαγγέλιον), salvation (σωτηρία), faith (πιστεύω, πίστις), Jew ('Ιουδαῖος)/gentile ("Ελλην), righteousness (δικαιοσύνη), living/life (ζάω). From the perspective of the Reformers, justification/righteousness was considered to be *the* dominant theme of Romans, though the New Perspective obviously brings the Jew/gentile social dynamics to the forefront as well.[3] But it ought not to go unnoticed how often Paul refers to faith, trust, and believing in this letter: the obedience of faith (1:5; also 16:26), the Romans' faith (1:8), mutual encouragement of faith (1:12), the πίστις of God (3:3), faith in/of Jesus (3:22–26), the "law of faith [πίστεως]" (3:27), justification of both circumcised and uncircumcised by faith (3:30), believing Abraham (4:3, 9, 16–20), Israel's failure pertaining to faith (9:30–32), and the necessity of faith (10:9).[4] It is reasonable, then, to observe that what Paul writes about faith in 1:16–17 is rather significant, and his appeal to Hab 2:4 is notably fundamental in his support of this. Thus, this chapter devotes attention to Paul's engagement with and use of Hab 2:4, with these questions in view:

Why does Paul quote Hab 2:4?
What purpose does it serve for Romans?
Is this a prooftext or a responsible use of Old Testament Scripture?

---

2. See Richard N. Longenecker, *The Epistle to the Romans*, New International Greek Testament Commentary (Grand Rapids: Eerdmans, 2016), 157; Robert Jewett, *Romans*, Hermeneia (Minneapolis: Fortress, 2007), 135–36; cf. Mark Reasoner, *Romans in Full Circle* (Louisville: Westminster John Knox, 2005), 1–10.

3. On the former, see, e.g., Peter Stuhlmacher, *Paul's Letter to the Romans: A Commentary* (Louisville: Westminster John Knox, 1994); on the latter, A. Katherine Grieb, *The Story of Romans: A Narrative Defense of God's Righteousness* (Grand Rapids: Eerdmans, 2002).

4. We could also add references to measures of faith (12:3, 6) and the so-called weak in faith (14:1–2).

The study of the intertextual dynamics of Rom 1:16–17 and Hab 2:4 is fraught with disagreement. Many scholars presume that Paul was prooftexting, drawing from a pithy Old Testament text in order to support his law-free gospel; if that were the case, Paul ostensibly had no interest in the original historical or literary context of Habakkuk. Others think that Paul not only plucked Hab 2:4 to use as a prooftext but also intentionally defied the original use of faith language in Habakkuk, away from the meaning associated with faithfulness to God and toward his own faith-and-not-works perspective. And others argue that Paul reads Hab 2:4 christocentrically, treating "the Righteous One" as a reference to Christ and *his* perfect πίστις. This raises a crucial question—whose πίστις is in view according to the original text of Hab 2:4 according to popular assumptions in Second Temple Judaism and Paul's own conception?[5]

Romans 1:16–17: A Brief Exegetical Analysis

> Οὐ γὰρ ἐπαισχύνομαι τὸ εὐαγγέλιον, δύναμις γὰρ θεοῦ ἐστιν εἰς σωτηρίαν παντὶ τῷ πιστεύοντι, Ἰουδαίῳ τε πρῶτον καὶ Ἕλληνι. δικαιοσύνη γὰρ θεοῦ ἐν αὐτῷ ἀποκαλύπτεται ἐκ πίστεως εἰς πίστιν, καθὼς γέγραπται· ὁ δὲ δίκαιος ἐκ πίστεως ζήσεται. (Rom 1:16–17)

The way this passage commences is often taken for granted because it is simply presumed that this is an instance of litotes.[6] This assumption downplays the natural concerns that Paul would have faced related to the suffering and shame associated with his gospel and his ministry. Halvor Moxnes's study of Romans is crucial. Moxnes argues that Paul had to reframe his readers' view of honor, especially for gentiles associating with Judaism who may have

---

5. I leave aside proposals that Paul used faith language in relation to Roman conceptions of *fides* and loyalty to the empire; pace Christian Strecker, "Fides-Pistis-Glaube: Kontexte und Konturen einer Theologie der 'Annahme' bei Paulus," in *Lutherische und Neue Paulusperspektive*, ed. Michael Bachmann, Wissenschaftliche Untersuchungen zum Neuen Testament 182 (Tübingen: Mohr Siebeck, 2005), 223–50.

6. George Kennedy, *New Testament Interpretation through Rhetorical Criticism* (Chapel Hill: University of North Carolina Press, 1984), 153; Leander Keck, *Romans*, Abingdon New Testament Commentary (Nashville: Abingdon, 2011), 50; Luke Timothy Johnson, *Reading Romans* (Macon, GA: Smyth & Helwys, 2001), 26.

been led to believe that one receives honor by Torah observance (3:27–28; 4:13) or circumcision (4:9–10). For Paul, "the question of honour and shame is now a question of their relationship to Christ. Christ now defines what is honour and what is shame."[7] On the matter of shame, Moxnes points to the common perplexity and problem among early Christians as they faced opprobrium from persecutors and critics of various kinds. Paul could use a text like Isa 28:16 ("behold, I am laying in Sion a stone that will make men stumble, a rock that will make them fall; and he who believes in him will not be put to shame") to reinforce this notion that "the righteous ask God to save them, to grant them justice so that they might be saved with honour and their enemy left with shame."[8] In his introduction to the powerful gospel that he proclaims, argues Moxnes, Paul seeks to reshape how they think about glory and honor: "Power in weakness, confidence of honour while seemingly put to shame—that was the paradox of Christian existence in a Jewish and Graeco-Roman environment."[9]

The gospel that Paul preaches is good news for all people, not just one privileged group or another; all have equal access to it through faith in Jesus. What is revealed in the gospel of the crucified and risen Jesus Christ is δικαιοσύνη θεοῦ, perhaps best understood as the fulfillment of God's promised "right-wising" activity in Christ.[10] Graham Stanton points out similarities in how Paul talks about the inexplicably nature and power of the gospel in Rom 1:16–17 and 1 Cor 1:18, where in the latter the foolish message of the cross happens to be the saving power of God. It is perhaps because of this superficial foolishness, in the folly of the cross, that Paul must point out that faith is required to see the righteousness of God at work despite the façade of shame and scandal. So, Paul writes in Rom 4 that Abraham did not give in to doubt, nor did he break trust with God, when the promise of a child was confronted with the reality that his and Sarah's old bodies were too dead to produce new life (4:18–19).[11]

---

7. Halvor Moxnes, "Honour and Righteousness in Romans," *Journal for the Study of the New Testament* (1988): 61–77 at 72.

8. Moxnes, "Honour and Righteousness," 72.

9. Moxnes, "Honour and Righteousness," 73.

10. I am indebted to Graham Stanton for some of this language and the subsequent connections to 1 Cor 1:18; see *Studies in Matthew and Early Christianity*, ed. Markus Bockmuehl and David Lincicum, Wissenschaftliche Untersuchungen zum Neuen Testament 309 (Tübingen: Mohr Siebeck, 2013), 284.

11. See Mark Seifrid, "Paul's Use of Habakkuk 2:4 in Romans 1:17: Reflections on

AND THE RIGHTEOUS WILL LIVE BY TRUST

To support the trust dimension of Paul's gospel, he cites Hab 2:4, approximating the text of the Septuagint:

ὁ δὲ δίκαιος ἐκ πίστεώς μου ζήσεται. (Hab 2:4 LXX)

ὁ δὲ δίκαιος ἐκ πίστεως ζήσεται. (Rom 1:17b)

Clearly Paul is especially interested in the terms πίστις and δίκαιος, but the meanings of both words—in the context of Hab 2:4 *and* in Rom 1:17—are debated (as also ζάω). What we can say with confidence is that Paul appealed to this brief line in Habakkuk to reinforce the centrality and productivity of a πίστις-determined way of living with God. To see what connection Hab 2:4 may have for Paul, we will first look at the message of Hab 2 in its original context and its reception into Paul's time.

The Background of Habakkuk 2:4 and Its Early Reception

Traditionally, Habakkuk is set within the twilight of the Assyrian Empire. The prophet wrestles with the problem of God supporting the violent conquest of the Chaldeans (cf. 1:5–11a: "I am rousing the Chaldeans" in 1:6 NRSV). Habakkuk recognizes that the Lord does this to reprove his wayward people (1:12). But he feels justified in questioning this divine act: "Your eyes are too pure to behold evil, and you cannot look at wrongdoing; why do you look on the treacherous, and are silent when the wicked swallow those more righteous than they?" (1:13 NRSV; cf. 2:1). The Lord responds by telling Habakkuk to record a vision. The people of God must wait for the "appointed time" that will demonstrate the justice of God (the *righteousness of God*!) that will come at *just the right time*. Theodore Hiebert succinctly summarizes the central concerns of this prophetical book:

> At a time when the wicked are in control, when the vision describing God's intention to reestablish justice has not yet become a reality, Habakkuk is called in the interim to trust God's assurances and to remain faithful.... Habakkuk is directed to maintain a faithful commitment to God's justice

---

Israel's Exile in Romans," in *History and Exegesis: New Testament Essays in Honor of Dr. E. Earle Ellis for His 80th Birthday*, ed. Sang-Won Son (Edinburgh: T&T Clark, 2006), 133–49 at 143.

Faith Language in Romans 1:16–17

and to persist in its principles, even when such justice appears to be absent in the world around him. Such is the message of God's second response.[12]

Given that what is *visible* to Israel is oppression and bloodshed, they are called upon to trust God despite appearances (hence the focus on *vision* in 2:2–3). So to summarize, "Those who do not lose faith, who remain faithful, even when there seems to be no reason to do so" will survive and see God's righteousness prevail.[13]

What is the meaning of אמונה in 2:4? Daniel Harrington makes the sensible case that it refers to "trust in God," not simply as a belief, but as a whole-life reliance on the righteousness of God and the surety of his promises of deliverance.[14]

The Septuagint text of 2:4 reads a bit differently than the Masoretic Text: ὁ δὲ δίκαιος ἐκ πίστεώς μου ζήσεται. This refers to the righteous one living by *my* (μου) faithfulness/trust.[15] Desta Heliso explains that the Masoretic Text/Septuagint difference may have resulted from a Hebrew *Vorlage* actually including the first-person pronoun. Alternatively it may have been a mechanical error, as the Hebrew suffixes *yod* and *waw* look similar. Or the difference may have been deliberate—after all, it is rather common for the Old Testament to refer to *God's* faithfulness (Deut 32:4; Ps 36:5; Isa 11:5; 25:1; Lam 3:23).[16]

The Qumranic Habakkuk Pesher refers to Hab 2:4b and apparently follows the Masoretic Text: "And the righteous will live by *his* trust." 1QpHab 7.17–8.3 offers this interpretation: this statement "concerns all those who observe Torah in the House of Judah, whom God will save from the house of

---

12. Theodore Hiebert, "The Book of Habakkuk," in *The New Interpreter's Bible*, ed. Leander E. Keck (Nashville: Abingdon, 1997), 7:623–55 at 642.

13. Donald Gowan, "Habakkuk, Book of," in *The New Interpreter's Dictionary of the Bible*, ed. Katharine Doob Sakenfeld (Nashville: Abingdon, 2006–9), 2:708.

14. Daniel J. Harrington, "Paul's Use of the Old Testament in Romans," *Studies in Christian-Jewish Relations* 4 (2009): 1–8 at 2–3; cf. also Arland J. Hultgren, *Paul's Letter to the Romans* (Grand Rapids: Eerdmans, 2011), 79: "In both texts the accent is on faith as fidelity and/or trust in God (Habakkuk) or the righteousness of God (Paul) as a means to life in its fullest sense."

15. See D.-A. Koch, "Der Text von Hab 2:4b in der Septuaginta und im Neuen Testament," *Zeitschrift für die neutestamentliche Wissenschaft* 76 (1985): 68–85.

16. See Desta Heliso, *Pistis and the Righteous One: A Study of Romans 1:17 against the Background of Scripture and Second Temple Jewish Literature*, Wissenschaftliche Untersuchungen zum Neuen Testament 235 (Tübingen: Mohr Siebeck, 2007), 52–53.

judgment on account of their tribulation and their fidelity to the Righteous Teacher."[17] In the early rabbinic literature, Hab 2:4b was used as a cornerstone for Jewish covenantal fidelity:

> R. Simlai said, "Six hundred and thirteen commandments were given to Moses.... Then David came and reduced them to eleven [Ps 15]. Then came Isaiah and reduced them to six [Isa 33:15]. Then came Micah and reduced them to three [Mic 6:8]. Then Isaiah [Isa 56:1]. Then came Amos, and reduced them to one, as it is said, 'Seek me and live' [Amos 5:4]. Or one may then say, then came Habakkuk [2:4] and reduced them to one, as it is said, 'The righteous shall live by his faith[fulness].'" (b. Mak. 23b)[18]

And, of course, we see Hab 2:4b three times in the New Testament; besides Rom 1:17 it is also cited by Paul in Gal 3:11 pertaining to the way of trust represented by Abraham (3:9), in contrast to the way of Torah works, which bears a curse (3:10-11). Paul explicitly states that Torah is not ἐκ πίστεως; rather the Abrahamic πίστις way comes with the promise of the Spirit (3:14).[19]

In Heb 10 the author calls the readers to persevere in faith (10:22-23) and to turn away from sin (10:26). He reminds them of their initial courage and resilience in the midst of persecution (10:32-34). So they are reminded to persevere, and Hab 2:3-4 is cited. The focus is on the righteous one not "shrinking back" (10:39). The text of Heb 10:38 is similar to Hab 2:4 LXX:

ὁ δὲ δίκαιός μου ἐκ πίστεως ζήσεται. (Heb 10:38)

ὁ δὲ δίκαιος ἐκ πίστεώς μου ζήσεται. (Hab 2:4 LXX)

---

17. As cited in James H. Charlesworth, "Revelation and Perspicacity in Qumran Hermeneutics?" in *The Dead Sea Scrolls and Contemporary Culture*, ed. Adolfo D. Roitman, Lawrence H. Schiffman, and Shani Tzoref (Boston: Brill, 2011), 161-80 at 174; see Timothy Lim, *Pesharim* (London: Continuum, 2002), 85.

18. As cited in M. Eugene Boring, *Mark*, New Testament Library (Louisville: Westminster John Knox, 2006), 344n33; see too Geza Vermes, *The Religion of Jesus the Jew* (Minneapolis: Fortress, 1993), 44.

19. J. Louis Martyn makes much of the way Paul contrasts Lev 18:5 and Hab 2:4 where the former supports "the route to life . . . in observance of the Law" and the latter faith leading to life; see "Paul's Understanding of the Textual Contradiction between Hab 2:4 and Lev 18:5," in *The Quest for Context and Meaning*, ed. Craig A. Evans and Shemaryahu Talmon (Boston: Brill, 1997), 465-74 (esp. 465-71).

Μου appears with ὁ δὲ δίκαιος such that it reads "my righteous one" rather than "my faith(fulness)."[20] Ultimately the point that Hebrews is making is rather transparent: "The righteous one is the Christian who demonstrates faithfulness to God as he moves toward the goal of life, eschatologically understood."[21]

Whose Πίστις?

Before discussing the meaning of πίστις in Rom 1:16–17, we must address the matter of the referent for ὁ δίκαιος. Most Romans interpreters take this as a generic reference to the believer who demonstrates faith. However, there is some support for a messianic reading of Hab 2:4 by Paul whereby this "Righteous One" refers to Jesus.[22] Richard Hays, for example, argues that ὁ δίκαιος was a title in Paul's time associated with the Messiah figure.[23] Furthermore, he posits that a messianic/christological reading of ὁ δίκαιος would fit Paul's "apocalyptic hermeneutic."[24]

In support, some appeal to 1 Enoch 38:2, which refers to "the Righteous One" who will come in judgment. In Acts as well "Righteous One" is used as a christological title (see 3:13–15; 7:51–53). Hays explains:

---

20. For a discussion of the placement of μου in various Septuagint manuscripts, see Gert J. Steyn, *A Quest for the Assumed LXX Vorlage of the Explicit Quotations in Hebrews* (Göttingen: Vandenhoeck & Ruprecht, 2011), 317 (esp. nn118–22).

21. William Lane, *Hebrews 9–13*, World Biblical Commentary 47B (Grand Rapids: Zondervan, 1991), 305. For insight into the importance of πίστις in Hebrews, see Luke Timothy Johnson, *Hebrews*, New Testament Library (Louisville: Westminster John Knox, 2006), 273; and Matthew C. Easter, *Faith and the Faithfulness of Jesus in Hebrews*, Society for New Testament Studies Monograph 160 (Cambridge: Cambridge University Press, 2014).

22. Many trace the beginnings of modern scholarly support for this to A. T. Hanson, *Studies in Paul's Technique and Theology* (London: SPCK, 1974), 39–45; cf. also C. H. Dodd, *According to the Scriptures* (London: Nisbet, 1952), 49–51; Richard B. Hays, "'The Righteous One': An Eschatological Deliverer: A Case Study in Paul's Apocalyptic Hermeneutics," in *Apocalyptic and the New Testament*, ed. Joel Marcus and Marion L. Soards, Journal for the Study of the New Testament Supplement 24 (Sheffield: JSOT Press, 1988), 191–215; and Leander Keck, *Romans*, Abingdon New Testament Commentary (Nashville: Abingdon, 2005), 54.

23. Hays, "Righteous One," 192.

24. Hays, "Righteous One," 192.

The term occurs *only* in speeches addressed to Jewish audiences—indeed, only to Jewish audiences in Jerusalem—and in every case the term is used without explanation, as though its meaning were presumed to be self-evident to the hearers. Luke does not use this title in his redactional framework or in constructive Christological formulations elsewhere; there is no reason to regard it as a Lukean theologoumenon.[25]

Other New Testament texts are notable as well for using "Righteous One" as a christological description (1 Pet 3:18; Jas 5:6; 1 John 2:1, 29; 3:7b). Returning to Rom 1:16-17, Hays argues that Paul's defense of the covenantal faithfulness of God aligns with key questions that are raised in Habakkuk: "How can God allow the wicked to oppress the righteous? Has God abandoned his people?"[26] Hays sees the πίστις of Jesus Christ (the Righteous One) as the manifestation of God's own righteousness.[27]

Hays's messianic/christological reading of Hab 2:4b in Rom 1:17 is possible, but it is not convincing.[28] First, Paul's (probably intentional) omission of the personal pronoun gives the saying a generic quality, and, obviously, Paul is quite insistent about Christian πίστις in Romans (1:8, 12). Craig Keener notes how Rom 4:5 echoes the Hab 2:4b/Rom 1:17 thesis: "But to one who without works trusts him who justifies the ungodly, such faith is reckoned as righteousness" (NRSV).[29] Wolfgang Kraus rejects the accusation that this places the salvific emphasis on human faith (and not divine deliverance):[30]

---

25. Hays, "Righteous One," 197.
26. Hays, "Righteous One," 207.
27. Hays, "Righteous One," 208-9.
28. Heliso is very attracted to the messianic reading of Hab 2:4b in Rom 1:17, but nevertheless is forced to concede that "no pre-Pauline Jewish writing cites Hab 2:4 in such a way that the citation can be understood messianically" (though he believes the Septuagint text could be understood this way); *Pistis and the Righteous One*, 164.
29. Craig Keener, *Romans*, New Covenant Commentary Series (Eugene, OR: Wipf & Stock, 2009), 30; also Wolfgang Kraus, "Πίστις ist zwar für Paulus stets mit Jesus verbunden, aber für Paulus hat der Glaube an Jesus Christus nach Gal 3 und insbesondere Rom 4 die gleiche Struktur wie das Vertrauen, das Abraham in Gott setzte"; see "Hab 2,3-4 in der hebräischen und griechischen Texttradition mit einem Ausblick auf das Neue Testament," in *Die Septuaginta und das frühe Christentum*, ed. Thomas S. Caulley and Hermann Lichtenberger, Wissenschaftliche Untersuchungen zum Neuen Testament 277 (Tübingen: Mohr Siebeck, 2011), 153-73 at 170.
30. For such accusation, see Douglas A. Campbell, "Romans 1:17—A *Crux Inter-*

"Faith/trust in Hab 2:4 is indeed not a prerequisite for attaining righteousness, but a response to God's promise, and thus the mode that leads to life."[31]

Richard Carlson makes the case that Paul intentionally presents Hab 2:4b in a malleable way, able to represent the right way of life for the righteous one. Thus, God will prove faithful, Christ is the manifestation of that fidelity, and true faith is modeled by Abraham and "lived out by all Christians in relationship to each other."[32]

Trust, Faith, or Faithfulness? Translating and Interpreting אמונה and Πίστις

Looking back at the original context of Hab 2:4b, surely "the righteous one will live by faith" did not refer to *Christian* faith. The Hebrew term אמונה often involved commitment to the covenantal relationship with God. Yet some scholars believe Paul was *not* intending to appeal to the original context of the book of Habakkuk, but rather found the key words in the Greek text of Hab 2:4b to be supportive of his gospel message.[33] Mark Seifrid, for example, argues that Paul *redefined* the meaning of πίστις for his Roman readers. If, Seifrid notes, the Septuagint presumes the Hebraic sense of faithfulness, this is recognizably different than Paul's use of πίστις: "In contrast with Jewish tradition, Paul does not understand 'faith' as a human quality or virtue. The context makes it clear. In proclamation ('from faith') God's saving righteousness is *revealed* and thus effects faith."[34]

---

pretum for the ΠΙΣΤΙΣ ΧΡΙΣΤΟΥ Debate," *Journal of Biblical Literature* 113 (1994): 265–85.

31. Kraus, "Hab 2,3–4 in der hebräischen und griechischen Texttradition," 170 (my translation).

32. Richard Carlson, "Whose Faith? Reexamining the Habakkuk 2:4 Citation with the Communicative Act of Romans 1:1–17," in *Raising Up a Faithful Exegete: Essays in Honor of Richard D. Nelson*, ed. K. L. Noll and Brooks Schramm (Winona Lake, IN: Eisenbrauns, 2010), 293–324 at 324.

33. See, e.g., John Barton, *Oracles of God* (Oxford: Oxford University Press, 2007), 245.

34. Mark Seifrid, "Romans," in *Commentary on the New Testament Use of the Old Testament*, ed. G. K. Beale and D. A. Carson (Grand Rapids: Baker, 2007), 608. Seifrid goes on to explain that "living by faith" for Paul does not point to the activity of the believer as a central concern but rather the notion of sharing in salvation and participating in the gospel.

Douglas Moo does not propose as strong of a difference between the original meaning of Hab 2:4b and Paul's concerns in Rom 1:17 but nevertheless emphasizes that faith for Paul was about believing in God rather than relying on "human abilities, activities, or assurances."[35]

Given the importance of Hab 2:4 in early Judaism and also for Paul (as well as the author of Hebrews), it is unlikely that Paul was shoehorning this text to support a gospel of faith (versus works). Rather, what both Hab 2:4b and Paul's concerns in Rom 1:16–17 have in common is the emphasis on *unqualified trust in God*. Rikki Watts cogently explains how Habakkuk and Romans share the concern to justify "God's mysterious actions":[36]

> Lamenting the Law's apparent failure to restrain wickedness, the prophet had appealed for Yahweh's righteous intervention only to face the scandalous prospect of his apparent injustice in seemingly favoring the wicked Chaldeans over his own people. It is thus in response to the question of theodicy that the issue of faith and faithfulness arises. Likewise reflecting on the ineffectiveness of the Law, Paul too is well aware of the problematic implications of his gospel. But as with Habakkuk, and as he outlines in his thesis statement (Rom 1:16–17), salvation is again to be found through faith in the faithfulness of the surprising and now eschatological revelation of righteous Yahweh's saving power.[37]

The point is not works or faith, nor is it faith versus faithfulness.[38] For Paul the gospel does not summon believers either to *beliefs* or to *obedient actions* per se. Rather, it is a call for *trust*. Again, Watts concludes that the power beyond the intertexture of Hab 2:4 and Rom 1:17 is the concern both for "God's covenantal faithfulness and [for] the reciprocal need for the obedience of faith and perseverance on the part of the hearer as the path to life."[39]

---

35. Douglas J. Moo, *The Epistle to the Romans*, New International Commentary on the New Testament (Grand Rapids: Eerdmans, 1996), 79.

36. Rikki Watts, "'For I Am Not Ashamed of the Gospel': Romans 1:16–17 and Habakkuk 2:4," in *Romans and the People of God: Essays in Honor of Gordon D. Fee*, ed. Sven K. Soderlund and N. T. Wright (Grand Rapids: Eerdmans, 1999), 3–25 at 3.

37. Watts, "For I Am Not Ashamed," 3–4.

38. Ray Clendenen leaves unsubstantiated his statement that faith and faithfulness are two clearly distinct concepts, with the former being passive and the latter being active; see "Salvation by Faith or by Faithfulness in the Book of Habakkuk," *Bulletin for Biblical Research* 24 (2014): 505–15 at 512.

39. Watts, "For I Am Not Ashamed," 25. Similarly, Paul Sampley underscores

Karl Barth's interpretation of faith language in Rom 1:17 does justice to *both* that sense of "believing the unbelievable," daring to put faith in the foolish gospel, and also the necessity of grasping and holding tight the invisible God, the *deus absconditus*. Barth is cogently able to describe what I call "trusting faith," which includes both "believing faith" (tuning hearts and minds into the gospel frequency of faith to see with faith instead of sight) and "obeying faith" (leaning human wills into a commitment to live and act in trust and obedience).

Regarding the ability to see wisdom in the folly of the gospel, Barth draws from the thought of Luther:

> Faith directs itself towards the things that are invisible. Indeed, only when that which is believed on is hidden, can it provide an opportunity for faith. And moreover, those things are most deeply hidden which most clearly contradict the obvious experience of the senses. Therefore, when God makes alive, He kills; when He justifies, He imposes guilt; when He leads us to heaven, He thrusts us down into hell.

That is, faith *inverts* reality, as it were, to "rightside" the upside-down gospel. But this requires much more than belief, if by this we mean assenting to doctrines. In Barth's view, Paul claims this: "The believer is the man who puts his trust in God, in God Himself, and in God alone; that is to say, the man who, perceiving the faithfulness of God in the very fact that He has set us within the realm of that which contradicts the course of this world, meets the faithfulness of God with a corresponding fidelity, and with God says 'Nevertheless' and 'In spite of this.'"[40]

Paul's concern with trusting faith and the reception of the gospel: "Faith is the touchstone for Jews and gentiles. Faith relativizes the question whether one is circumcised or not, whether one is a Jew or not, whether one is a gentile or not. Decision has become the criterion of admission, not ancestry, and not the keeping of certain ritual performance"; see "Romans and Galatians: Comparison and Contrast," *Understanding the Word*, ed. J. T. Butler et al. (Sheffield: JSOT Press, 1985), 315–39 at 327–28.

40. Karl Barth, *The Epistle to the Romans*, trans. Edwyn C. Hoskyns (London: Oxford University Press, 1968), 39.

From Πίστις to Πίστις

Related to all of this is the much debated phrase ἐκ πίστεως εἰς πίστιν (Rom 1:17), which obviously sets up the Hab 2:4b quotation. There are four major views on the interpretation of this phrase. One option could be called the *continuative* view, where Paul is showing a continuation from Old Testament style faith to New Testament faith. This view was popular among patristic theologians; so Origen wrote: "The first people were in the faith because they believed God and Moses his servant, from which faith they have now gone over to the faith of the gospel."[41]

Another possible reading is *progressive*; that is, something like "starting with faith and ending with faith." This view is often attributed to John Calvin, as he explained this phrase as denoting "the daily progress of every believer."[42]

A third view treats each πίστις as in reference to a different partner in the covenantal relationship, that is, from divine πίστις to human πίστις. So Ambrosiaster explains this *covenantal* reading: "What does this mean, except that 'the faith of God' is in him because he promises, and 'the faith of man' is in him because he believes the one who promises?"[43] This view is also taken up by Karl Barth and James Dunn.[44]

Lastly, a very popular view is the *rhetorical* reading, which does not try to read each instance of πίστις in isolation but in light of its literary effect; thus, it could be translated as something like *"faith and only faith."* What is being communicated is the purity or exclusiveness of faith.[45]

---

41. As cited in Longenecker, *Romans*, 177; Origen, *Ad Romanos*, in Patrologia Graeca, ed. Jacques-Paul Migne (Paris, 1857–86), 14:861; see also Tertullian, *Adversus Marcionem* 5.13.

42. John Calvin, *Commentary on Romans 1–16* (Grand Rapids: Baker, 1993), 28; see similarly John W. Taylor, "From Faith to Faith: Romans 1.17 in the Light of Greek Idiom," *New Testament Studies* 50 (2004): 337–48; cf. C. Kruse, *Paul's Letter to the Romans*, Pillar New Testament Commentary (Grand Rapids: Eerdmans, 2012), 75–78.

43. Ambrosiaster, *Ad Romanos*, in Patrologia Latina, ed. Jacques-Paul Migne (Paris, 1844–64), 17:56 and in Corpus Scriptorum Ecclesiasticorum Latinorum 81:3; as cited in Longenecker, *Romans*, 177.

44. Cf. Barth, *Romans*, 41.

45. So C. E. B. Cranfield, *A Critical and Exegetical Commentary on the Epistle to the Romans*, International Critical Commentary (Edinburgh: T&T Clark, 1975), 1:99–100; C. K. Barrett, *The Epistle to the Romans*, Black's New Testament Commen-

These options are difficult to adjudicate, which probably attests to the ambiguity of Paul's phrasing. I find least likely the covenantal view, because it requires a parsing out of πίστις between two separate parties without explication. The interpretation of ἐκ πίστεως εἰς πίστιν depends on one's reading of Paul's use of Hab 2:4, which follows in Romans. But the use of πιστεύω in 1:16 also contributes to this discussion. My inclination is to see the faith language and the Hab 2:4b quote primarily pertaining to *human* faith and trust. Because Rom 1:17 begins with a focus on the *new* revelation of God's righteousness in the gospel (ἐν αὐτῷ), I incline toward the rhetorical view; that is, Paul underscores the absoluteness of πίστις, trust. One might paraphrase 1:17 in this way: *In this gospel God's righteousness has been brought to full light that expects complete and exclusive truth, just as it has been written in Scripture, "The righteous will live by trust."*

Conclusion

In Paul's use of Hab 2:4b in Rom 1:17, he is not merely prooftexting the prophetic text, nor is he distorting a Jewish understanding of *emunah* by transposing into a so-called Pauline faith (i.e., over and against works). Rather, we have here a comprehensive use of πίστις that we might call "trusting faith." Paul attests that he is bold in his proclamation of the gospel because it is powerful and effective for salvation for everyone who believes. What is expected is not commitment to Torah but rather trust in God, plain and simple. This is captured exquisitely by Elizabeth Achtemeier's reading of Habakkuk:

> Habakkuk . . . makes the affirmation that the relationship with God is fulfilled by "faithfulness." That does not mean moral steadfastness, rectitude, and earnestness. It does not signify the proper performance of ethical or cultic duties. Rather, faithfulness here means trust, dependence, clinging to God; it means living and moving and having one's being in him alone; it means relying on him for the breath one draws, for the direction one takes, for the decisions one makes, for the goals one sets, and for the outcome of one's living. . . . Faithfulness means placing one's whole life in God's hands

---

tary (Peabody, MA: Hendrickson, 1991), 31; and Joseph Fitzmyer, *Romans*, Anchor Bible 33 (New York: Doubleday, 1993), 263.

and trusting him to fulfill it, despite all outward and inward circumstances; despite all personal sin and guilt; despite all psychological and social and physical distortions. Faithfulness is life by God's power rather than by one's own. And there it is truly life, because it draws its vitality from the living God who is the source of life.[46]

---

46. Elizabeth Achtemeier, *Nahum–Malachi*, Interpretation (Louisville: Westminster John Knox, 1986), 46; as cited in Clendenen, "Salvation by Faith," 515.

10 Revisiting "The Faith of Christ"

Πίστις Χριστοῦ and the Christ-Relation in Paul

The so-called πίστις Χριστοῦ debate is one of those scholarly feuds that experiences periodical revival and renewed energy every few years. All agree that it is not really a make-or-break issue in Pauline studies, but it continues to be an enigma in search of a satisfactory solution. Before offering my take on the issue, here is a brief summary of the matter for the uninitiated.[1]

Paul has a routine way that he refers to the source or essence of the Christian life: πίστις Χριστοῦ, woodenly translated "faith of Christ." There are at least two possible meanings/translations of this phrase based on one's interpretation of the genitive form Χριστοῦ and its relationship to the head-noun πίστις:

1. faith *in* Christ
2. Christ's faithfulness/the faithfulness shown by Christ

The first option takes the phrase as referring to the faith that Christians have *in* Christ. The second option views πίστις as something that Christ *himself* has or shows. Most scholars recognize that πίστις can mean faith (i.e., belief) or faithfulness (i.e., loyalty, obedience, commitment). If Χριστοῦ is an objective genitive, then the phrase refers to belief *in* Christ. If it is subjective, then it is communicating the faithfulness *of* Christ. The phrase "faith of Christ"

---

1. There are many helpful discussions of the debate; see Debbie Hunn, "Debating the Faithfulness of Jesus Christ in Twentieth-Century Scholarship," in *The Faith of Jesus Christ: Exegetical, Biblical, and Theological Studies*, ed. Michael F. Bird and Preston M. Sprinkle (Peabody, MA: Hendrickson, 2009), 15–31; Matthew Easter, "The Pistis Christou Debate: Main Arguments and Responses in Summary," *Currents in Biblical Research* 9 (2010): 33–47; and Chris Kugler, "ΠΙΣΤΙΣ ΧΡΙΣΤΟΥ: The Current State of Paul and the Key Arguments," *Currents in Biblical Research* 14 (2016): 244–55.

appears in its πίστις + Χριστοῦ (faith + of Christ) form in six main texts in Paul: Rom 3:22, 26; Gal 2:16 (twice); 3:22; Phil 3:9.

How does one decide which option is exegetically stronger? Scholars appeal to syntactical clues to make their case (such as the presence of the article or certain genitive patterns), but these factors have proven inconclusive.[2] Several other features are spotlighted in hopes of resolution:

- the absolute use of πίστις in Galatians
- the parallel phrase "works of the law"
- Paul's use of ἐκ πίστεως in Gal 3 (and Rom 1)
- the appeal to Abraham as the model of πίστις
- similar language in the New Testament outside of the undisputed Pauline letters
- early reception history[3]

Perhaps most importantly of all, scholars make their case based on the flow and best reading of those wider passages where πίστις Χριστοῦ appears. Unfortunately (1) both readings *can* make sense in all of the relevant passages and (2) because Paul *could* have expressed either sentiment in a more straightforward fashion, it leaves readers to wonder why he fixated on this particular phrasing.

Perhaps the strongest point of the objective genitive view is the simple fact that Paul *does* refer ubiquitously to "faith/believing in Christ," such that this theological concept is concretely established in his letters. What many find most attractive about the subjective genitive view is the way in which it places Paul's soteriological focus on the person and work of Christ and not on human πίστις.[4] The objective interpretation is more compelling, especially because Paul never clearly and explicitly appeals to Christ's

---

2. See Easter, "*Pistis Christou* Debate," 34.

3. See Roy Harrisville, "ΠΙΣΤΙΣ ΧΡΙΣΤΟΥ: Witness of the Fathers," *Novum Testamentum* 36 (1994): 233–41; Mark W. Elliott, "Πίστις Χριστοῦ in the Church Fathers and Beyond," in *The Faith of Jesus Christ*, ed. Bird and Sprinkle, 279–90; and Michael R. Whitenton, "After ΠΙΣΤΙΣ ΧΡΙΣΤΟΥ: Neglected Evidence from the Apostolic Fathers," *Journal of Theological Studies* 61 (2010): 82–109. For a broader study of reception, see Benjamin Schliesser, "'Exegetical Amnesia' and ΠΙΣΤΙΣ ΧΡΙΣΤΟΥ: The 'Faith *of* Christ' in Nineteenth-Century Pauline Scholarship," *Journal of Theological Studies* 66 (2015): 61–89.

4. See, classically, Richard B. Hays, "Πίστις and Pauline Christology: What Is at Stake?" in *The Faith of Jesus Christ* (Grand Rapids: Eerdmans, 2002), 272–98.

faithfulness to God (though his obedience is praised; e.g., Phil 2:5–11; Rom 5:19).[5] Furthermore, it skews the conversation from the start to refer to the objective genitive as the "anthropological view" and the subjective genitive view as the "christological view," because this appears to imply that the former deemphasizes the dominant agency of Christ. But that is certainly not implied by Paul in Gal 3:26, where he clearly highlights human "faith in Christ" (πάντες γὰρ υἱοὶ θεοῦ ἐστε διὰ τῆς πίστεως ἐν Χριστῷ Ἰησοῦ). That is, no responsible interpreter of Paul concludes that here human faith is *the* prime factor in self-identification as a son of God; rather, faith is the given human *means* of receiving and living within this status *in and through Christ Jesus*. The objective genitive and subjective genitive proponents sometimes establish a rigid either/or that seems to diminish either the platform of human belief *or* the centrality of the model loyalty of Christ. And thus we are reminded that the πίστις Χριστοῦ formulation itself is frustratingly obscure in Paul.

Other Possible Readings of Πίστις Χριστοῦ

The objective and subjective views are obviously the most popular options and those given the most attention in scholarship. But other possible readings are as well. For example, Shuji Ota argues that πίστις Χριστοῦ is a subjective genitive, but the orientation of Christ's faithfulness in the Pauline phrase is toward *humanity*, not God. One of his best cases for this reading is Gal 2:20, where Paul explains how his new postcrucified self lives by πίστις in the Son of God. Ota argues that here it is not by his *own* faith, nor by Christ's faithfulness to God, but according to *Christ's faithfulness to Paul* that he is able to live.[6] Notice how the verse ends: "who loved *me* and gave himself for *me*" (NRSV).

Another possible reading is sometimes called the "third view" or the "eschatological event" view.[7] For this view, the focus is on Gal 3:23–26, where

---

5. See Jouette Bassler, *Navigating Paul* (Louisville: Westminster John Knox, 2007), 23–34.

6. Shuji Ota, "ΠΙΣΤΙΣ ΧΡΙΣΤΟΥ: Christ's Faithfulness to Whom?" *Hitotsubashi Journal of Arts and Sciences* 55 (2014): 15–26 at 26.

7. See Benjamin Schliesser, "'Christ-Faith' as an Eschatological Event (Galatians 3.23–26): A 'Third View' on Πίστις Χριστοῦ," *Journal for the Study of the New Testa-*

Paul refers to the coming of πίστις.⁸ It would have been natural (or expected) for Paul to state that at the time of fulfillment *Christ* came—so why πίστις? Preston Sprinkle makes the case that here the most sensible way to interpret πίστις is to view it as a synonym for the "gospel." This seems to make sense in Gal 1:23, but does not explain why Paul seems to have preferred faith terminology. Benjamin Schliesser also supports the third view but gives more direct attention to the Pauline word choice. With Gal 3:23, 25 in view, Schliesser argues that πίστις functions as a summary word for (quoting Dieter Lührmann) "an entire large complex."⁹ Put another way, it refers to more than human faith or Christ's faithfulness per se; rather, it points to "the event of salvation, God's redemptive eschatological act."¹⁰ Schliesser focuses on participationistic language by asserting that Paul imagines this event to involve uniting with Christ through faith. Thus, Schliesser argues in favor of what he calls a "relational genitive," which he describes in spatial terms as entering into the realm of Christ.¹¹

Πίστις Χριστοῦ and the Centrality of the Christ-Relation

I have long defended the objective genitive view of πίστις Χριστοῦ, but as I concluded my research for this book, I became more sympathetic toward the "third view." Ultimately, the nature of this debate reinforces the notion that πίστις Χριστοῦ (and Paul's πίστις language in general) is hard to pin down to very specific referents and actions. It is right to associate Pauline πίστις with the gospel and with participation in Christ. For Paul, πίστις Χριστοῦ refers to the fact and experience of the Christ-relation. This involves Christ's connection with God, of course, and it involves human faith, but it also involves Christ's outstretched hand toward believers. Accordingly, I am sympathetic to Schliesser's proposal. The Christ-relation is by the grace of God and initiated by Christ, but believers participate in it *by faith*. Both sides of the relationship are in view, but probably for Paul πίστις Χριστοῦ

---

ment 38 (2016): 277–300; and Preston Sprinkle, "Πίστις Χριστοῦ as an Eschatological Event," in *The Faith of Jesus Christ*, ed. Bird and Sprinkle, 166–84.
    8. Schliesser, "Christ-Faith," 284.
    9. Schliesser, "Christ-Faith," 285.
    10. Schliesser, "Christ-Faith," 285.
    11. Schliesser credits Morna Hooker with inspiring this spatial-transmigration concept.

is a placeholder that simply stands for the agency of Christ, especially as a platform or mediation that relates God's people to God in a personal and transformative fashion.

Ota comes to a similar conclusion. He argues that the absolute use of πίστις cannot refer to the belief of an individual human. Rather, it "refers to an *objective dispensation or system of salvation by God* comparable with the Torah of Judaism."[12] Ota argues that this is not an individual reality (or personal, individualized faith) but a collective-communal one given by the grace of God. This new reality is focused on neither human faith nor Christ's faithfulness to God. Rather, it includes human faith plus the fidelity of the believed Christ as well as "the word of proclamation that creates their relationship."[13]

The Translation Question

One of the biggest challenges for the third view (in whatever version) is the matter of translation: *what is the easiest rendering in plain English?* Neither "faith in Christ" nor "faithfulness of Christ" does justice to this perspective. While it may not be elegant, I suggest the "Christ-relation(ship)," which is properly Christ centered, respecting the relational aspect of πίστις, but leaving understated *who is doing what.*

Importance of Human Faith in the Christ-Relation

It is easy, in this debate, to treat the objective genitive view as a kind of works-oriented approach—in this case the human work happens to be faith. Thus, some on the subjective-genitive side can claim a kind of higher chris-

---

12. Shuji Ota, "The Absolute Use of ΠΙΣΤΙΣ and ΠΙΣΤΙΣ ΧΡΙΣΤΟΥ in Paul," *Annual of the Japanese Biblical Institute* 23 (1997): 64–82 at 76.

13. Ota, "Absolute Use of ΠΙΣΤΙΣ and ΠΙΣΤΙΣ ΧΡΙΣΤΟΥ," 76; cf. 82. Ota is correct in general, but I demur when he argues that the inclusion of a genitive modifier (Χριστοῦ) explicates in a given case more clearly the focus of this reality. Πίστις Χριστοῦ does not especially refer to Christ's faithfulness but the reality of the "Christ-relation" without getting into further specification. What is most important to Paul is that Christ is always the center—the center of faith, the center of salvation, the center of the relationship with God.

tological agency. But we must be careful not to sell human faith in Paul too short. Paul presses his converts to continually *choose* to think with the mind of Christ and to see with the eyes of faith. For example, in 2 Corinthians Paul is insistent that the Corinthians chose worldly or carnal spectacles. They evaluated based on appearances and outward glory. Instead, they ought to be like Paul, who learned how to disregard the fleshly perspective (κατὰ σάρκα) and instead walk by πίστις and not εἶδος (5:7). Paul did not boast in this or consider it a form of self-aggrandizing merit. To *choose* to live by faith is to recognize one's own poverty of vision and discernment. It requires denying self and depending on Christ.[14] "Faith in Christ" is no more than a call to be rescued by the "faithfulness *of* Christ."

---

14. See Jeanette Hagen, "Faith as Participation: An Exegetical Study of Some Key Pauline Texts" (PhD diss., Durham University, 2016).

11 Faith beyond Belief

Synthesis and Conclusion

Anthony Thiselton reflects at length on the uniqueness of the terminology of faith (and πίστις in particular) in the Bible. His observations are very much in line with the points I make in this book. Thiselton explains that πίστις is polymorphous and, therefore, cannot be brought into English with one static term like "faith."[1] In his recent book, *Doubt, Faith, and Certainty*, Thiselton isolates no less than thirteen meanings for faith, including belief, mental assent, spiritual disposition, the gospel, faithfulness, and reason.[2] It is not so important that all the meanings are neatly distinguished and exhaustively catalogued. What matters most is that one can recognize the somewhat unusual way that πίστις can shift and blend into different semantic domains. One might call this polyvalence, using the idea of *modulation*. It is as if πίστις falls on a spectrum from believing (cognitive/epistemological) faith to obeying (volitional/social/practical) faith. Depending on the context, the pragmatic meaning can be plotted somewhere on this continuum, with some cases where it appears to fall to one extreme or the other. And sometimes Paul used πίστις in a more comprehensive or all-encompassing sense, where it could be called trusting faith.

This fundamental insight into the nature of πίστις needs to be more widely recognized and appreciated because English Bible translations have been notoriously rigid in their treatment of this noun and concept. In all but the rarest of occasions, it is assumed that πίστις means only belief. But there is ample reason to hold that it deserves a broader understanding and vocabulary.

---

1. Anthony Thiselton, *The First Epistle to the Corinthians*, New International Greek Testament Commentary (Grand Rapids: Eerdmans, 2000), 223.
2. Anthony Thiselton, *Doubt, Faith, and Certainty* (Grand Rapids: Eerdmans, 2017), 10–11.

Obeying Faith

On many occasions in Paul (e.g., 1 Thessalonians and Philippians), πίστις means faithfulness or loyalty—that is, it operates as something like a social virtue. There is almost endless evidence of the use of πίστις in ancient Hellenistic political and military literature, where it appears in relation to social concord and relational commitment. In 1 Thessalonians, for example, there is good reason to expect this use of πίστις, since Paul was concerned with their respective perseverance and endurance in the midst of persecution and societal pressures that tested their commitment to Christ and the Christ-following community. In such cases, πίστις as a virtue was fundamentally social and embodied in an active way.[3] It would be going too far to translate πίστις as "obedience." It can easily be related to obedience (hence Rom 1:5), but it is not exactly the same thing (correlation, not equation). If obedience is fully active, then obeying πίστις is "preobedience." It is the faith that dovetails with obedience; it is the energy that produces the movement that becomes outward obedience. One could make the case that πίστις blends *into* ὑπακοή, but they are not synonyms.

Believing Faith

One could make the equal and opposite mistake of concluding that πίστις, since it so often means faithfulness in ancient literature, *always* means faithfulness.[4] But, again, this neglects the primary point that πίστις is a dynamic word capable of shifting shades of meaning based on use and context. There are some situations where it certainly makes good sense to translate πίστις as faith or belief. This kind of meaning was certainly present in ancient literature and can be demonstrated in the New Testament (cf. Jas 5:15). It is often assumed that for Paul faith was about correct beliefs about Jesus. This has some truth to it in a broad sense and follows a certain pattern of usage

---

3. Scholars sometimes refer to this as the passive use of πίστις; presumably this means it is considered a state or perhaps a trait. But given that it is a social habit, it can be confusing to call it passive, especially given the connotations it might have that complicate questions about faith/works and agency (see below).

4. This is, perhaps, the flaw in Gordon Zerbe, "Believers as Loyalists: The Anatomy of Paul's Language of *Pistis*," in *Citizen: Paul on Peace and Politics* (Winnipeg: CMU Press, 2012), 26–47.

established by the verb πιστεύω (cf. 1 Cor 15:2-11). But as far as Paul is concerned, his faith language is not primarily focused on correct knowledge as much as it is about the correct way of looking at all of reality.[5] To use a computer metaphor, faith is not about having the right data or even the right software; it is about using the right operating system. While this notion of believing faith can be found in many of his letters (including 1 Thessalonians and Philippians), 1-2 Corinthians are crucially important case studies. This is because here, more than anywhere else, Paul focuses extensively on *epistemology*.[6] He sought to convince the Corinthians that, although they craved spiritual wisdom, they could reach divine revelation only through faith in the foolishness of the cross of Christ. In 2 Corinthians, Paul borrows from a Jewish tradition of anti-idol polemic to demonstrate that it can be easy to focus on forms, *what the eye sees*, but true life and power happen to come from what is unseen; thus believers are called to walk *by faith* (πίστις), and not by sight (5:7).

Trusting Faith

Finally, Paul's faith language in Galatians and Romans (1:16-17; cf. Hab 2:4) is interesting because he sometimes uses πίστις in an absolute sense, that is, without descriptors (Gal 1:23; 3:23, 25). In these cases it is as if πίστις stands for something *like* Christianity, Christ, the Christian life, and so on. Just as Jews used πίστις to refer to their relationship with God (in, e.g., Josephus and Septuagint), Paul employed faith language in reference to the human-divine relation. But instead of articulating a model of πίστις mediated by Torah, Paul saw Christ as the conduit or agent of this. From the New Perspective, Dunn and Hooker see the same pattern in Paul of grace and obligation as was true of the Judaism of his time. And yet something is clearly wrong with labeling Paul a "covenantal nomist." *Nomism* was precisely what Paul repudiates in Galatians, if by nomism this means Torah agency of the divine-human relationship. Rather, "covenantal *pistism*" is the more accurate term to indicate a divine-human relationship that includes both expectation and

---

5. See Mary Healy, "Knowledge of the Mystery: A Study of Pauline Epistemology," in *The Bible and Epistemology*, ed. Mary Healy and Robin A. Parry (Eugene, OR: Wipf & Stock, 2007), 134-58, esp. 149-56.

6. See Ian Scott, *Paul's Way of Knowing* (Grand Rapids: Baker, 2008); on the Corinthian correspondence in particular, see 23-48, 59-68.

goodwill (hence covenantal) but mediates by πίστις in Christ. In Paul's mind there is no *intermediating* agency (by, e.g., Torah or anything else) for divine salvation and vitality—except the Christ-relation. In Paul's mind, the unique role and status of Christ somehow meant that, although he clearly serves as a mediator, Christ *directly* connects believers to the one God (3:19–20). His preferred word for this new type of relationship with God is πίστις, hence covenantal *pistism*.

An important πίστις moment occurs in Rom 1:17, where Paul quotes Hab 2:4 in expression of one of the main ideas in his letter. Paul draws attention to the essence of πίστις that had become for him a way of identifying the heart of a trusting relationship with God. The dream of Israel was to have and maintain this intimate relationship of trust with God, but the corruption, waywardness, and doubts of Israel made this seem frustrated and elusive. With Christ as Paul's inspiration, he reimagines a new way to appropriate the Hab 2:4 vision to establish this living and intimate link between God and his people, a link established *in Christ* and represented by the unique word πίστις.

Πίστις as a Tensive Symbol in Early Christian Discourse

This book points out the problem with rigidly using the word "faith" to translate the Greek word πίστις, especially when we bring certain anachronistic and culturally loaded ideas to the English word that would not have been in Paul's mind. At the risk of making the matter too convoluted, I propose that πίστις is a remarkably dynamic word that can move along a spectrum of meaning such that one can use a number of words to translate it depending on the context. Again, this could appear to be overloading πίστις with too much theological weight, and I certainly don't want to make this more complex than is necessary.

Most of the time in Paul, we know pretty well what he means when he uses a word (as in any prose writing). But there are situations where certain words are more vibrant; this is often the case with foundational words.[7] Πίστις in Paul appears to fit this category. The ongoing conversation about the language of the "kingdom of God" in the study of Jesus and the Gospels will help us think through how this works. Norman Perrin, drawing

---

7. To give a linguistic example, it is widely recognized that "to be" verbs are usually irregular in English, Greek, Hebrew, French, German, Latin, and so on.

Synthesis and Conclusion

from the work of Amos Wilder, Paul Riceour, and Phillip Wheelwright, famously distinguishes between steno-symbols and tensive symbols. With a steno-symbol, essentially the concept relates directly to its referent. But a tensive symbol has a "set of meanings that can neither be exhausted nor adequately expressed by any one referent."[8] A tensive symbol, then, becomes a headword for a complex of interrelated ideas; naturally, then, the symbol can appear somewhat amorphous and difficult to define. This is obviously the case with the phrase "kingdom of God," but it is a helpful concept in application to Pauline πίστις as well. And, furthermore, this helps to make sense of how πίστις could function as a circumlocution for "Christianity" or "the gospel."[9]

This raises the question of *translation*. If πίστις is a tensive symbol, how should it be translated, given all the possibilities? One tactic would be to simply translate it with one catchword, "faith"—and that is the most popular approach among English translations of the Pauline corpus. The problem here is that "faith" has certain connotations in modern English that ought not to be read into Paul's letters, especially faith as thoughtless or irrational or faith as essentially nonactive. My suggestion is to translate with three categories in mind:

- "Faith" could be retained and used for those occasions where Paul seems to be talking about "believing faith."
- "Trust" could be employed in those many cases where πίστις refers to a relationship of trust in God. When it appears that Paul was using πίστις to refer to Christianity/the gospel, we might render this "trust," capturing the sense that sometimes Paul *was* using πίστις in a semitechnical way or as insider jargon. This can seem awkward, but we should keep in mind when Paul used πίστις in this absolute way (with no stated referent), it would also come across as unusual, peculiar, or unnatural to an outsider.[10]

---

8. Norman Perrin, *Jesus and the Language of the Kingdom: Symbol and Metaphor in New Testament Interpretation* (Philadelphia: Fortress, 1976), 30.

9. I thank Jonathan Pennington for drawing my attention (in personal conversation) to this idea of "tensive symbol" and how it might relate to πίστις in Paul.

10. Imagine someone in the first century, unacquainted with the development of the Jesus followers and Christianity, reading Paul's statement "now that πίστις has come" (Gal 3:25)—what could this possibly mean? Πίστις in what? Is πίστις an event? A person? A new relationship?

- "Faithfulness" and "loyalty" work well in those occasions where the social value of commitment, devotedness, or loyalty seems to be involved. Some translations, like the CEB (and to a lesser degree the NLT) show more openness to allowing for this translation in relation to *human* πίστις.

The potential downside to this variation in translation involves the simple fact that the (English) reader might not recognize that these words (faith, trust, faithfulness) all come from a single Greek word πίστις; they might not pick up on, for example, wordplay or a consistent thematic emphasis. But this is a problem not just with πίστις.

Take for example the challenge of translating σῴζω in the Synoptic Gospels. When Jesus performed a healing, the evangelists often used σῴζω. In Luke 8:48 Jesus says to a young woman who was brought back to life: ἡ πίστις σου **σέσωκέν** σε. Given that the context is a healing, it makes good sense to translate "your faith has *healed* you" (so NIV). The exact same wording is found in Luke 7:50 in connection with a sinful woman forgiven by Jesus (ἡ πίστις σου **σέσωκέν** σε), but in that situation it makes little sense to translate "your faith has healed you." Rather, most translations rightly render this "your faith has *saved* you" (NRSV). By contextualizing the translation and tailoring the meaning to the literary context, translators naturally prioritize ease of understanding over things like verbal consistency or thematic repetition. My recommendation is that translators do the same for πίστις, recognizing its polyvalence and dynamic semiotic nature.

Influences on Pauline Πίστις Language

A key concern of this book is the investigation of not only the *uses* of πίστις by Paul, but also the major influences on his πίστις language. Again, many readers of Paul, I presume, imagine that Paul had some kind of "aha" moment and promoted faith over and against works as a religious conviction. There indeed must have been some important epiphanies for Paul in his understanding of religion and a proper relationship with God in Jesus Christ, but Paul's Jewish heritage and the Jewish scriptures seem to have played a formative role as well (perhaps partly only in retrospect for him as he [re] interpreted Scripture from a christological lens).

Let's begin with Hellenistic Jewish literature. While Jews of the Second Temple period did not rely on πίστις as a common religious term (see chap.

3), there is enough evidence (e.g., from the Septuagint and Josephus) to suggest that this word group *could* serve as a contributor to discourse about life with God in community. Obviously it did not function as a reference or substitute to the word "covenant," but it is a kind of circumlocution or perhaps a simplistic way of talking about a relationship of dependence, obligation, and mutuality. This would make sense in light of the way pagans used πίστις in relation to pledges, agreements, and social bonds at personal, group, and national levels.

And not to be neglected is the way πιστεύω was central to Paul's theology and his important connections with the Septuagint, especially Gen 15:16 (cf. Gal 3:6; Rom 4:3). Psalm 115:1 LXX ("I believed, therefore I spoke" [NETS]; cf. 2 Cor 4:13) and, more widely in the New Testament, Isa 53:1 ("who has believed our message?" [NRSV]; cf. John 12:38) focus on revelation and the epistemological transformation required to make sense of Jesus Christ and his cruciform way.

The Jesus tradition would have inspired Paul to use faith language (see 58–76). While some distance Paul from Jesus theologically, it seems difficult to argue that Jesus's faith language had no effect on the apostle. Jesus made a choice to emphasize faith language in his proclamation, so much so it became a fixture in the Jesus tradition (e.g., Mark 1:15; 5:36; 9:23–24; cf. Matt 21:22; Luke 7:9). The particular way that Jesus did this makes it seem that he was drawing especially from the prophetic use of belief terminology to turn God's people's attention to fresh ways of perceiving the work of the Lord. Paul, the religious leader with no temple, priesthood, or cult statues, would certainly have felt it was appropriate to encourage gentile followers of Jesus to dare to believe in the invisible God and revere a crucified Lord.

What Has Works to Do with Faith?

Throughout this book, I dispel the notion that Paul treated faith (πίστις) and works as opposites or alternatives. Yes, indeed there is a clear juxtaposition of these in Paul, but to what end? What did Paul have against works? What did Paul mean by faith, and what was it about this term that made it so central and totalizing?

First, no one in the ancient Hellenistic world would have thought of πίστις as kinetically passive (as in nonactive). In fact, it was often considered something you *do*—you *do* πίστις (e.g., Matt 23:23). The matter of πίστις involved faith and trust of course, but especially as a virtue it was active, energized, propelling. Second, Paul had no problem with works per se. His letters are highly oriented toward doing what is good and right as a matter of obligation (e.g., 1 Thess 5:15–22; Gal 6:9–10), and he spends ample time in his letters preparing his gentile converts for the return of the Lord, implying moral purity and upright behavior (Rom 15:6). Not only could Paul emphasize the importance of good works (1 Cor 3:13–15), but even in Galatians Paul brought together the language of faith (πίστις) and work(s) (ἔργον) in reference to the *telos* of life: "The only thing that counts is faith working through love [πίστις δι' ἀγάπης ἐνεργουμένη]" (5:6 NRSV).

If Paul were not antiworks, what was it about works that caused him to establish a faith/works binary? There have been attempts at arguing that Paul was not critiquing works per se but works *of the law/Torah* in particular (in relation to the establishment of in-group Jewish identity). There are certainly many occasions where Torah is in view, but sometimes it appears works (qua *works*) are a clear point of focus (Rom 4:2–5; 9:32). For Paul, there was indeed a problem with a narrow emphasis on works, but not because it was too active or because it presumed self-righteousness. Rather, for Paul, works *as* works became problematic when they replaced or detracted from πίστις. For Paul, (1) πίστις had a relational core and (2) the Christ-relation is central to this relational dynamic. This can explain how Paul could use πίστις as a kind of shorthand to talk about Christianity, the way of Christ, the religious experience of Jesus followers, the gospel of Jesus Christ, trust in Christ, and so on.

This is a good opportunity to revisit Luther's interpretation of faith and Christology in Paul, because the Reformer's interpretation of Paul has been a topic of intensified discussion especially over the last forty years (with even *more* interest in the last few)—and yet there is still much misunderstanding of Luther. (To riff off of Mark Twain, I am afraid Luther's writings are in danger of becoming a classic: something everyone wants to cite, but that few actually *read*.) Chapter 2 demonstrates that Luther's interpreters make two common mistakes when they articulate his Pauline-oriented soteriology. First of all, there is an assumption that Luther had *one way* of looking at Paul, that is, that Luther had a coherent and consistent soteriology (focused on justification by faith). This is not demonstrably the case, certainly not in the way it was true for more systematic theologians like Calvin. Luther himself never sought out to articulate a coherent systematic theology. We must be cautious especially with his polemical writings, because he is less theologically consistent on such occasions. When it comes to his teachings on *faith* in particular, it is often presumed that for Luther the emphasis fell on imputation, repudiation of self-centered works-righteousness, and justification. Obviously all of these were important pieces of Luther's theo-logic, as it were, but he would have been immensely troubled if any of these terms took center stage. For Luther, what stood at the center of his theology was not an idea or a doctrine but *Christ*. Imputation assumes *identification with Christ*. Repudiation of works righteousness assumes rejection of self-centered justification and *relocation within Christ*. Even "justification by faith" implies a righteous standing before God *through Christ*. Of course a focus on works leads to arrogance, self-delusion, and idolatry—that much he makes clear. But Luther never states that works, as active earning of righteousness by merit, are the opposite of faith, as if faith were something nonactive. Rather, Luther talked about faith as a tethering of self to Christ through belief and trust.

Luther was not entirely consistent in the way he articulated his Pauline soteriology, but this particular piece—the centrality of the Christ-relation as the essence of faith—is substructural in Luther's thought, and in this area Luther got Paul right.

Returning then to Paul, we can start with this assumption about the relational core of Pauline faith and reconsider the works question. What is the problem with works? For Paul, the problem with works is not that they are bad or too self-active, but simply that they do not constitute the core; the core is the Christ-relation. The negativity toward Torah works has nothing to do with those works in and of themselves, except insofar as they become a point of focus or potentially damage the core relationship of faith and trust. For Paul, both faith and works matter, but there can be only one center—Christ, who is received and bonded to the believer by faith. Faith is the adhesive that connects believers to Christ (and through Christ to God).

Divine and Human Agency: Believing, Trusting, and Doing

How does Paul's faith language relate to broader guild questions about divine and human agency in Paul? Πίστις has become tangled up in this debate and been used to argue for different positions.

Richard Hays, for example, has engaged extensively in the πίστις Χριστοῦ debate over the years and, thus, has some important thoughts on this subject. But in one essay in particular he narrows his interest to faith and human/divine agency in Galatians.[11] Hays argues that Pauline faith ought not to be

11. Richard B. Hays, "Jesus' Faith and Ours: A Rereading of Galatians 3," in *Con-*

focused on the importance of the human operation of belief, but on Christ: "Nowhere in Galatians 3 does Paul place an emphasis on the salvific efficacy of the individual activity of 'believing.'"[12] Hays also observes that Paul never appeals to human belief/faith in Gal 3 at all. In this essay Hays rearticulates his position that a "faithfulness of Christ" reading of πίστις Χριστοῦ does right by Paul and Galatians by placing the theological weight on Christ and not on human belief. He sees this position as in opposition to Luther, who urged that "all we need to do in order to be forgiven by God and reconciled to him is to hear and believe."[13] So Hays affirms that for the apostle, Christ saves and justifies, not belief.[14]

While Hays's essay is mostly about Gal 3, he also mentions the use of πίστις in 2:20 (δὲ νῦν ζῶ ἐν σαρκί, ἐν πίστει ζῶ τῇ τοῦ υἱοῦ τοῦ θεοῦ). Here, argues Hays, Paul "is affirming that the acting subject is Christ, whose faithfulness is here closely linked with his loving self-sacrifice. The whole context portrays Christ as the active agent and Paul as the instrument through whom and for whom Christ acted and acts. This assertion of the priority of Christ's faithfulness over our willing and acting is the theological heartbeat of the whole letter."[15]

Hays should be given credit for placing Paul's emphases in the right place. It is obvious that Paul did not put much stock in the justifying power of the human capacity to believe. But I still detect in Hays's discussion an unfortunate either-or framework of thinking. *If πίστις is about the faithfulness of Christ, it denies or rejects the significance of human faith.* If one adheres to a faith-in-Christ interpretation, for Hays this immediately implies human agency that downgrades divine agency. This binary is unnecessary, and at the end of the day, regardless of the πίστις Χριστοῦ formulation, Paul underscores the importance both of divine rescue, as it were, *and* human belief, even though both of these are not equal.

My desire is to move beyond a simplistic zero-sum approach to divine and human agency whereby the math that makes divine agency thoroughgoing must by necessity reduce human agency to zero. As convenient as such a formulation would be for understanding Paul's thought, there are enough

---

flict and Context: Hermeneutics in the Americas, ed. Mark Lau Branson and C. René Padilla (Grand Rapids: Eerdmans, 1986), 257–68.

    12. Hays, "Jesus' Faith and Ours," 261.
    13. Hays, "Jesus' Faith and Ours," 257.
    14. Hays, "Jesus' Faith and Ours," 261.
    15. Hays, "Jesus' Faith and Ours," 264.

Synthesis and Conclusion

nuances and complexities in Paul to make this untenable. When it comes to Paul, to argue for a high level of divine agency does not necessarily tip the scale away from human agency. Rather, Paul seems to affirm *both*.[16]

We already engaged Barth's interpretation of Pauline faith language (28–29 and 167–68). But here we can also briefly bring Barth's Philippians commentary into view. Throughout, Barth repeatedly affirms that Paul in no way promoted the efficacy of human will or faith per se. Perseverance (Phil 1:6) is not a matter of human grit, but of divine empowerment:

> In *him* [God] Paul's confidence is placed. It was not Paul who "began the good work" in Philippi, nor did the Philippians themselves do so by becoming converted. God began it. That strips them and him [Paul] of *all* glory, *all* self-assurance, but precisely therewith also of all despondency, all inquisitorial deliberation as to whether everyone in Philippi is still as much in earnest as ever and will always remain so; whether they will keep faith and not perhaps forsake the way upon which they have entered. It is a question of *God's* earnestness, *God's* good faith, *God's* way.[17]

Later, in relation to 1:27 ("striving . . . for the faith of the gospel"), Barth offers the same point. Here he explicitly states that Paul uses a subjective genitive (τῇ πίστει τοῦ εὐαγγελίου). Quoting Fritz Horn, Barth writes, "Faith is not mine, but God's. If I struggle for my faith, then I do not know what I am striving after, nor even whether it is lasting and worthwhile. If I struggle for God's faithfulness, then I slay Goliath."[18] Despite Barth's ostensible allergic reaction to any interpretation of faith language that smacks of mortal contribution, he nevertheless can articulate a formative dimension to human faith as well.

In his discussion of 3:9, Barth presumes that τὴν ἐκ θεοῦ δικαιοσύνην ἐπὶ τῇ πίστει refers to Christian faith. Here Barth explains that human faith is crucially important, but not as any kind of soteriological agency in the way that Christ rescues. Nevertheless, and paradoxically, Barth refers to faith as

---

16. Jeanette Hagen offers an appropriately nuanced approach to Pauline faith language that argues the apostle tended to use πίστις to communicate both self-negating and self-involving dependence on Christ; see "Faith as Participation: An Exegetical Study of Some Key Pauline Texts"(PhD diss., Durham University, 2016).

17. Karl Barth, *The Epistle to the Philippians* (Louisville: Westminster John Knox, 2002 [originally 1947]), 17.

18. Barth, *Philippians*, 47.

a decisive act that in and of itself *is* the "collapse of every effort of one's own capacity and will, and the recognition of the absolute necessity of that collapse."[19] Put another way, for Barth (reading Paul), mortal faith is not about asserting power but quite the opposite, *actively* negating oneself so as to relocate oneself in the righteousness of God. The paradox that Barth raises defies a mathematical formula of divine and human agency: "For the understanding of the concept of *pistis* (faith), everything depends on whether the supposed Object [of faith], God, is understood as in fact the effecting Subject."[20] And Barth shares with Luther the same use of the language of "apprehend/apprehension" in relation to faith: "To believe means to apprehend God and go on repeatedly apprehending God in *his* righteousness as the acting Subject, to give God the *glory* in self-surrender."[21] Faith is not actively justifying, but it is active denial of oneself and active willingness to believe in the God who alone can justify—and to believe even *this* belief comes from God.

J. Louis Martyn also advocates the subjective genitive (faithfulness of Christ) understanding of πίστις Χριστοῦ. In his Galatians commentary, Martyn clearly presses for the priority and prominence of the rectifying work of Christ. He leaves no room for an understanding of Paul whereby the believer weighs salvific options and then *chooses* Christ "autonomously."[22] But, Martyn argues, neither is the believer merely a puppet dancing around by divine compulsion. Martyn asserts that priority must be given to the (for lack of a better word) prevenient work of Christ, which makes human faith possible. Faith in Christ is not about human capacity to choose God (i.e., freedom of the will) but rather "God's freeing of the will." Put in Martyn-style apocalyptic terms: "In Christ, the Son of God whose faith is engagingly enacted in his death, God invaded the human orb and commenced a battle for the liberation of the human will itself. And in the case of believers, that apocalyptic invasion is the mysterious genesis of faith in Christ."[23]

It is somewhat subtle, but Martyn's use of "mysterious" is telling in regard to the divine and human agency question. Faithfulness of Christ and

---

19. Barth, *Philippians*, 101.

20. Barth, *Philippians*, 101–2.

21. Barth, *Philippians*, 101. See the interpretation of Barth's faith language in Francis Watson's preface to Barth's *Philippians* titled "Philippians as Theological Exegesis," esp. xliv–xlv.

22. J. Louis Martyn, *Galatians*, Anchor Yale Bible 33A (New Haven: Yale University Press, 1997), 276.

23. Martyn, *Galatians*, 277.

faith *in* Christ are not equal, but neither do they serve as opposites whereby one cancels out or substitutes for the other. While Christ's rectifying work or obedience is prior and powerful, it is incomplete. However we conceive of human faith, it is the necessary way in which believers *engage* with the work of God in Christ. "Agency" may not be the best word; one might prefer "participation" or "association" in order to move the discussion away from assumptions about "contribution" or "merit."

I don't want to belabor the point, but this retrospective discussion of the divine-and-human-agency question, with special interest in faith language, can help to reconceive of the matter as more than a formula (*what amount of divine or human contribution equals salvation?*). This is a nonstarter for Paul. *Christ is all in all!*, he would say. But we cannot discount the way πίστις functions for Paul anthropologically, epistemologically, and socially as the *way* believers relate to God through the Christ-relation, which is necessarily thoughtful and participatory (socially, volitionally, existentially, etc.).

Biblical faith language is connected to the concept of covenant (15–17 and 49–50 on the Septuagint and 141–54 on Galatians). This is controversial,[24] but if we make the association at the broadest and simplest level, we can profit from it without giving hostages to fortune. In his book *The Covenanted Self*, Walter Brueggemann does a masterful job of articulating the dynamic nature of covenantal participation according to Scripture.[25] He represents the drama of "life with God" as dynamic, as the nature of the relationship changes in different situations and contexts. For example, Brueggemann argues that in the situation of lament, humans dare to take a (seemingly inappropriate) position of addressing God "in insistent imperative,"[26] whereas in praise worshipers humbly respect God as lord of all. As strange as all this may be, it is necessary because "live communion with an initiating and responsive Thou requires precisely such vitality, energy, freedom, and courage."[27] This relationship has boundaries, and one must avoid either extreme of *self-denial* or *self-indulgence*. Brueggemann presses for a model of divine and human relationship, a life of communion, that involves "intentional, dialectical interaction."[28] This relates

---

24. See Lester Grabbe, "Covenant in Philo and Josephus," in *The Concept of the Covenant in the Second Temple Period* (Boston: Brill, 2003), 251–66.

25. Walter Brueggemann, *The Covenanted Self: Explorations in Law and Covenant* (Minneapolis: Fortress, 1999).

26. Brueggemann, *Covenanted Self*, 18.

27. Brueggemann, *Covenanted Self*, 18.

28. Brueggemann, *Covenanted Self*, 19.

to a Jewish style of what he calls "*interactionalism,* marked by a sort of mutuality, even if not commensurability."²⁹ This is exactly the kind of dynamic relational perspective that is missing from many discussions of divine and human agency in Paul. Faith for Paul is not a work, something to boast in, something to rely on for justification or salvation; indeed, unless someone draws attention to it, it invisibly operates as the mode of engagement or orientation toward God. We are compelled to recognize faith for Paul as a gift of God's grace; after all, Paul affirms that it is the Creator God who let light shine in the darkness of human hearts to reveal the gospel in the person of Jesus (2 Cor 4:6). But we must also recognize the many times that Paul makes direct appeal to the πίστις of his converts (all quotations from NRSV):

> Your faith is proclaimed throughout the world. (Rom 1:8; cf. 1 Thess 1:8)

> Stand firm in your faith. (1 Cor 16:13)

> Your faith increases. (2 Cor 10:15)

> The sacrifice and the offering of your faith. (Phil 2:17)

> We pray most earnestly that we may see you face to face and restore whatever is lacking in your faith. (1 Thess 3:10)

> Your faith is growing abundantly. (2 Thess 1:3)

While Paul never pats them on the back for their πίστις as if it is self-generated, still these texts make it rather obvious that human faith was instrumental to a healthy and thriving relationship with God through Jesus Christ.³⁰ From this perspective, Hays's fear can be put to rest that human faith will be "a new kind of work."³¹

---

29. Brueggemann, *Covenanted Self,* 19.
30. In *Homilies on Romans* 7 (on Rom 3:22), Chrysostom writes: "In order to stop anyone from asking: 'How can we be saved without contributing anything at all to our salvation?' Paul shows that in fact we do contribute a great deal toward it—we supply our faith!"; in Gerald L. Bray, ed., *Romans,* Ancient Christian Commentary on Scripture (Downers Grove, IL: InterVarsity, 1998), 100.
31. Hays, "Christ's Faith and Ours," 260.

Synthesis and Conclusion

How Did Christians Come to Be Called Believers?

This is a complicated question, but it is an inquiry that is important historically and theologically. Undoubtedly Paul offers our earliest record of this usage (1 Thess 1:7), and his usage and Luke's Acts make up the vast majority of occurrences of this language.[32]

Paul Trebilco has done important work on this topic in his monograph *Self-Designations and Group Identity in the New Testament*.[33] He argues that (1) the label "believers" (versus unbelievers) would have had an important social boundary and social identity role and (2) the language of "believer" pointed to faith and identification with Christ.[34] Some scholars have attempted to move away from "believer" language to something more social like "loyalists."[35] The point of this—an admirable one, I admit—is to acknowledge the holistic nature of πίστις and its relational quality. But this robs Peter to pay Paul, so to speak. To call Christians believers implies a close relationship with the object, Christ. But *another* key reason that *this* became foundational terminology for Christians is the unique nature of their religious experience and expressions. The early Christians were odd religionists by ancient standards. They (like Jews) did not use cult statues. Christians did not visit temples regularly. *And* the venerated, death-defying, divine savior (Jesus) was invisible by the time this group gained traction.

My hunch is that "belief" became an important word for people who worshiped an unseeable deity and placed special emphasis on the later *hope* of seeing him with their own eyes in the end age. For the time being, they had to fix their eyes on a reality that is unseen, to an invisible reality beyond visual perception (2 Cor 4:18). While 1 Peter is obviously not written by Paul, 1:8 touches nicely on the way belief language captures this sense of faith and hope in a truth and power beyond forms: "Although you have not seen him, you love him; and even though you do not see him now, you believe in him and rejoice with an indescribable and glorious joy" (NRSV). And similarly

---

32. The one exception is 1 Pet 1:21, although the Johannine writings frequently use belief language.

33. Paul Trebilco, *Self-Designations and Group Identity in the New Testament* (Cambridge: Cambridge University Press, 2012).

34. Trebilco, *Self-Designations*, 68–121.

35. See Zerbe, "Believers as Loyalists"; also Matthew Bates, *Salvation by Allegiance Alone: Rethinking Faith, Works, and the Gospel of Jesus the King* (Grand Rapids: Baker, 2017).

the words of the Johannine Jesus: "Blessed are those who have not seen and yet have come to believe" (John 20:29 NRSV). Of course Christians came to be marked by their death-accepting devotion to Jesus—and hence loyal or faithful to their deity—but they also were distinct for their unusual beliefs and practices, not least of which claiming temples of bodies and communities, inward *pneuma* possession, and belief in an all-reigning unseen Lord who will come from the clouds in judgment and redemption. For Paul this was a religion beyond belief.

Bibliography

Achtemeier, Elizabeth. *Nahum–Malachi*. Interpretation. Louisville: Westminster John Knox, 1986.
Arzt-Grabner, Peter. "Zum alltagssprachlichen Hintergrund von Πίστις." Pages 241–49 in *Glaube: Das Verständnis des Glaubens im frühen Christentum und in seiner jüdischen und hellenistisch-römischen Umwelt*. Edited by Jörg Frey, Benjamin Schliesser, and Nadine Kessler. Wissenschaftliche Untersuchungen zum Neuen Testament 373. Tübingen: Mohr Siebeck, 2017.
Ashton, John. *Understanding the Fourth Gospel*. Oxford: Oxford University Press, 1991.
Aune, David E. *Revelation*. 3 vols. World Biblical Commentary 52A–C. Grand Rapids: Zondervan, 1997.
Babut, Daniel. "Du scepticisme au depassement de la raison: Philosophie et foi religieuse chez Plutarque." Pages 549–81 in *Parerga: Choix d'articles de D. Babut (1974–1994)*. Lyon: Maison de L'Orient Méditerranéen, 1994.
Bagnall, Roger S., and Raffaella Cribiore. *Women's Letter from Ancient Egypt, 300 BC–AD 800*. Ann Arbor: University of Michigan Press, 2006.
Baird, William. "Abraham in the New Testament: Tradition and the New Identity." *Interpretation* 42 (1988): 367–79.
Bammel, Ernst. "Galater i.23." *Zeitschrift für die neutestamentliche Wissenschaft* 59 (1968): 108–12.
Barclay, John M. G. "2 Corinthians." Pages 1353–73 in *Eerdmans Commentary on the Bible*. Edited by James D. G. Dunn. Grand Rapids: Eerdmans, 2003.
———. *Flavius Josephus: Translation and Commentary*, vol. 10: *Against Apion*. Boston: Brill, 2007.
———. *Obeying the Truth: The Study of Paul's Ethics in Galatians*. Edinburgh: T&T Clark, 1988.
———. *Paul and the Gift*. Grand Rapids: Eerdmans, 2015.

Barclay, John M. G., and Simon J. Gathercole, eds. *Divine and Human Agency in Paul and His Cultural Environment*. London: T&T Clark, 2006.
Barrett, C. K. *The Epistle to the Romans*. Black's New Testament Commentary. Peabody, MA: Hendrickson, 1991.
———. *The First Epistle to the Corinthians*. Black's New Testament Commentary. Peabody, MA: Hendrickson, 1968.
———. *The Second Epistle to the Corinthians*. Black's New Testament Commentary. Peabody, MA: Hendrickson, 1991.
Barth, Gerhard. "Glaube und Zweifel in den synoptischen Evangelien." *Zeitschrift für Theologie und Kirche* 72 (1975): 269–92.
———. "Pistis in hellenistischer Religiosität." *Zeitschrift für die neutestamentliche Wissenschaft* 73 (1982): 110–26.
Barth, Karl. *Church Dogmatics*, vol. 4: *The Doctrine of Reconciliation*. Edited by G. W. Bromiley and T. F. Torrance. Edinburgh: T&T Clark, 1956.
———. *Dogmatics in Outline*. New York: Harper, 1959.
———. *The Epistle to the Philippians*. Louisville: Westminster John Knox, 2002 (originally 1947).
———. *The Epistle to the Romans*. Translated by Edwyn C. Hoskyns. London: Oxford University Press, 1968.
Barth, Markus. *The Letter to Philemon*. Eerdmans Critical Commentary. Grand Rapids: Eerdmans, 2010.
Barton, John. *Oracles of God*. Oxford: Oxford University Press, 2007.
Barton, Stephen C. *The Spirituality of the Gospels*. Peabody, MA: Hendrickson, 1992.
Bassler, Jouette. *Navigating Paul*. Louisville: Westminster John Knox, 2007.
Bates, Matthew W. *Salvation by Allegiance Alone: Rethinking Faith, Works, and the Gospel of Jesus the King*. Grand Rapids: Baker, 2017.
Bauer, David. *Structure of Matthew's Gospel: A Study in Literary Design*. London: Bloomsbury, 2015.
Beale, G. K. *The Book of Revelation*. New International Greek Testament Commentary. Grand Rapids: Eerdmans, 1999.
———. "The Old Testament Background of Reconciliation in 2 Corinthians 5–7 and Its Bearing on the Literary Problem of 2 Corinthians 6:14–7:1." *New Testament Studies* 35 (1989): 550–81.
———. *The Temple and the Church's Mission*. Downers Grove, IL: InterVarsity, 2005.
Beavis, Mary Ann. "Mark's Teaching on Faith." *Biblical Theology Bulletin* 16 (1986): 139–42.

Becker, Siegbert. *The Foolishness of God: The Place of Reason in the Theology of Martin Luther*. Milwaukee: Northwest Publishing, 1999.

Begg, Christopher T. *Josephus' Account of the Early Divided Monarchy (AJ 8,212–420)*. Leuven: Peeters, 1993.

Beker, J. Christaan. *Paul the Apostle: The Triumph of God in Light and Thought*. Philadelphia: Fortress, 1994.

Best, Ernest. *A Commentary on the First and Second Epistles to the Thessalonians*. Black's New Testament Commentary. Peabody, MA: Hendrickson, 1972.

Blackwell, Ben C., John K. Goodrich, and Jason Maston, ed. *Paul and the Apocalyptic Imagination*. Minneapolis: Fortress, 2016.

Blomberg, Craig L. "Quotations, Allusions, and Echoes of Jesus in Paul." Pages 129–43 in *Studies in Pauline Epistles*. Edited by Dane C. Ortlund and Matthew S. Harmon. Grand Rapids: Zondervan, 2014.

Bloomquist, L. Gregory. "Subverted by Joy: Suffering and Joy in Paul's Letter to the Philippians." *Interpretation* 61 (2007): 270–82.

Blumenthal, David. "The Place of Faith and Grace in Judaism." Pages 104–14 in *A Time to Speak*. Edited by James Rudin and Marvin R. Wilson. Grand Rapids: Eerdmans, 1987.

Boda, Mark J. *"Return to Me": A Biblical Theology of Repentance*. Downers Grove, IL: InterVarsity, 2015.

Boespflug, Mark. "Is Augustinian Faith Rational?" *Religious Studies* 52 (2016): 63–79.

Böhm, Martina. "Zum Glaubensverständnis des Philo von Alexandrien." Pages 159–81 in *Glaube: Das Verständnis des Glaubens im frühen Christentum und in seiner jüdischen und hellenistisch-römischen Umwelt*. Edited by J. Frey, B. Schliesser, and N. Ueberschaer. Wissenschaftliche Untersuchungen zum Neuen Testament 373. Tübingen: Mohr Siebeck, 2017.

Boring, M. Eugene. *1 and 2 Thessalonians*. New Testament Library. Louisville: Westminster John Knox, 2015.

———. *Mark*. New Testament Library. Louisville: Westminster John Knox, 2006.

———. *Revelation*. Interpretation. Louisville: Westminster John Knox, 2011.

Bornkamm, Günther. *Paul*. Translated by D. M. G. Stalker. New York: Harper & Row, 1971.

Bowman, John W. "Three Imperishables: A Meditation on 1 Corinthians 13." *Interpretation* 13 (1959): 433–43.

Bray, Gerald L., ed. *Romans*. Ancient Christian Commentary on Scripture. Downers Grove, IL: InterVarsity, 1998.

Bridges, Linda M. "2 Corinthians 4:7–15." *Interpretation* 86 (1989): 391–96.

Brockington, Leonard H. *Ezra, Nehemiah, and Esther*. New Century Bible. London: Nelson, 1969.

Brown, Alexandra. *The Cross and Human Transformation: Paul's Apocalyptic Word in 1 Corinthians*. Minneapolis: Fortress, 1995.

Brown, Raymond E. *The Gospel according to John I–XII*. Anchor Bible 29. Garden City, NY: Doubleday, 1966.

Bruce, F. F. *The Epistle to the Galatians*. New International Greek Testament Commentary. Grand Rapids: Eerdmans, 1982.

Brueggemann, Walter. *The Covenanted Self: Explorations in Law and Covenant*. Minneapolis: Fortress, 1999.

———. *Reverberations of Faith*. Louisville: Westminster John Knox, 2002.

Bruner, F. Dale. *Matthew*, vol. 2: *The Churchbook*. Grand Rapids: Eerdmans, 2004.

Bülow-Jacobsen, Adam. "Private Letters." Pages 317–465 in *Didymoi: Une garnison romaine dans le désert oriental d'Égypte*, vol. 2: *Les textes*. Fouilles de l'Ifao 67. Cairo: Institut français d'archéologie orientale, 2012.

Bultmann, Rudolf. "*Pisteuō*." Pages. 849–57 in *Theological Dictionary of the New Testament: Abridged Edition*. Edited by Gerhard Kittel and Gerhard Friedrich. Translated by Geoffrey W. Bromiley. Grand Rapids: Eerdmans, 1985.

———. *Theology of the New Testament*. Translated by K. Grobel. 2 vols. New York: Scribner, 1951, 1955. German original: *Theologie des Neuen Testament*. Tübingen: Mohr Siebeck, 1948–53.

Calvin, John. *Commentary on Romans 1–16*. Grand Rapids: Baker, 1993.

———. *Institutes of the Christian Religion*. Translated by H. Beveridge. 2 vols. Repr., Grand Rapids: Eerdmans, 1964 (originally 1845).

Campbell, Douglas A. "2 Corinthians 4:13: Evidence in Paul That Christ Believes." *Journal of Biblical Literature* 128 (2009): 337–56.

———. *The Quest for Paul's Gospel: A Suggested Strategy*. London: T&T Clark, 2005.

———. "Romans 1:17—A *Crux Interpretum* for the ΠΙΣΤΙΣ ΧΡΙΣΤΟΥ Debate." *Journal of Biblical Literature* 113 (1994): 265–85.

Campbell, William S. *Unity and Diversity in Christ*. Cambridge: James Clarke, 2017.

Carey, Greg. "Revelation as Counter-Imperial Script." Pages 157–76 in *In the Shadow of Empire: Reclaiming the Bible as a History of Faithful Resistance*. Edited by R. A. Horsley. Louisville: Westminster John Knox, 2008.

Carlson, Richard. "Whose Faith? Reexamining the Habakkuk 2:4 Citation with the Communicative Act of Romans 1:1–17." Pages 293–324 in *Raising Up a*

Faithful Exegete: Essays in Honor of Richard D. Nelson. Edited by K. L. Noll and Brooks Schramm. Winona Lake, IN: Eisenbrauns, 2010.

Carson, D. A. "Matthew." Pages 23–670 in *Matthew and Mark.* New Expositor's Bible Commentary. Edited by Tremper Longman III and David E. Garland. Grand Rapids: Zondervan, 2005.

Catchpole, David. "The Son of Man's Search for Faith (Luke 18:8)." *Novum Testamentum* 19 (1973): 81–104.

Charlesworth, James H. "Revelation and Perspicacity in Qumran Hermeneutics?" Pages 161–80 in *The Dead Sea Scrolls and Contemporary Culture.* Edited by Adolfo D. Roitman, Lawrence H. Schiffman, and Shani Tzoref. Boston: Brill, 2011.

Chester, Stephen. *Reading Paul with the Reformers.* Grand Rapids: Eerdmans, 2017.

Chiraparamban, Varghese P. "The Translation of Πίστις and Its Cognates in the Pauline Epistles." *Bible Translator* 66 (2015): 176–89.

Chroust, Anton-Hermann. "Treason and Patriotism in Ancient Greece." *Journal of the History of Ideas* 15 (1954): 280–88.

Clendenen, Ray. "Salvation by Faith or by Faithfulness in the Book of Habakkuk." *Bulletin for Biblical Research* 24 (2014): 505–15.

Collange, J. F. *Énigmes de la deuxième épitre aux Corinthiens: Étude exegetique de 2 Cor.* Cambridge: Cambridge University Press, 1972.

Collins, Raymond F. *First Corinthians.* Sacra Pagina 7. Collegeville, MN: Liturgical Press, 1999.

Cousar, Charles B. "1 Corinthians 2:1–13." *Interpretation* 44 (1990): 169–73.

Cox, Steven L. "1 Corinthians 13—An Antidote to Violence: Love." *Review and Expositor* 93 (1996): 529–36.

Cranfield, C. E. B. *A Critical and Exegetical Commentary on the Epistle to the Romans.* 2 vols. International Critical Commentary. Edinburgh: T&T Clark, 1975.

Crook, Zeba. *Reconceptualising Conversion: Patronage, Loyalty, and Conversion in the Religions of the Ancient Mediterranean.* Beihefte zur Zeitschrift für die neutestamentliche Wissenschaft 130. Berlin: de Gruyter, 2004.

Culpepper, R. Alan. *Mark.* Smyth & Helwys Biblical Commentary. Macon, GA: Smyth & Helwys, 2007.

Danker, Frederick W., Walter Bauer, William F. Arndt, and F. Wilbur Gingrich. *A Greek-English Lexicon of the New Testament and Other Early Christian Literature.* 3rd ed. Chicago: University of Chicago Press, 2000.

Das, Andrew A. *Galatians.* Concordia Commentary. St. Louis: Concordia, 2014.

Davies, W. D., and Dale C. Allison. *Matthew*. International Critical Commentary. 3 vols. Edinburgh: T&T Clark, 1988–97.
de Boer, Martinus. *Galatians*. Louisville: Westminster John Knox, 2011.
Deissmann, Adolf. *St. Paul: A Study in Social and Religious History*. New York: Hodder & Stoughton, 1912.
deSilva, David A. *Galatians: A Handbook on the Greek New Testament*. Baylor Handbook on the Greek New Testament. Waco, TX: Baylor University Press, 2014.
———. *Honor, Patronage, Kinship, and Purity: Unlocking New Testament Culture*. Downers Grove, IL: InterVarsity, 2012.
———. *An Introduction to the New Testament*. Downers Grove, IL: InterVarsity, 2004.
———. "Measuring Penultimate against Ultimate: An Investigation of the Integrity and Argumentation of 2 Corinthians." *Journal for the Study of the New Testament* 52 (1993): 41–70.
Dio Chrysostom. *Orations*. Translated by James W. Cohoon. LCL 385. Cambridge: Harvard University Press, 1971.
Dionysius of Halicarnassus. *Roman Antiquities*. Translated by Earnest Cary. LCL 338. Cambridge: Harvard University Press, 1950.
Dodd, C. H. *According to the Scriptures*. London: Nisbet, 1952.
Donahue, John R. *The Gospel in Parable: Metaphor, Narrative, and Theology in the Synoptic Gospels*. Minneapolis: Fortress, 1988.
Dunn, James D. G. *1 Corinthians*. Sheffield: Sheffield Academic Press, 1995.
———. "The Christian Life from the Perspective of Paul's Letter to the Galatians." Pages 1–18 in *The Apostle Paul and the Christian Life*. Edited by S. McKnight and J. B. Modica. Grand Rapids: Baker, 2016.
———. "Epilogue." Pages 208–20 in *Paul and Judaism: Crosscurrents in Pauline Exegesis and the Study of Jewish-Christian Relations*. Edited by Reimund Bieringer and Didier Pollefeyt. London: T&T Clark, 2012.
———. "ΕΚ ΠΙΣΤΕΩΣ: A Key to the Meaning of ΠΙΣΤΙΣ ΧΡΙΣΤΟΥ." Pages 351–66 in *The Word Leaps the Gap*. Edited by J. Ross Wagner, C. Kavin Rowe, and A. Katherine Grieb. Grand Rapids: Eerdmans, 2008.
———. *The Epistle to the Galatians*. Black's New Testament Commentary. Peabody, MA: Hendrickson, 1993.
———. *Jesus Remembered*. Grand Rapids: Eerdmans, 2003.
———. "The New Perspective on Paul." *Bulletin of the John Rylands University Library of Manchester* 65 (1983): 95–122.
———. *The New Perspective on Paul*. Grand Rapids: Eerdmans, 2008.

———. "The Theology of Galatians." Pages 1:138–46 in *Pauline Theology*. Edited by J. M. Bassler. Minneapolis: Fortress, 1991.

———. *The Theology of Paul the Apostle*. Grand Rapids: Eerdmans, 1998.

———. *The Theology of Paul's Letter to the Galatians*. New Testament Theology. Cambridge: Cambridge University Press, 1993.

———. *Unity and Diversity in the New Testament*. Philadelphia: Westminster, 1977.

———. "What's Right about the Old Perspective on Paul?" Pages 214–29 in *Studies in the Pauline Epistles*. Edited by Matthew S. Harmon and Jay E. Smith. Grand Rapids: Zondervan, 2014.

Easter, Matthew C. *Faith and the Faithfulness of Jesus in Hebrews*. Society for New Testament Studies Monograph 160. Cambridge: Cambridge University Press, 2014.

———. "The *Pistis Christou* Debate: Main Arguments and Responses in Summary." *Currents in Biblical Research* 9 (2010): 33–47.

Ehrman, Bart. *The Apostolic Fathers*, vol. 1: *I Clement, II Clement, Ignatius, Polycarp, Didache*. LCL 24. Cambridge: Harvard University Press, 2003.

Eichrodt, Walther. "Covenant and Law." *Interpretation* 20 (1966): 302–21.

Elliott, Mark W. "Πίστις Χριστοῦ in the Church Fathers and Beyond." Pages 279–90 in *The Faith of Jesus Christ: Exegetical, Biblical, and Theological Studies*. Edited by Michael F. Bird and Preston M. Sprinkle. Peabody, MA: Hendrickson, 2010.

Evans, Craig A. "Prophet, Sage, Healer, Messiah: Types and Identities of Jesus." Pages 1219–22 in *Handbook for the Study of the Historical Jesus*. Edited by T. Holmén and Stanley E. Porter. Leiden: Brill, 2010.

Fee, Gordon D. *The First Epistle to the Corinthians*. Revised edition. New International Commentary on the New Testament. Grand Rapids: Eerdmans, 2014.

———. *Paul's Letter to the Philippians*. New International Commentary on the New Testament. Grand Rapids: Eerdmans, 1995.

Feldman, Louis H. *Judaism and Hellenism Reconsidered*. Boston: Brill, 2006.

Findlay, George G. *The Epistle to the Galatians*. New York: Armstrong, 1902.

Finney, Mark T. *Honour and Conflict in the Ancient World: 1 Corinthians in Its Greco-Roman Setting*. Library of New Testament Studies. London: T&T Clark, 2012.

Fitzmyer, Joseph. *The Gospel according to Luke*. 2 vols. Anchor Yale Bible 28. Garden City, NY: Doubleday, 1981–85.

———. *Pauline Theology: A Brief Sketch*. Englewood Cliffs, NJ: Prentice-Hall, 1967.

———. *Romans*. Anchor Yale Bible 33. New York: Doubleday, 1993.

Fosdick, Harry Emerson. *The Meaning of Faith*. New York: Association Press, 1917.
France, R. T. *The Gospel according to Matthew*. New International Commentary on the New Testament. Grand Rapids: Eerdmans, 2007.
———. *The Gospel of Mark*. New International Greek Testament Commentary. Grand Rapids: Eerdmans, 2002.
Frazier, Françoise. "Returning to 'Religious' ΠΙΣΤΙΣ: Platonism and Piety in Plutarch and Neoplatonism." Pages 189–208 in *Saint Paul and Philosophy*. Edited by Gert-Jan van der Heiden, George van Kooten, and Antonio Cimino. New York: de Gruyter, 2017.
Frey, Jörg, Benjamin Schliesser, and Nadine Ueberschaer, eds. *Glaube: Das Verständnis des Glaubens im frühen Christentum und in seiner jüdischen und hellenistisch-römischen Umwelt*. Wissenschaftliche Untersuchungen zum Neuen Testament 373. Tübingen: Mohr Siebeck, 2017.
Furnish, Victor P. *II Corinthians*. Anchor Yale Bible 23A. Garden City, NY: Doubleday, 1984.
———. *Jesus according to Paul*. Cambridge: Cambridge University Press, 1993.
———. *Theology and Ethics in Paul*. Louisville: Westminster John Knox, 2009.
———. *The Theology of the First Letter to the Corinthians*. New Testament Theology. Cambridge: Cambridge University Press, 1999.
Garland, David E. *2 Corinthians*. New American Commentary. Nashville: Broadman & Holman, 1999.
———. *First Corinthians*. Baker Exegetical Commentary on the New Testament. Grand Rapids: Baker, 2003.
Garlington, Don. Review of *Paul and Judaism Revisited*. *Journal of the Evangelical Theological Society* 57 (2014): 442–46.
Gaventa, Beverly R. *First and Second Thessalonians*. Interpretation. Louisville: Westminster John Knox, 1998.
———. "Galatians." Pages 1374–84 in *Eerdmans Commentary on the Bible*. Edited by J. W. Rogerson and James D. G. Dunn. Grand Rapids: Eerdmans, 2003.
Geoffrion, Timothy. *The Rhetorical Purpose and the Political and Military Character of Philippians: A Call to Stand Firm*. Lewiston, NY: Mellen, 1993.
Georgi, Dieter. "God Upside Down." Pages 148–57 in *Paul and Empire: Religion and Power in Roman Imperial Society*. Edited by R. A. Horsley. Harrisburg, PA: Trinity, 1997.
Gorman, Michael J. *Becoming the Gospel: Paul, Participation, and Mission*. Grand Rapids: Eerdmans, 2015.
———. *The Death of the Messiah and the Birth of the Covenant*. Eugene, OR: Wipf & Stock, 2014.

Goulder, Michael. "2 Cor. 6:14–7:1 As An Integral Part of 2 Corinthians." *Novum Testamentum* 36 (1994): 49–57.

Gowan, Donald. "Habakkuk, Book of." Pages 2:705–9 in *The New Interpreter's Dictionary of the Bible*. Edited by Katharine Doob Sakenfeld. Nashville: Abingdon, 2006–2009.

Grabbe, Lester. "Covenant in Philo and Josephus." Pages 251–66 in *The Concept of the Covenant in the Second Temple Period*. Boston: Brill, 2003.

Grieb, A. Katherine. *The Story of Romans: A Narrative Defense of God's Righteousness*. Grand Rapids: Eerdmans, 2002.

Grindheim, Sigurd. "'Everything Is Possible for One Who Believes': Faith and Healing in the New Testament." *Trinity Journal* 26 (2005): 11–17.

Gundry, Robert. *Matthew: A Commentary on His Literary and Theological Art*. Grand Rapids: Eerdmans, 1982.

Gupta, Nijay K. *1–2 Thessalonians*. Eugene, OR: Wipf & Stock, 2015.

———. *1-2 Thessalonians*. Zondervan Critical Introductions to the New Testament. Grand Rapids: Zondervan, 2019.

———. "Fighting the Good Fight: The Good Life in Paul and the Giants of Philosophy." In *Paul and the Giants of Philosophy*. Edited by David Briones and Joseph R. Dodson. Downers Grove, IL: InterVarsity, 2019.

———. "Mirror-Reading Moral Issues in Paul's Letters." *Journal for the Study of the New Testament* 34 (2012): 361–81.

———. "Paul and the *Militia Spiritualis* Topos in 1 Thessalonians." Pages 13–32 in *Paul and the Greco-Roman Philosophical Tradition*. Edited by J. R. Dodson and A. W. Pitts. London: T&T Clark, 2017.

Guthrie, George. *2 Corinthians*. Baker Exegetical Commentary on the New Testament. Grand Rapids: Baker, 2015.

Hagen, Jeanette. "Faith as Participation: An Exegetical Study of Some Key Pauline Texts." PhD diss., Durham University, 2016.

Hagner, Donald A. "Matthew: Christian Judaism or Jewish Christianity?" Pages 263–82 in *The Face of New Testament Studies: A Survey of Recent Research*. Edited by S. McKnight and G. Osborne. Grand Rapids: Baker, 2004.

———. *Matthew*. 2 vols. World Biblical Commentary 33A–B. Grand Rapids: Zondervan, 1993–1995.

Han, Paul. *Swimming in the Sea of Scripture: Paul's Use of the Old Testament in 2 Corinthians 4:7–13:13*. Library of New Testament Studies. London: T&T Clark, 2014.

Hanson, A. T. *Studies in Paul's Technique and Theology*. London: SPCK, 1974.

Harrington, Daniel J. *The Gospel of Matthew*. Sacra Pagina 1. Collegeville, MN: Liturgical, 1991.

———. "Paul's Use of the Old Testament in Romans." *Studies in Christian-Jewish Relations* 4 (2009): 1–8.

Harris, Murray J. *The Second Epistle to the Corinthians*. New International Greek Testament Commentary. Grand Rapids: Eerdmans, 2005.

Harrison, James. *Paul and the Imperial Authorities at Thessalonica and Rome*. Wissenschaftliche Untersuchungen zum Neuen Testament 273. Tübingen: Mohr Siebeck, 2011.

Harrisville, Roy A. *1 Corinthians*. Minneapolis: Fortress, 1987.

———. "Paul and the Psalms: A Formal Study." *Word and World* 5 (1985): 168–79.

———. "ΠΙΣΤΙΣ ΧΡΙΣΤΟΥ: Witness of the Fathers." *Novum Testamentum* 36 (1994): 233–41.

Hawthorne, Gerald F. "Faith: The Essential Ingredient of Effective Christian Ministry." Pages 249–59 in *Worship, Theology, and Ministry in the Early Church*. Edited by M. H. Wilkins and T. Paige. Journal for the Study of the New Testament Supplement 87. Sheffield: JSOT Press, 1992.

Hay, David. "Pistis as 'Ground for Faith' in Hellenized Judaism and Paul." *Journal of Biblical Literature* 108 (1989): 461–76.

Hays, Richard B. *1 Corinthians*. Interpretation. Louisville: Westminster John Knox, 1997.

———. "Jesus' Faith and Ours: A Rereading of Galatians 3." Pages 257–68 in *Conflict and Context: Hermeneutics in the Americas*. Edited by Mark Lau Branson and C. René Padilla. Grand Rapids: Eerdmans, 1986.

———. "The Letter to the Galatians." Paegs 11:181–348 in *The New Interpreter's Bible*. Edited by Leander E. Keck. Nashville: Abingdon, 2000.

———. "Lost in Translation: A Reflection on Romans in the Common English Bible." Pages 83–101 in *The Unrelenting God*. Edited by David Downs and Matthew Skinner. Grand Rapids: Eerdmans, 2014.

———. "Πίστις and Pauline Christology: What Is at Stake?" Pages 272–98 in *The Faith of Jesus Christ*. Grand Rapids: Eerdmans, 2002.

———. "'The Righteous One': An Eschatological Deliverer: A Case Study in Paul's Apocalyptic Hermeneutics." Pages 191–215 in *Apocalyptic and the New Testament*. Edited by Joel Marcus and Marion L. Soards. Journal for the Study of the New Testament Supplement 24. Sheffield: JSOT Press, 1988.

———. "Three Dramatic Roles: The Law in Romans 3–4." Pages 151–64 in *Paul and the Mosaic Law*. Edited by James D. G. Dunn. Grand Rapids: Eerdmans, 2000.

———. "Wisdom according to Paul." Pages 111–23 in *Where Shall Wisdom Be Found?* Edited by S. C. Barton. Edinburgh: T&T Clark, 1998.

Healy, Mary. "Knowledge of the Mystery: A Study of Pauline Epistemology." Pages 134–58 in *The Bible and Epistemology*. Edited by Mary Healy and Robin A. Parry. Eugene, OR: Wipf & Stock, 2007.

Heliso, Desto. *Pistis and the Righteous One: A Study of Romans 1:17 against the Background of Scripture and Second Temple Jewish Literature*. Wissenschaftliche Untersuchungen zum Neuen Testament 235. Tübingen: Mohr Siebeck, 2007.

Hellerman, Joseph. *Reconstructing Honor in Roman Philippi*. Society for New Testament Studies Monograph 132. Cambridge: Cambridge University Press, 2005.

Herman, Gabriel. *Ritualised Friendship and the Greek City*. Cambridge: Cambridge University Press, 2002.

Hiebert, Theodore. "The Book of Habakkuk." Pages 7:623–55 in *The New Interpreter's Bible*. Edited by Leander E. Keck. Nashville: Abingdon, 1997.

Hill, H. "Dionysius of Halicarnassus and the Origins of Rome." *Journal of Roman Studies* 51 (1961): 88–93.

Hirsch-Luipold, Rainer. "Religiöse Tradition und individuelle Glaube: Πίστις und Πιστεύειν bei Plutarch." Pages 251–73 in *Glaube: Das Verständnis des Glaubens im frühen Christentum und in seiner jüdischen und hellenistisch-römischen Umwelt*. Edited by Jörg Frey, Benjamin Schliesser, and Nadine Kessler. Wissenschaftliche Untersuchungen zum Neuen Testament 373. Tübingen: Mohr Siebeck, 2017.

Holloway, Paul. *Philippians*. Hermeneia. Minneapolis: Fortress, 2017.

Holmes, Michael W. *The Apostolic Fathers in English*. Grand Rapids: Baker, 2006.

———. *The Apostolic Fathers: Greek Texts and English Translations*. 3rd ed. Grand Rapids: Baker, 2007.

Hooker, Morna D. *From Adam to Christ: Essays on Paul*. Eugene, OR: Wipf & Stock, 1990.

———. "Phantom Opponents and the Real Source of Conflict." Pages 377–95 in *Fair Play: Diversity and Conflict in Early Christianity*. Edited by Heikki Raïsanen, Ismo Dunderberg, C. M. Tuckett, and Kari Syreeni. Novum Testamentum Supplement 103. Leiden: Brill, 2002.

Hopper, David H. *Divine Transcendence and the Culture of Change*. Grand Rapids: Eerdmans, 2010.

Horsley, Richard. *Wisdom and Spiritual Transcendence in Corinth*. Eugene, OR: Wipf & Stock, 2008.

Houghton, Myron J. "A Reexamination of 1 Corinthians 13:8–13." *Bibliotheca Sacra* 153 (1996): 344–56.

Hultgren, Arland J. *Paul's Letter to the Romans*. Grand Rapids: Eerdmans, 2011.

Hunn, Debbie. "Debating the Faithfulness of Jesus Christ in Twentieth-Century Scholarship." Pages 15–31 in *The Faith of Jesus Christ: Exegetical, Biblical, and Theological Studies*. Edited by M. F. Bird and P. M. Sprinkle. Peabody, MA: Hendrickson, 2009.
Hunter, A. M. *Paul and His Predecessors*. London: SCM, 1961.
Inkelaar, Harm-Jan. *Conflict over Wisdom: The Theme of 1 Corinthians 1–4 Rooted in Scripture*. Leuven: Peeters, 2011.
Jansen, Joseph "Greek Oath Breakers?" *Mnemosyne* 67 (2014): 122–30.
Jervis, L. Ann. *At the Heart of the Gospel*. Grand Rapids: Eerdmans, 2007.
Jewett, Robert. *Romans*. Hermeneia. Minneapolis: Fortress, 2007.
Johnson, Andy. "Response to Witherington." *Ex Auditu* 24 (2008): 176–80.
Johnson, Dru. *Biblical Knowing: A Scripture Epistemology of Error*. Eugene, OR: Wipf & Stock, 2013.
Johnson, Elizabeth. "Paul's Reliance on Scripture in 1 Thessalonians." Pages 143–61 in *Paul and Scripture: Extending the Conversation*. Edited by Christopher D. Stanley. Atlanta: Society of Biblical Literature, 2011.
Johnson, Luke Timothy. *The Creed*. New York: Doubleday, 2003.
———. *The Gospel of Luke*. Sacra Pagina 3. Collegeville, MN: Liturgical Press, 1991.
———. *Hebrews*. New Testament Library. Louisville: Westminster John Knox, 2006.
———. *Reading Romans*. Macon, GA: Smyth & Helwys, 2001.
Kaiser, Walter C. *The Christian and the Old Testament*. Pasadena, CA: William Carey Library, 1998.
Käsemann, Ernst. *Perspectives on Paul*. Translated by M. Kohl. London: SCM, 1971.
Kauppi, Lynn Allan. *Foreign but Familiar Gods: Greco-Romans Read Religion in Acts*. Library of New Testament Studies. London: T&T Clark, 2006.
Keck, Leander. *Paul and His Letters*. Philadelphia: Fortress, 1979.
———. *Romans*. Abingdon New Testament Commentary. Nashville: Abingdon, 2005.
Keener, Craig S. *1–2 Corinthians*. Cambridge: Cambridge University Press, 2005.
———. "Paul and the Corinthian Believers." Pages 46–62 in *Blackwell Companion to Paul*. Edited by Stephen Westerholm. Oxford: Blackwell, 2011.
———. *Romans*. New Covenant Commentary Series. Eugene, OR: Wipf & Stock, 2009.
Kennedy, George. *New Testament Interpretation through Rhetorical Criticism*. Chapel Hill: University of North Carolina Press, 1984.

Bibliography

Kim, Yung Suk. *Truth, Testimony, and Transformation*. Eugene, OR: Wipf & Stock, 2014.

Kingsbury, Jack D. *The Christology of Mark's Gospel*. Philadelphia: Fortress, 1983.

Knowles, Michael P. "Paul's 'Affliction' in Second Corinthians: Reflection, Integration, and a Pastoral Theology of the Cross." *Journal of Pastoral Theology* 15 (2005): 64–77.

Koch, D.-A. "Der Text von Hab 2:4b in der Septuaginta und im Neuen Testament." *Zeitschrift für die neutestamentliche Wissenschaft* 76 (1985): 68–85.

Koester, Craig. *Revelation and the End of All Things*. 2nd ed. Grand Rapids: Eerdmans, 2018.

———. *The Word of Life: A Theology of John's Gospel*. Grand Rapids: Eerdmans, 2008.

Konstan, David. "Trusting in Jesus." *Journal for the Study of the New Testament* 40 (2018): 247–54.

Kraftchick, Steve J. "Death in Us, Life in You: The Apostolic Medium." Pages 2:156–81 in *Pauline Theology: 1 and 2 Corinthians*. Edited by David M. Hay. Atlanta: Society of Biblical Literature, 2002.

Kraus, Wolfgang. "Hab 2,3–4 in der hebräischen und griechischen Texttradition mit einem Ausblick auf das Neue Testament." Pages 153–73 in *Die Septuaginta und das frühe Christentum*. Edited by Thomas S. Caulley and Hermann Lichtenberger. Wissenschaftliche Untersuchungen zum Neuen Testament 277. Tübingen: Mohr Siebeck, 2011.

Krauter, Stefan. "'Glaube' im Zweiten Makkabäerbuch." Pages 207–18 in *Glaube: Das Verständnis des Glaubens im frühen Christentum und in seiner jüdischen und hellenistisch-römischen Umwelt*. Edited by Jörg Frey, Benjamin Schliesser, and Nadine Ueberschaer. Wissenschaftliche Untersuchungen zum Neuen Testament 373. Tübingen: Mohr Siebeck, 2017.

Krentz, Edgar. "Military Language and Metaphors in Philippians." Pages 105–27 in *Origins and Method: Towards a New Understanding of Judaism and Christianity*. Edited by B. H. McLean. Sheffield: JSOT Press, 1993.

Kruse, Colin. *Paul's Letter to the Romans*. Pillar New Testament Commentary. Grand Rapids: Eerdmans, 2012.

Kugler, Chris. "ΠΙΣΤΙΣ ΧΡΙΣΤΟΥ: The Current State of Paul and the Key Arguments." *Currents in Biblical Research* 14 (2016): 244–55.

Kurek-Chomycz, Dominika A. "The Scent of (Mediated) Revelation?" Pages 69–107 in *Theologizing in the Corinthian Conflict: Studies in the Exegesis and Theology of 2 Corinthians*. Edited by Reimund Bieringer et al. Leuven: Peeters, 2013.

Lambrecht, Jan. "The Fragment 2 Cor 6:14–7:1: A Plea for Its Authenticity." *Miscellanea neotestamentica* 2 (1978): 143–61.

———. "A Matter of Method (II): 2 Cor 4,13 and the Recent Studies of Schenck and Campbell." *Ephemerides Theologicae Lovanienses* 86 (2010): 441–48.

———. "Reconcile Yourselves . . . : A Reading of 2 Corinthians 5:11–21." Pages 363–412 in *Studies in 2 Corinthians*. Edited by Reimund Bieringer and Jan Lambrecht. Leuven: Leuven University Press, 1994.

Lampe, Peter. "Theological Wisdom and the 'Word about the Cross': The Rhetorical Scheme in 1 Corinthians 1–4." *Interpretation* 44 (1990): 117–31.

Land, Christopher. *The Integrity of 2 Corinthians and Paul's Aggravating Absence*. Sheffield: Sheffield Phoenix Press, 2015.

Lane, William. *Hebrews 9–13*. World Biblical Commentary 47B. Grand Rapids: Zondervan, 1991.

LaSor, William S., David A. Hubbard, and F. W. Bush. *Old Testament Survey*. Grand Rapids: Eerdmans, 1982.

Law, T. Michael. *When God Spoke Greek*. Oxford; Oxford University Press, 2013.

Lendon, Jon E. *Empire of Honour*. Oxford: Oxford University Press, 1997.

Lenski, Richard C. H. *The Interpretation of St. Paul's Epistle to the Galatians*. Minneapolis: Fortress, 2008 (originally 1946).

Levenson, Jon D. "The Conversion of Abraham to Judaism, Christianity, and Islam." Pages 3–40 in *The Idea of Biblical Interpretation*. Edited by H. Najman and J. H. Newman. Boston: Brill, 2004.

———. *The Love of God: Divine Gift, Human Gratitude, and Mutual Faithfulness in Judaism*. Princeton: Princeton University Press, 2015.

Lim, Timothy. *Pesharim*. London: Continuum, 2002.

Lincoln, Andrew T. *Truth on Trial: The Lawsuit Motif in the Fourth Gospel*. Peabody, MA: Hendrickson, 2000.

Lindgård, Fredrik. *Paul's Line of Thought in 2 Corinthians 4:16–5:10*. Wissenschaftliche Untersuchungen zum Neuen Testament 189. Tübingen: Mohr Siebeck, 2005.

Lindsay, Dennis R. *Josephus and Faith: Πίστις and Πιστεύειν as Faith Terminology in the Writings of Flavius Josephus and in the New Testament*. Boston: Brill, 1993.

———. "Πίστις in Flavius Josephus and the New Testament." Pages 183–205 in *Glaube: Das Verständnis des Glaubens im frühen Christentum und in seiner jüdischen und hellenistisch-römischen Umwelt*. Edited by Jörg Frey, Benjamin Schliesser, and Nadine Ueberschaer. Wissenschaftliche Untersuchungen zum Neuen Testament 373. Tübingen: Mohr Siebeck, 2017.

Bibliography

Lohse, Bernhard. *Martin Luther's Theology: Its Historical and Systematic Development*. Minneapolis: Fortress, 1999.

Longenecker, Bruce W. *The Triumph of Abraham's God*. Edinburgh: T&T Clark, 1998.

Longenecker, Richard N. *The Epistle to the Romans*. New International Greek Testament Commentary. Grand Rapids: Eerdmans, 2016.

———. *Galatians*. World Biblical Commentary 41. Grand Rapids: Zondervan, 1990.

Louw, Johannes P., and Eugene Albert Nida. *Greek-English Lexicon of the New Testament: Based on Semantic Domains*. 2 vols. New York: United Bible Societies, 1996.

Lührmann, Dieter. "Pistis im Judentum." *Zeitschrift für die neutestamentliche Wissenschaft* 64 (1973): 19–38.

Luther, Martin. *Commentary on the Epistle to the Galatians*. Translated by T. Graebner. Grand Rapids: Zondervan, 1965.

———. *Luther's Works*. Edited by Jaroslav Pelikan and Helmut T. Lehmann. Philadelphia: Fortress, 1900–1986.

Luz, Ulrich. *Matthew 21–28*. Hermeneia. Minneapolis: Fortress, 2005.

———. *The Theology of the Gospel of Matthew*. New Testament Theology. Cambridge: Cambridge University Press, 1995.

Mannermaa, Tuomo. *Christ Present in Faith: Luther's View of Justification*. Minneapolis: Fortress, 2005.

Marincola, John. "Xenophon's Anabasis and Hellenica." Pages 103–18 in *The Cambridge Companion to Xenophon*. Edited by Michael A. Flower. Cambridge: Cambridge University Press, 2016.

Marshall, Christopher D. *Faith as a Theme in Mark's Narrative*. Cambridge: Cambridge University Press, 1994.

Martin, Ralph P. *2 Corinthians*. World Biblical Commentary 40. 2nd ed. Grand Rapids: Zondervan, 2014.

Martyn, J. Louis. *Galatians*. Anchor Yale Bible 33A. New Haven: Yale University Press, 1997.

———. "The Gospel Invades Philosophy." Pages 13–36 in *Paul, Philosophy, and the Theopolitical Vision*. Edited by Douglas Harink. Eugene, OR: Wipf & Stock, 2010.

———. "Paul's Understanding of the Textual Contradiction between Hab 2:4 and Lev 18:5." Pages 465–74 in *The Quest for Context and Meaning*. Edited by C. A. Evans, and S. Talmon. Boston: Brill, 1997.

Maston, Jason. *Divine and Human Agency in Second Temple Judaism and Paul:*

A Comparative Study. Wissenschaftliche Untersuchungen zum Neuen Testament 297. Tübingen: Mohr Siebeck, 2010.

Matera, Frank. *New Testament Ethics: The Legacies of Jesus and Paul.* Louisville: Westminster John Knox, 1996.

Matlock, R. Barry. "Detheologizing the ΠΙΣΤΙΣ ΧΡΙΣΤΟΥ Debate: Cautionary Remarks from a Lexical Semantic Perspective." *Novum Testamentum* 42 (2000): 13–15.

McGrath, Alister. *Studies in Doctrine.* Grand Rapids: Zondervan, 1997.

Mearns, Chris. "The Identity of Paul's Opponents at Philippi." *New Testament Studies* 33 (1987): 194–204.

Meier, John P. *Matthew.* Wilmington, DE: Glazier, 1980.

Moltmann, Jürgen. *The Way of Jesus Christ: Christology in Messianic Dimensions.* Minneapolis: Fortress, 1993.

Moo, Douglas J. *The Epistle to the Romans.* 2nd ed. New International Commentary on the New Testament. Grand Rapids: Eerdmans, 2018.

———. *The Epistle to the Romans.* New International Commentary on the New Testament. Grand Rapids: Eerdmans, 1996.

———. *Galatians.* Baker Exegetical Commentary on the New Testament. Grand Rapids: Baker, 2013.

———. "Genesis 15:6 in the New Testament." Pages 147–62 in *From Creation to New Creation: Biblical Theology and Exegesis.* Edited by D. M. Gurtner and B. L. Gladd. Peabody, MA: Hendrickson, 2013.

Morgan, Richard. "Faith, Hope, and Love Abide." *Churchman* 101 (1987): 128–39.

Morgan, Teresa. *Roman Faith and Christian Faith: Pistis and Fides in the Early Roman Empire and the Early Churches.* Oxford: Oxford University Press, 2015.

Morris, Leon. *1 and 2 Thessalonians.* Tyndale New Testament Commentary. Grand Rapids: Eerdmans, 1984.

———. *The Gospel according to Matthew.* Grand Rapids: Eerdmans, 1992.

Moulton, James H., and George Milligan. *The Vocabulary of the Greek Testament.* Repr., Peabody, MA: Hendrickson, 1997 (originally 1930).

Moxnes, Halvor. "Honour and Righteousness in Romans." *Journal for the Study of the New Testament* (1988): 61–77.

Muraoka, Takamitsu. *A Greek-English Lexicon of the Septuagint.* Louvain: Peeters, 2009.

Murphy-O'Connor, Jerome. "Relating 2 Corinthians to Its Context." *New Testament Studies* 33 (1987): 272–75.

———. *The Theology of the Second Letter to the Corinthians.* New Testament Theology. Cambridge: Cambridge University Press, 1991.

Bibliography

Murphy, Frederick J. Review of *Paul and Variegated Nomism*. Catholic Biblical Quarterly 65 (2003): 148–50.
Murray, John. *The Epistle to the Romans*. Grand Rapids: Eerdmans, 1997 (originally 1968).
Nash, R. Scott. *First Corinthians*. Smyth & Helwys Biblical Commentary. Macon, GA: Helwys, 2009.
Nave, Guy D. *The Role and Function of Repentance in Luke-Acts*. Leiden: Brill, 2002.
Neirynck, Frans. "The Sayings of Jesus in 1 Corinthians." Pages 141–76 in *The Corinthian Correspondence*. Edited by R. Bieringer. Leuven: Peeters, 1996.
Nolland, John. *The Gospel of Matthew*. New International Greek Testament Commentary. Grand Rapids: Eerdmans, 2005.
Noss, Philip, and Kenneth Thompson. *A Handbook on Ezra and Nehemiah*. New York: United Bible Societies, 2005.
O'Day, Gail R. "The Ethical Shape of Pauline Spirituality." *Brethren Life and Thought* 32 (1987): 81–92.
Oakes, Peter. *Galatians*. Paideia. Grand Rapids: Baker, 2015.
———. *Philippians: From People to Letter*. Society for New Testament Studies Monograph 110. Cambridge: Cambridge University Press, 2001.
———. "Πίστις as Relational Way of Life in Galatians." *Journal for the Study of the New Testament* 40 (2018): 255–75.
Oropeza, B. J. *Jews, Gentiles, and the Opponents of Paul*. Eugene, OR: Wipf & Stock, 2012.
Osborne, Grant. *Romans*. Downers Grove, IL: InterVarsity, 2004.
Ota, Shuji. "The Absolute Use of ΠΙΣΤΙΣ and ΠΙΣΤΙΣ ΧΡΙΣΤΟΥ in Paul." *Annual of the Japanese Biblical Institute* 23 (1997): 64–82.
———. "ΠΙΣΤΙΣ ΧΡΙΣΤΟΥ: Christ's Faithfulness to Whom?" *Hitotsubashi Journal of Arts and Sciences* 55 (2014): 15–26.
Perkins, Pheme. *First Corinthians*. Paideia. Grand Rapids: Baker, 2012.
———. *Introduction to the Synoptic Gospels*. Grand Rapids: Eerdmans, 2009.
Perrin, Norman. *Jesus and the Language of the Kingdom: Symbol and Metaphor in New Testament Interpretation*. Philadelphia: Fortress, 1976.
Peterlin, Davorin. *Paul's Letter to the Philippians in the Light of Disunity in the Church*. Novum Testamentum Supplement 79. Leiden: Brill, 1995.
Plutarch, *Moralia*, vol. 6. Translated by W. C. Helmbold. LCL 337. Cambridge: Harvard University Press, 1939.
———. *Moralia*, vol. 9. Translated by E. L. Minar Jr., F. H. Sandbach, and W. C. Helmbold. LCL 425. Cambridge: Harvard University Press, 1971.

Przybylski, Benno. *Righteousness in Matthew and His World of Thought.* Cambridge: Cambridge University Press, 1980.

Rabens, Volker. "'Indicative and Imperative' as the Substructure of Paul's Theology-and-Ethics in Galatians? A Discussion of Divine and Human Agency in Paul." Pages 285–305 in *Galatians and Christian Theology.* Edited by Mark W. Eliott et al. Grand Rapids: Baker, 2014.

———. "Paul's Rhetoric of Demarcation: Separating from 'Unbelievers' (2 Cor 6:14–7:1) in the Corinthian Conflict." Pages 229–53 in *Theologizing in the Corinthian Conflict: Studies in the Exegesis and Theology of 2 Corinthians.* Edited by R. Bieringer et al. Leuven: Peeters, 2013.

Rainbow, Paul A. *Johannine Theology: The Gospels, the Epistles, and the Apocalypse.* Downers Grove, IL: InterVarsity, 2014.

Reasoner, Mark. *Romans in Full Circle.* Louisville: Westminster John Knox, 2005.

Rensberger, David. *1 John, 2 John, 3 John.* Abingdon New Testament Commentary. Nashville: Abingdon, 1997.

———. "2 Corinthians 6:14–7:1—A Fresh Examination." *Studia Biblica et Theologica* 8 (1978): 25–49.

Reumann, John. *Philippians.* Anchor Yale Bible 33B. New Haven: Yale University Press, 2008.

Rhoads, David M. *Reading Mark.* Minneapolis: Fortress, 2004.

Rist, John M. "Plutarch's *Amatorius*: A Commentary on Plato's Theories of Love." *Classical Quarterly* 51 (2001): 557–75.

Rosner, Brian S. "Paul and the Law: What He Does Not Say." *Journal for the Study of the New Testament* 32 (2010): 405–19.

———. *Paul and the Law: Keeping the Commandments of God.* Downers Grove, IL: InterVarsity, 2013.

Rosner, Brian, and Roy Ciampa. *The First Letter to the Corinthians.* Pillar New Testament Commentary. Grand Rapids: Eerdmans, 2010.

Sampley, Paul. "The First Letter to the Corinthians." Pages 10:771–1003 in *The New Interpreter's Bible.* Edited by Leander E. Keck. Nashville: Abingdon, 2002.

———. "Romans and Galatians: Comparison and Contrast." Pages 315–39 in *Understanding the Word.* Edited by J. T. Butler et al. Sheffield: JSOT Press, 1985.

Sanders, E. P. *Paul and Palestinian Judaism.* Minneapolis: Fortress, 1977.

Savage, Timothy B. *Power through Weakness: Paul's Understanding of the Christian Ministry in 2 Corinthians.* Society for New Testament Studies Monograph 86. Cambridge: Cambridge University Press, 2004.

Schlatter, Adolf. *Der Glaube im Neuen Testament.* Stuttgart: Calwer, 1883.

Schliesser, Benjamin. "'Christ-Faith' as an Eschatological Event (Galatians 3.23–26): A 'Third View' on Πίστις Χριστοῦ." *Journal for the Study of the New Testament* 38 (2016): 277–300.

———. "'Exegetical Amnesia' and ΠΙΣΤΙΣ ΧΡΙΣΤΟΥ: The 'Faith *of* Christ' in Nineteenth-Century Pauline Scholarship." *Journal of Theological Studies* 66 (2015): 61–89.

———. "Faith in Early Christianity." Pages 1–50 in *Glaube: Das Verständnis des Glaubens im frühen Christentum und in seiner jüdischen und hellenistisch-römischen Umwelt*. Edited by Jörg Frey, Benjamin Schliesser, and Nadine Ueberschaer. Wissenschaftliche Untersuchungen zum Neuen Testament 373. Tübingen: Mohr Siebeck, 2017.

———. *Was Ist Glaube? Paulinische Perspektiven*. Zurich: Theologischer Verlag, 2011.

Schreiner, Thomas R. *Galatians*. Zondervan Exegetical Commentary on the New Testament. Grand Rapids: Zondervan, 2010.

———. "Justification apart from and by Works: At the Final Judgment Works Will Confirm Justification." Pages 71–98 in *Four Views on the Role of Works at the Final Judgment*. Edited by Alan P. Stanley. Grand Rapids: Zondervan, 2013.

———. *Magnifying God in Christ: A Summary of New Testament Theology*. Grand Rapids: Baker, 2010.

Scott, Ian. *Paul's Way of Knowing*. Grand Rapids: Baker, 2008.

Seifrid, Mark. "Paul's Use of Habakkuk 2:4 in Romans 1:17: Reflections on Israel's Exile in Romans." Pages 133–49 in *History and Exegesis: New Testament Essays in Honor of Dr. E. Earle Ellis for His 80th Birthday*. Edited by S.-W. Son. Edinburgh: T&T Clark, 2006.

———. "Romans." Pages 607–94 in *Commentary on the New Testament Use of the Old Testament*. Edited by G. K. Beale and D. A. Carson. Grand Rapids: Baker, 2007.

Senior, Donald. *Jesus: A Gospel Portrait*. Mahwah, NJ: Paulist, 1992.

Sierksma-Agteres, Suzan. "The Metahistory of Δικη and Πιστις." Pages 209–30 in *Saint Paul and Philosophy*. Edited by Gert-Jan van der Heiden, George van Kooten, and Antonio Cimino. New York: de Gruyter, 2017.

Skehan, Patrick, and Alexander A. Di Lella. *The Wisdom of Ben Sirach*. Anchor Yale Bible 39. New Haven: Yale University Press, 2007.

Skinner, Matthew L. "'She Departed to Her House': Another Dimension of the Syrophoenician Mother's Faith in Mark 7.24–30." *Word and World* 26 (2006): 14–21.

Soards, Marion. *1 Corinthians*. New International Biblical Commentary. Peabody, MA: Hendrickson, 1999.

Spicq, Ceslas. *Agape in the New Testament*. St. Louis: Herder, 1963.

———. "L'Image sportive de 2 Cor 4:7–9." *Ephemerides Theologicae Lovanienses* 13 (1937): 209–29.

———. *Theological Lexicon of the New Testament*. Translated and edited by J. D. Ernest. 3 vols. Peabody, MA: Hendrickson, 1994.

Spilsbury, Paul. "Josephus." Pages 241–60 in *Justification and Variegated Nomism: The Complexities of Second Temple Judaism*. Edited by D. A. Carson, Peter T. O'Brien, and Mark Seifrid. Grand Rapids: Baker, 2001.

Sprinkle, Preston. *Paul and Judaism Revisited: A Study of Divine and Human Agency in Salvation*. Downers Grove, IL: InterVarsity, 2013.

———. "Πίστις Χριστοῦ as an Eschatological Event." Pages 166–84 in *The Faith of Jesus Christ: Exegetical, Biblical, and Theological Studies*. Edited by Michael F. Bird and Preston M. Sprinkle. Peabody, MA: Hendrickson, 2009.

Stanton, Graham. *Studies in Matthew and Early Christianity*. Edited by M. Bockmuehl and D. Lincicum. Wissenschaftliche Untersuchungen zum Neuen Testament 309. Tübingen: Mohr Siebeck, 2013.

Stegman, Thomas. "'Ἐπίστευσα, διὸ ἐλάλησα (2 Corinthians 4:13): Paul's Christological Reading of Psalm 115:1a LXX." *Catholic Biblical Quarterly* 69 (2007): 725–45.

Steinmann, Andrew E. *Ezra and Nehemiah*. St. Louis: Concordia, 2010.

Stendahl, Krister. *Paul among Jews and Gentiles*. Philadelphia: Fortress, 1976.

Steyn, Gert. *A Quest for the Assumed LXX Vorlage of the Explicit Quotations in Hebrews*. Göttingen: Vandenhoeck & Ruprecht, 2011.

Still, Todd D. *Conflict in Thessalonica*. Journal for the Study of the New Testament Supplement 183. Sheffield: JSOT Press, 1999.

Strecker, Christian. "Fides-Pistis-Glaube: Kontexte und Konturen einer Theologie der 'Annahme' bei Paulus." Pages 223–50 in *Lutherische und Neue Paulusperspektive*. Edited by M. Backmann. Wissenschaftliche Untersuchungen zum Neuen Testament 182. Tübingen: Mohr Siebeck, 2005.

Stuhlmacher, Peter. *Paul's Letter to the Romans: A Commentary*. Louisville: Westminster John Knox, 1994.

Talbert, Charles H., and J. A. Whitlark. "Paul, Judaism, and the Revisionists." Pages 11–34 in *Getting "Saved": The Whole Story of Salvation in the New Testament*. Grand Rapids: Eerdmans, 2011.

Taylor, John W. "From Faith to Faith: Romans 1.17 in the Light of Greek Idiom." *New Testament Studies* 50 (2004): 337–48.

Tellbe, Mikael. *Between Synagogue and State: Christians, Jews, and Civic Au-

thorities in 1 Thessalonians, Romans, and Philippians. Stockholm: Almqvist & Wiksell, 2001.

Theissen, Gerd. *The Miracle Stories of the Early Christian Tradition*. Translated by F. McDonagh. Edited by John Riches. Edinburgh: T&T Clark, 1983.

Thiselton, Anthony. *1 Corinthians: A Shorter Exegetical and Pastoral Commentary*. Grand Rapids: Eerdmans, 2011.

———. *Doubt, Faith, and Certainty*. Grand Rapids: Eerdmans, 2017.

———. *The First Epistle to the Corinthians*. New International Greek Testament Commentary. Grand Rapids: Eerdmans, 2000.

———. *Thiselton on Hermeneutics*. Grand Rapids: Eerdmans, 2006.

Thomas Aquinas. *The Summa Theologica*. Translated by L. Shapcote and D. J. Sullivan. Chicago: Encyclopedia Britannica, 1909–1990.

Thompson, James W. *Moral Formation according to Paul: The Context and Coherence of Pauline Ethics*. Grand Rapids: Baker, 2011.

Torrance, T. F. "One Aspect of the Biblical Conception of Faith." *Expository Times* 68 (1957): 111–14.

Trebilco, Paul. *Self-Designations and Group Identity in the New Testament*. Cambridge: Cambridge University Press, 2012.

Twelftree, Graham. *Jesus the Miracle Worker*. Downers Grove, IL: InterVarsity, 1999.

Tyson, Joseph B. "Paul's Opponents at Philippi." *Perspectives in Religious Studies* 3 (1976): 83–96.

Ueberschaer, Frank. "Πιστις in der Septuaginta." Pages 79–107 in *Glaube: Das Verständnis des Glaubens im frühen Christentum und in seiner jüdischen und hellenistisch-römischen Umwelt*. Edited by Jörg Frey, Benjamin Schliesser, and Nadine Ueberschaer. Wissenschaftliche Untersuchungen zum Neuen Testament 373. Tübingen: Mohr Siebeck, 2017.

Verhoef, Eduard. *Philippi: How Christianity Began in Europe*. London: Bloomsbury, 2013.

Vermes, Geza. *The Religion of Jesus the Jew*. Minneapolis: Fortress, 1993.

Watson, Francis. "Constructing an Antithesis: Pauline and Other Jewish Perspectives on Divine and Human Agency." Pages 99–116 in *Divine and Human Agency in Paul*. Edited by John M. G. Barclay and Simon J. Gathercole. London: T&T Clark, 2006.

———. *Paul, Judaism, and the Gentiles: Beyond the New Perspective*. Grand Rapids: Eerdmans, 2007.

Watts, Rikki. "'For I Am Not Ashamed of the Gospel': Romans 1:16–17 and Habakkuk 2:4." Pages 3–25 in *Romans and the People of God: Essays in Honor of Gordon D. Fee*. Edited by Sven K. Soderlund and N. T. Wright. Grand Rapids: Eerdmans, 1999.

Weaver, Dorothy J. "Luke 18:1–8." *Interpretation* 56 (2002): 317–19.

Weima, Jeffrey A. D. "The Reason for Romans: The Evidence of Its Epistolary Framework (1:1–15; 15:14–16:27)." *Review and Expositor* 100 (2003): 17–33.

Weinfeld, Moshe. *Deuteronomy 1–11*. Anchor Bible 5. New York: Doubleday, 1991.

Weiss, Wolfgang. "Glaube-Liebe-Hoffnung: Zu der Trias bei Paulus," *Zeitschrift für die neutestamentliche Wissenschaft* 84 (1993): 197–217.

Wells, Kyle. *Grace and Agency in Paul and Second Temple Judaism: Interpreting the Transformation of the Heart*. Novum Testamentum Supplement 157. Leiden: Brill, 2014.

Westerholm, Stephen. *Understanding Matthew*. Grand Rapids: Baker, 2006.

White, Adam. *Where Is the Wise Man? Graeco-Roman Education as a Background to the Divisions in 1 Corinthians 1–4*. Library of New Testament Studies. London: T&T Clark 2015.

White, Horace. *The Roman History of Appian of Alexandria*. 2 vols. London: Macmillan, 1899.

Whitenton, Michael R. "After ΠΙΣΤΙΣ ΧΡΙΣΤΟΥ: Neglected Evidence from the Apostolic Fathers." *Journal of Theological Studies* 61 (2010): 82–109.

Wildberger, Hans. "Glauben, Erwägungen zu האמין." Pages 372–86 in *Hebräische Wortforschung: Festschrift für W: Baumgartner*. Vetus Testamentum Supplement 16. Leiden: Brill, 1967.

Wilkins, Michael. *The Concept of Disciple in Matthew's Gospel as Reflected in the Use of the Term Mathētēs*. Boston: Brill, 1988.

Williams, H. H. Drake. *The Wisdom of the Wise: The Presence and Function of Scripture within 1 Corinthians 1:18–3:23*. Boston: Brill, 2001.

Wilson, Marvin. *Our Father Abraham*. Grand Rapids: Eerdmans, 1989.

Wilson, Walter T. *Healing in the Gospel of Matthew: Reflections on Methods and Ministry*. Minneapolis: Fortress, 2014.

———. *The Sentences of Pseudo-Phocylides*. Berlin: de Gruyter, 2005.

Witherington III, Ben. *Conflict and Community in Corinth*. Grand Rapids: Eerdmans, 1995.

———. *Grace in Galatia: A Commentary on Paul's Letter to the Galatians*. Grand Rapids: Eerdmans, 1998.

———. *Paul's Letter to the Philippians*. Grand Rapids: Eerdmans, 2011.

Wolter, Michael. *Paul: An Outline of His Theology*. Waco, TX: Baylor University Press, 2015.

Wright, N. T. *The Climax of the Covenant*. Minneapolis: Fortress, 1993.

———. *Jesus and the Victory of God*. Minneapolis: Fortress, 1996.

———. *Paul and His Recent Interpreters*. Minneapolis: Fortress, 2015.
———. *Paul and the Faithfulness of God*. 2 vols. Minneapolis: Fortress, 2013.
Yeung, Maureen W. *Faith in Jesus and Paul*. Tübingen: Mohr Siebeck, 2002.
Yinger, Kent L. *Paul, Judaism, and Judgment according to Deeds*. Society for New Testament Studies Monograph 105. Cambridge: Cambridge University Press, 1999.
———. "*Reformation Redivivus*: Syngerism and the New Perspective." *Journal of Theological Interpretation* 3 (2009): 89–106.
———. Review of *Paul and Judaism Revisited*. *Bulletin for Biblical Research* 25 (2015): 580–82.
Zerbe, Gordon. "Believers as Loyalists: The Anatomy of Paul's Language of *Pistis*." Pages 26–47 in *Citizen: Paul on Peace and Politics* (Winnipeg: CMU Press, 2012).
Zetterholm, Magnus. *Approaches to Paul: A Student's Guide to Recent Research*. Minneapolis: Fortress, 2009.

Index of Names and Subjects

Abraham, 4, 9, 25, 30, 37, 51, 144, 145, 146, 150–51, 152, 159, 172
Achtemeier, Elizabeth, 169–70
Allison, D. C., 11
Aquinas, Thomas, 24

Baird, William, 151
Barclay, John M. G., 54–55, 116–17, 118
Barth, Karl, 1, 28–29, 156–67, 187–88
Barth, Markus, 8, 10, 11
Barton, Stephen, 71
Bassler, Jouette, 85n23
Bates, Matthew, 33
Bauer, David, 69
Beale, Gregory, 93
Beavis, Mary Ann, 60
Becker, Siegbert, 26n7
Beker, J. C., 118, 125
Best, Ernest, 82n12
Blumenthal, David, 1, 16
body, 102, 121–24, 125, 129
Boer, Martinus de, 139
Boespflug, Mark, 2
Boring, M. Eugene, 83n42
Bornkamm, Günther, 30
Bridges, Linda McKinnish, 124
Brown, Alexandra, 103, 104

Brown, Raymond, 73n52
Bruce, F. F., 150
Brueggemann, Walter, 6, 189
Bultmann, Rudolf, 28
Bush, Frederic William, 17n35

Calvin, John, 27–28
Campbell, Douglas, 46n15
Campbell, William S., 46n15
Carlson, Richard, 165
Carson, D. A., 69n39
Catchpole, David, 72
Chester, Stephen, 27n9
Christ-relation, 26, 37, 57, 143, 144, 146, 147–53, 174–75, 184, 185
Clendenen, Ray, 166
Collins, Raymond F., 101
Cousar, Charles, 107, 108
covenant, 6, 13, 15, 16, 17, 36–37, 49, 53–54, 57, 143, 165, 183
covenantal nomism, 140, 141, 142, 144, 155, 179
covenantal *pistism*, 141–42, 153–54, 155, 179
Cox, Steven, 111

Das, Andrew, 159
Davies, W. D., 11

Index of Names and Subjects

Deissmann, Adolf, 21, 30
deSilva, David, 118, 149
divine agency, 14–17, 35, 137–38, 139–40, 153–54, 185–90
Donahue, John, 72
Dunn, James D.G., 109, 110, 123, 141, 142, 145, 146, 149, 168

epistemology, 10, 32, 36, 59–60, 62, 73–75, 103, 104, 105, 107–8, 119, 130, 132

faith: as belief, 41, 51, 52; gift of, 108–9; healing faith, 63, 67, 71; as knowledge, 24, 29; as opinion, 2; as passive, 4–5, 6, 15, 135; seeking faith, 61–65
Fee, Gordon D., 88
Feldman, Louis, 46n15
Findlay, G. G., 135
Finney, Mark, 98
Fitzmyer, Joseph, 30
Fosdick, Harry Emerson, 77
France, R. T., 69
Furnish, Victor, 99, 123, 134

Garland, David, 10, 111n46
Georgi, Dieter, 88
Gorman, Michael, 32
Gundry, Robert, 69
Guthrie, George, 116

Hagner, Donald, 65
Harrington, Daniel, 66, 161
Hawthorne, Gerald, 62
Hay, David, 50
Hays, Richard B., 12, 13, 108, 111, 113, 152, 163–64, 185–86
Heliso, Desto, 161

Helmbold, W. C., 77
Hiebert, Theodore, 160
honor, 98, 133
Hooker, Morna D., 141n26, 142
hope, 81, 102, 111, 112, 131
Hopper, David H., 95
Horsley, Richard, 99
Houghton, Myron, 112
Hubbard, David Allan, 17n35
human agency, 14–17, 137–38, 139–40, 153–54, 185–90

idolatry, 119, 120, 121, 122, 128

Jervis, L. Ann, 85
Jesus and Paul, 75–76
Johnson, Luke Timothy, 3, 72n47

Kaiser, Walter, 4–5
Käsemann, Ernst, 29–30
Keck, Leander, 31, 134
Keener, Craig, 164
Kingsbury, Jack Dean, 60
Kraftchick, Steven, 128
Kraus, Wolfgang, 164–65

Lampe, Peter, 100
Lane, William, 163
LaSor, William S., 17n35
Lindsay, Dennis R., 52
Lohse, Bernhard, 26
Longenecker, Richard, 7–8
Louw, J. P., 18, 129–30
love, 9, 80, 81, 82, 83, 84, 111, 113
loyalty, 22, 25, 32–33, 39, 43, 47, 48, 51, 52, 68–70, 78, 80, 82, 92, 178
Luther, Martin, 4, 24–27, 95, 184–85
Luz, Ulrich, 11, 66

Index of Names and Subjects

Mannermaa, Tuomo, 27
Martyn, J. Louis, 138–39, 154, 188–89
Matera, Frank, 59
McGrath, Alister, 4
Meier, John, 66
Moltmann, Jürgen, 63
Moo, Douglas, 8, 31, 166
Morgan, Richard, 113
Morgan, Teresa, 33, 73, 130n31
Moxnes, Halvor, 158–59
Murphy-O'Connor, Jerome, 124, 126–27, 128

Nash, Scott, 101
New Perspective on Paul, 136, 140–41
Nida, Eugene, 18, 129–30

Oakes, Peter, 14, 145, 148
obedience, 10, 11, 25, 28, 34, 79
O'Day, Gail R., 108n33
Osborne, Grant, 5n7
Ota, Shuji, 173, 175

Perkins, Pheme, 101
Perrin, Norman, 180

Reumann, John, 87
revelation, 28, 74, 150
righteousness, 4, 25, 71, 153, 157, 159, 160–61, 164, 165, 169, 188

Sampley, Paul, 109
Sanders, E. P., 144
Schlatter, Adolf, 28n16
Schreiner, Thomas, 31
Seifrid, Mark, 165

Senior, Donald, 68
Spicq, Ceslas, 82, 112n47
Spilsbury, Paul, 55, 56
Spirit, 108–10
Sprinkle, Preston, 137
Stanton, Graham, 159
suffering and weakness, 86, 118, 125, 128, 158

Tennyson, Alfred, 115
Thiselton, Anthony, 97, 177
Thompson, James, 85
Tilling, Chris, 26
Torrance, T. F., 6n11
Trebilco, Paul, 191
trust, 6, 12–13, 31, 43, 45, 51, 65–68, 74, 114, 166, 169–70, 181

Watson, Francis, 142, 153, 154
Watts, Rikki, 166
Weaver, Dorothy Jean, 72
Weima, Jeffrey, 156
Weinfeld, Moshe, 83
Weiss, Wolfgang, 112n47
Westerholm, Stephen, 70n41
White, Adam, 99
White, Horace, 83
wisdom, 95, 96, 100, 101, 104, 105, 110
Witherington, Ben, III, 87
Wolter, Michael, 31
works and doing, 11, 24–27, 28, 29, 31, 93, 135, 136–37, 140, 148–150, 183–84
Wright, N. T., 32n43, 59n4

Yinger, Kent, 138

Index of Scripture and Other Ancient Texts

OLD TESTAMENT

Genesis
15:5	51
15:6	31, 151

Exodus
17:2	6

Leviticus
11:33	123
15:12	123
18:5	152

Deuteronomy
5:31	51
6:5	83
7:8	16
27:26	144
32:20	46–47

1 Samuel
20:8	53
26:30	47

2 Samuel
3:12	54

2 Kings
12:16	47
23:3	54

1 Chronicles
9:26	47
9:31	47

2 Chronicles
31:12–18	47
34:12	47
34:31	54

Nehemiah
9:38/10:1	15–16, 49

Psalms
32:4 LXX	47
115:2–8	119
116	125–28
116:10/Ps 115:1 LXX	126, 183

Proverbs
14:22 LXX	47
15:27 LXX	47
15:28 LXX	47

Isaiah
2:18 LXX	122
6:10	74
7:9 LXX	106
10:11 LXX	122
11:5	161
16:12 LXX	122
19:1 LXX	122
21:9 LXX	122
25:1	161
28:16 LXX	105, 159
29:14 LXX	105
29:15	123
31:7 LXX	122
33:18 LXX	105
38:3	6
40:4	67
40:13	106
43:10 LXX	106
45:9	123
46:6 LXX	122
49:11	67
52:13 LXX	131
52:14 LXX	131
53:1	36, 58, 74, 107, 131
53:2–3 LXX	131
54:10	67

Index of Scripture and Other Ancient Texts

64:4	106	8:13	62, 63	11:23	75		
64:8	123	8:26	60, 66	14:58	121		
		9:2–8	60, 61, 63				
Jeremiah		9:18–26	60, 61, 63	**Luke**			
9:2 LXX	47	9:21	63	5:20	71		
9:3 LXX	49	9:22	63	7:9	71		
34:15	59	9:27–31	60, 61, 64	7:50	71, 182		
		9:29	64	8:25	71		
Lamentations		10:1	70	8:48	71, 182		
3:23	161	10:8	70	11:42	69		
		10:14–39	70	12:42	151		
Ezekiel		13:46	65	17:5–6	71		
18:21	59	14:31	66	17:9	71		
		15:21–28	60, 61, 64	18:8	58, 71, 72		
Daniel		16:8	66	18:42	71		
5:4 LXX	122	16:16	65	22:31–32	71		
5:23 LXX	122	16:17	62n15	22:33	71		
6:28 LXX	122	16:20	65				
		17:8	65	**John**			
Hosea		17:14–21	66	6:47	74		
2:22	7	17:20	65, 66, 70, 75	11:26	74		
				12:11	74		
Habakkuk		21:18–22	60, 67	12:36	74		
1:5–11	160	21:21–22	65, 66	12:38	58		
1:12	160	21:23–27	68	12:38–41	74		
1:13	160	21:32	13	12:41	75		
2:2–3	161	23:23	11, 68, 70, 183	12:46	74		
2:4	5, 20, 36, 58, 144, 152, 157, 179	24:45	151	14:1	74		
				16:27	74		
		Mark		20:29	192		
NEW TESTAMENT		1:15	59, 183				
		2:1–12	60	**Acts**			
Matthew		4:40	60	3:13–15	163		
1:21	64	5:21–43	60	4:32	152		
1:27	68	5:36	183	7:51–53	163		
6:30	66	7:24–30	60	19:26	121		
7:7–8	67–68	9:23–24	183				
8:5–13	61	9:29	67	**Romans**			
8:8–9	61	11:20–26	60	1:5	28, 79, 157		

221

Index of Scripture and Other Ancient Texts

1:5–6	156	1:18–2:16	97–99	3:14	15
1:8	79, 157, 164, 190	1:19	105	4:1–5:10	120, 122–32
1:12	79, 157, 164	1:20	105	4:4	36, 118
1:15	156	1:21	96, 102–5	4:6	28, 190
1:16–17	20, 166	2:2	99	4:7–12	123–25
1:17	5, 20, 58	2:4	99	4:12	118, 125
3:3	7, 157	2:4–5	101	4:13	36, 183
3:21	62	2:5	96, 98, 100, 104	4:13–15	125–28
3:22–26	157	2:9	106	4:16–18	128
3:23	172	2:16	106	4:18	191
3:26	172	3:5	96	5:1	121
3:27	157	3:13–15	184	5:1–5	129
3:27–28	158–59	4:2	97	5:6–10	129–32
3:30	157	4:17	97	5:7	10, 36, 79, 112, 115–16, 176
4:2–5	184	7:25	97	5:13	118
4:3	157–83	10:13	96	6:16	120
4:5	8n16, 164	11:25	15	10:15	190
4:9	157	12:7–11	108	11:5	116
4:9–10	159	12:9	96, 97	11:13	116
4:13	159	13:2	75, 110, 111	11:16	118
4:16–20	157–59	13:7	96	12:11	116
5:19	173	13:12	112		
6:8	31	13:13	97, 102, 110–14	**Galatians**	
8:9–11	150	14:22	96, 151–52	1:23	31, 142, 147–48, 174, 179
8:24	112	15:2	96		
9:4	15	15:2–11	179	2:16	35, 139, 148–50, 172
9:30–32	157	15:11	96		
9:32	5, 184	15:12	102	2:17	150
10:9	31, 157	15:12–34	101–2	2:19	150
10:9–10	36	15:14	97, 102	2:20	150, 173, 186
11:27	15	15:17	97, 102	3:2	148
15:16	184	15:19	102	3:5	148
16:19	28	16:13	97, 190	3:6	139, 150, 151, 183
16:26	79, 157			3:7–14	136
		2 Corinthians		3:7–22	139
1 Corinthians		1:8–10	118	3:8	151
1:9	96	2:12–17	125	3:8–9	150–51
1:10–17	99	2:14	28	3:9	9n20, 162
1:18	103, 159	3:6	15		

3:10	144, 148, 149	2:5–11	172–73	10:32–34	162
3:10–11	162	2:14	87	10:38–39	162
3:11–12	143	2:14–16	90	11:1	10, 128
3:12	144, 148, 149, 152–53	2:17	88–89, 93, 190		
		2:25	80	**James**	
3:14	162	2:27	80	2:19	3
3:15	15	3:3–4	87	5:6	164
3:19	144	3:9	172, 187	5:15	178
3:19–20	152–53	3:21	129		
3:21	144, 149, 152	4:2	87	**1 Peter**	
3:22	144, 151–52, 172			1:8	130n30, 191
3:23	143–46, 174, 179	**Colossians**		3:18	164
		4:9	151	5:2	151
3:23–26	173–74				
3:25	143, 174, 179	**1 Thessalonians**		**1 John**	
3:26	25, 173	1:3	8, 81, 93, 113, 154	2:1	164
4:24	15	1:7	191	2:29	164
5:6	84, 140, 154, 184	1:8	81	3:7	164
5:12	120	3:2	84		
5:22–23	7, 69	3:5–8	85	**Revelation**	
6:9–10	184	3:10	190	2:9	92
6:10	32	4:14	31	2:13	92
		5:8	80, 82, 84	2:19	92, 93
Ephesians		5:15–22	184	2:20	92
2:8–9	5			2:23–24	92
2:12	15	**2 Thessalonians**		2:25	92
		1:3	190	13:10	93
Philippians		1:11	154		
1:3–7	91			**Deuterocanon-**	
1:6	187	**1 Timothy**		**ical Works**	
1:9	87	4:6	3		
1:13–14	87			**Judith**	
1:25	87–88	**Philemon**		8:18	121
1:26	88	5	8, 9		
1:27	31, 87, 88, 90, 187			**Wisdom of Solomon**	
		Hebrews		14:8	121
1:28	86, 88	9:11	121	15:1–16	130
1:29	86	10:22–23	162	15:7	124
2:1–2	87	10:26	162	15:8	124

Index of Scripture and Other Ancient Texts

15:13	124	**1 Enoch**		*On Dreams*	
15:15–17	124	38.2	163	1.68	52
Sirach		**Jubilees**		*On Drunkenness*	
1:27	48	24.11	150–51	40	50
15:15	39, 48–49	**Psalms of Solomon**		*On the Decalogue*	
22:23	49	14.1	83	15	36n52
27:16	49			172	50
45:4	85	**Pseudo-Phocylides**		*On the Life of Abraham*	
46:15	85	1.13	49, 50	268	51
Bel and the Dragon		1.218	77	273	50
4b–5	121	**Testament of Asher**		*On the Life of Joseph*	
7	124	7.7	49	100	36n52
				258	50
1 Maccabees		**Testament of Levi**		273	50
2:59	85	8.2	49	*On the Life of Moses*	
10:27	47			1.90	36n52
		Dead Sea Scrolls		1.280	52
2 Maccabees				*On the Migration of Abraham*	
1:2	151	**1QpHab**			
3 Maccabees		7.17–8.3	161–62	43	51
3:3	47	**Philo**		*Who Is the Heir?*	
4 Maccabees		*Allegorical Interpretation*		91	51
14:20	48			93	51
15:12	48, 85	3.208	50	**Josephus**	
15:14	85	*On the Change of Names*		*Against Apion*	
15:15	48			1.72	52–53
15:23	48	201	51	2.18	52–53
16:22	48	*On the Cherubim*		2.42–43	53
OT Pseudepigrapha		85	51	2.163	53
		On the Confusion of Tongues		2.165	32, 55
				2.166	55
2 Baruch				2.169	53
57.2	150–51	31	51	2.210	38

Index of Scripture and Other Ancient Texts

Jewish Antiquities

6.228	53
7.24	54
7.107	84
10.63	54
13.349	54
14.186	83
15.87	53
15.134	39
15.366	53
15.368	53
15.369	53
17.1	54
17.53	54
17.78	54
17.146	54
19.289	84

RABBINIC LITERATURE

b. Mak.

23b	162

GRECO-ROMAN WRITINGS

Appian of Alexandria

Mithridatic Wars

12.7.47	83

Cicero

Tusculan Disputations

1.22.52	123–24

Dio Chrysostom

On Trust, On Distrust

73.3	43
73.7	44
73.9	44
74.5	44

Dionysius of Halicarnassus

Roman Antiquities

11.11.15	40
11.34.5	40
11.49.4	40

Epictetus

Discourses

2.4	46

Plato

Republic

7.533E–534A	46

Plutarch

Dialogue on Love

756AB	41

763A	42
763C	42
767E	42, 43
768E	43
769B	43
770C	78

Moralia

503B	78
506C	78

Xenophon

Anabasis

3.2.4	89
3.2.6	89
3.2.7	89
3.2.8	89
3.2.11	89
3.3.2	89
3.3.4	89

DOCUMENTARY PAPYRI

O.Did 415	44
P.Bad. 2.35	45
P.Col. 4.64	45
P.Erasm. 1.1	45
P.Hib II 268	44
SB 14.12172	45

www.ingramcontent.com/pod-product-compliance
Lightning Source LLC
Chambersburg PA
CBHW020647300426
44112CB00007B/278